Laughs, Luck . . . and *Lucy*

How I Came to Create the Most Popular Sitcom of All Time

Jess Oppenheimer

With Gregg Oppenheimer

Syracuse University Press

First Paperback Edition 1999

99 00 01 02 03 04   6 5 4 3 2 1

Library of Congress Cataloging-in-Publication Data
Oppenheimer, Jess.
    Laughs, luck—and Lucy : how I came to create the most popular
sitcom of all time / Jess Oppenheimer, with Gregg Oppenheimer.
        p.   cm.—(The television series)
    Includes index.
    ISBN 0-8156-0406-8 (cloth : alk. paper)
    ISBN 0-8156-0584-6 (pbk :)
    1. Oppenheimer, Jess.   2. Television producers and directors—
United States—Biography.   3. I love Lucy (Television program)
I. Oppenheimer, Gregg.   II. Title.   III. Series.
PN1992.4.066A3   1996
791.45'0232'092—dc20
    [B]   96-20756

Manufactured in the United States of America

To Es

Jess Oppenheimer (1913–88), producer and head writer of 153 classic episodes of *I Love Lucy,* had an extensive broadcast career, beginning in radio's Golden Age, when he wrote for Fred Astaire, Jack Benny, Edgar Bergen and Charlie McCarthy, Al Jolson, Rudy Vallee, John Barrymore, and Fanny Brice, among others. His association with Lucille Ball began in 1948, when he signed on as head writer, producer, and director of her radio series, *My Favorite Husband.* After *I Love Lucy* he created and produced such TV series as *Angel, Glynis* (starring Glynis Johns), and *The Debbie Reynolds Show.* His other TV credits include *The General Motors 50th Anniversary Show, Ford Star Time, The U.S. Steel Hour, Get Smart,* and *Bob Hope's Chrysler Theater,* as well as specials for Danny Kaye, Lucille Ball, Bob Hope, and others. He received two Emmy awards and five Emmy nominations, a Sylvania Award, a Michael Award, the Writers' Guild Paddy Chayefsky Laurel Award for Television Achievement, and a Distinguished Service Award from the National Academy of Television Arts and Sciences, serving on the Academy's Board of Governors from 1955 to 1957.

Gregg Oppenheimer began his career as an amateur humorist in 1955, after being introduced by his father to Lucille Ball on the set of *I Love Lucy.* Lucy kneeled down and asked Gregg, then four years old, "Where did you get those big brown eyes?" Gregg's reply: "They came with the face." After a brief stint as a rehearsal cameraman on *The Debbie Reynolds Show,* Gregg left Hollywood and attended the Massachusetts Institute of Technology, receiving a degree in Art and Design, and then the Boalt Hall School of Law at the University of California at Berkeley. Gregg has been a partner in the international law firm of O'Melveny and Myers since 1986. Last January, after completing this book, Gregg decided to give up practicing law in order to pursue writing and other creative endeavors, and to spend more time with his wife, Debbie, and his ten-year-old daughter, Julie.

Contents

Illustrations / ix

Foreword, Gregg Oppenheimer / xiii

Acknowledgments, Gregg Oppenheimer / xv

Preface, Jess Oppenheimer / xvii

1. Baby Boom / 3

2. Look at It This Way . . . / 9

3. Perfect Timing / 22

4. Radio Days / 34

5. The Passports / 46

6. Handcuffs and Other Mishaps / 56

7. Going Hollywood / 74

8. Dancing on the Air / 84

9. The Eyes Have It / 98

10. My Favorite Comedienne / 114

11. The TV Audition / 132

12. Three Cameras or Four? / 148

13. The Ideal Cast / 163

14. Anatomy of a Lucy Script / 180

15. Straight to the Top / 192

16. Lucy Is "Enceinte" / 198

Afterword / 212

Appendixes:

    A.   A Character Is Born / 219

    B.   The Unperformed *I Love Lucy* / 249

    C.   "The Freezer" / 259

    D.   "Vitameatavegamin" / 273

    E.   Compact Disc Contents / 275

    F.   My *Favorite Husband* Outtakes / 279

Index / 281

Illustrations

Jess Oppenheimer directing Lucille Ball in
   My Favorite Husband   *frontispiece*

I Love Lucy, created by Jess Oppenheimer   2

Lucille Ball, Desi Arnaz, Vivian Vance, William Frawley, and
   Hans Conried in "Lucy Hires an English Tutor"   6

Lucille Ball, Gregg Oppenheimer, and Jo Oppenheimer   7

Stella, Jess, and Janice Oppenheimer   11

Fourth grade class portrait   25

James Oppenheimer   29

Harrison Holliway   42

Jess Oppenheimer and Ralph Freud in *The Bat*   60

Jess Oppenheimer in *Judgment Day*   61

Letters from John Steinbeck and James Thurber   70

Letter from Edna Ferber   72

Jess Oppenheimer at typewriter   82

Young and Rubicam Christmas party   86

U.S. Coast Guard group photograph   101

Jess and Estelle Oppenheimer on honeymoon   108

Fanny Brice as Baby Snooks   112

Lucille Ball, Jess Oppenheimer, Madelyn Pugh Davis, and Bob
   Carroll, Jr.   118

Lucille Ball and Richard Denning rehearsing *My Favorite
   Husband*   120

My Favorite Husband advertisement   121

Richard Denning, Jess Oppenheimer, and Lucille Ball with
   Jell-O cake   123

Bea Benaderet and Gale Gordon   125

Page from *My Favorite Husband* script   127

Jess Oppenheimer in control booth   128

Jess Oppenheimer, Edgar Bergen, and Dario Soria   129

First page of *I Love Lucy* audition script   135

Lucille Ball and Desi Arnaz rehearsing *I Love Lucy* audition   137

Jess Oppenheimer and Karl Freund   146

Jess Oppenheimer and William Frawley   149

Flat lighting on *I Love Lucy* set   151

I Love Lucy set and cameras   152

Lucille Ball, Jess Oppenheimer, Karl Freund, Marc Daniels,
    Emily Daniels, Ken Morgan, and Johnny Jacobs   153

Advertisement for *I Love Lucy* premiere   154

Jess Oppenheimer at dress rehearsal   156

Bud Molin and Dann Cahn with "three-headed monster"   158

Jess Oppenheimer, Harry Ackerman, and Hal Hudson   160

"Lucy's Italian Movie"   166

Jess Oppenheimer, Desi Arnaz, and Lucille Ball   167

Lucille Ball in putty nose for "L.A. at Last"   168

Lucille Ball in "The Great Train Robbery"   169

Clowning around on the set   176

Jess Oppenheimer contract, page two   178

Publicity shot for "Ricky Thinks He Is Getting Bald"   182

I Love Lucy writing staff: Jess Oppenheimer, Bob Weiskopf,
    Madelyn Pugh Davis, Bob Schiller, and Bob Carroll, Jr.   186

Lucille Ball, Desi Arnaz, and Jess Oppenheimer at Emmy
    Awards banquet   190

"The Man Behind the Ball" trophy   193

Alfred Lyons, Jess Oppenheimer, Marc Daniels, and
    Milton Biow   199

Monsignor Joseph Devlin, Jess Oppenheimer, Lucille Ball, and
    Desi Arnaz   200

Rerun authorization document   202

Lucille Ball, Jess Oppenheimer, and Desi Arnaz with "So Long
    Till August" cake   203

Jayo Viewer   206
"Vitameatavegamin"   209
Farewell party for Jess Oppenheimer   214
Lucille Ball accepting her "Oppy Award"   214
Lucille Ball kissing Jess Oppenheimer   215

Foreword

GREGG OPPENHEIMER

MY FATHER, Jess Oppenheimer, was a consummate storyteller. Of course, many of his tales are familiar to countless millions of *I Love Lucy* fans all over the world. But successful as he was at writing comedy for radio and television, I think his greatest joy came from hearing friends and acquaintances laugh one at a time as he recounted his stories to them.

And he had a lot of stories to tell—everything from his first encounter with Lucille Ball and the creation of *I Love Lucy* to his experiences with such stars as Jack Benny, Fred Astaire, and Groucho Marx.

I loved listening to and laughing at my father's stories as much as he enjoyed telling them—maybe more. Growing up, I heard them so many times that I knew most of them by heart. But for some reason he always resisted setting them down on paper. Finally, at age seventy-two, after years of urging by family and friends, he began writing his memoirs.

He died in 1988, before the project was completed. After his death, I took eight weeks off from my law practice to go through the six metal filing cabinets full of his notes and papers that still sat in his office in the basement of my mother's house in Brentwood. In a file labeled "Memoirs" I found an eighty-five-page typewritten manuscript, the beginnings of a book. I had seen an earlier version of this manuscript more than a year before, when he had given it to me to edit. That was the only time that we ever collaborated on a writing project, an experience I still cherish. But as I went through his files, I found additional passages that I had never seen before, together with his notes for additional stories—stories that I knew well.

As I dug deeper into his files, I came up with even more treasures: his journal from his 1934 trip around the world; the text of a television comedy writing seminar he gave in 1953; a three-hour-long taped interview that he gave in 1961; the manuscript of an article he wrote about Lucy having TV's first baby; and a one-page typewritten sheet of paper, registered with the Writers' Guild in 1951 for $1.00, containing "an idea for a radio and/or television program incorporating characters named Lucy and Ricky Ricardo." I made a decision then and there—someday I would finish the book my father had started.

Over the next three years I spent much of my spare time accumulating everything that I could find that my father ever wrote or recorded— every interview, every quote in a news clipping, every letter, every magazine article he authored, every radio or TV program, every script. When I decided that I had enough material, together with my memories of his stories, to begin writing in earnest, I obtained permission from my law firm to take a year's leave to complete the project.

When I began, my primary motivation was to share with others the wonderful stories that I had enjoyed all of my life. But as I progressed, I started to see patterns and relationships that I had never noticed before. I gained insight into how my father's experiences shaped his life and his work, and led him to be the unique and remarkable person that he was. Writing this book has been a tremendously rewarding experience for me, and I hope that reading it will be an enjoyable one for you.

Acknowledgments

GREGG OPPENHEIMER

IN THE SEVEN YEARS since I began work on this book, I've accumulated an enormous debt of gratitude to a great many people who helped make it possible.

I am particularly indebted to CBS Entertainment, especially to Marty Garcia, for permission to reproduce the *My Favorite Husband* and *I Love Lucy* scripts, photographs, and audio recordings.

I would like to thank my father's friends Bill Asher, True Boardman, Walter Bunker, Dann Cahn, Sue Chadwick, Saul Chaplin, Eliot Daniel, Ralph Edwards, Mayfair Freud, Charlie Isaacs, Felice Kolda, Mercedes Manzanares, Anne Nelson, Sam Perrin, Austin Peterson, Al Simon, Glenhall Taylor, Pat Weaver, Bob Weiskopf, and the late Jerry Hausner for generously sharing their time and their memories with me. Thanks especially to Norman Tyre, my father's attorney, for giving me access to his correspondence files, which proved to be a valuable resource.

A personal note of thanks to my aunt, Janice Wolk, for sharing her memories of Grandma; and to my uncle, Jack Brown, Steve Sheldon, Graydon Murrell, and everyone else at Rainbo Records, for producing a wonderful CD.

I am grateful to Bart Andrews, whose voluminous research materials, correspondence files, and notes from conversations with my father were a real lifesaver; and also to Tom Watson—both for keeping such good notes of his interviews, and for making them available to me. And I'd like to express my special appreciation to Mike McClay, who generously put his enormous stockpile of *I Love Lucy* photographs at my disposal.

Special thanks to Richard Fliegel, Leslie and Steve Schatzberg, Glenn Padnick, and Owen Olpin for their encouragement and insightful suggestions; to Elsa Cameron for her boundless enthusiasm and help with everything from research to publishing leads; and to Leonard Maltin for his interest, support, and advice along the way.

Thanks also to Tom Gilbert, John and Larry Gassman, Stuart Shostak, Marty Halperin, and Ron Wolf, all of whom gave me invaluable help in the course of my research.

An especially important note of appreciation to my former law partners Warren Christopher, Chuck Bender, and Larry Preble for supporting my request for a sabbatical to pursue this project; and to Dale Cendali for her sage advice on the legal aspects of the book business.

Also deserving of recognition and appreciation are my agents, B. J. Robbins and Ken Sherman, who shared my belief that there was a publishable book here; Bob Thompson at Syracuse University and Robert Mandel at Syracuse University Press, who agreed with them; and Tom Schatz at University of Texas, who not only recommended publication but offered valuable suggestions for improving the manuscript.

My special thanks go to Ming-Lee Chow and Diane Phillips for spending their free time transcribing taped interviews and to Beryl Arbit for her careful proofreading.

I would like to express my sincere appreciation to Stuart Rosen, Trustee of the Edna Ferber Literary Trust, and to Ms. Ferber's great-niece, Julie Gilbert, for permission to reprint the letters from Edna Ferber; to McIntosh and Otis, Inc. and Julie Fallowfield for permission to reprint the letter from John Steinbeck; and to Rosemary Thurber for permission to reprint the letter from James Thurber; to Ron Simon and Ellen O'Neill of the Museum of Television and Radio for permission to reprint my father's essay, "Producing Lucy," first published in the Museum of Television and Radio's 1984 exhibition catalogue, *Lucille Ball: First Lady of Comedy*, from which portions of chapters 11 and 12 were adapted; to the *Hollywood Reporter* for permission to reprint the Dan Jenkins and Leo Guild columns; to *Variety* for permission to reprint the piece by Frank Scully; to Kraft General Foods, Inc. for permission to use the Jell-O commercial and jingle; to John Schneider for the photograph of Harrison Holliway; and especially to Ray Stark, both for his generous efforts on behalf of this project and for permission to reprint *Baby Snooks* dialogue.

And, finally, my special heartfelt thanks to Mom for keeping after Dad to write his memoirs until he finally gave in; to my wife, Debbie, for all her editing help and her willingness to let me read manuscript drafts to her for hours on end; and to my daughter, Julie, now ten years old, who was too young to read when this project began, but who recently called my attention to several grammatical errors in the manuscript.

Preface

JESS OPPENHEIMER

IT WAS A LONG BATTLE, but in the end I lost. My family exacted my solemn promise: I would write my memoir.

I had always resisted writing about my life because I didn't feel that I was important or interesting enough for other people to sit down and read about. Besides, I didn't really have anything in particular to say. My life offers little to inspire or teach anyone. And I certainly have no particularly strong points of view. About as controversial a position as I've ever taken is to support the Golden Rule—under some circumstances.

But I've lived through and been a part of a particularly exciting era: from the start of radio through the development and maturation (of a sort) of television. And I've worked with many people—everyone from Marlene Dietrich to Lucille Ball—who *are* of great interest to the public. So, as a reporter rather than autobiographer, I could see my family's rationale for wanting me to set these things down on paper.

"After all," they kept saying, "you keep telling these stories over and over again, and people seem to enjoy them." It sounded logical enough, but I suspected that part of their motivation was that with a book to refer people to, they would never again have to sit and listen to me.

The first thing I realized after promising to write my memoir was that I didn't know, except in the vaguest way, what the word *memoir* meant. So I looked it up. The dictionary gave me a choice of meanings: either "a narrative composed from personal experience," or "a biography written without special regard for completeness."

Combining parts of both, I pieced together my own personal definition, which made it possible for me to undertake this project: Memoir: An incomplete history of episodes in my life.

A word of warning. Almost everything reminds me of a story. If I were talking to you in person (and when I write, I feel as though I am), I would digress and tell you these stories as they came to mind, which is just what I'll do as this memoir unfolds. My brain works much like a kaleidoscope. Ideas, memories, bits, pieces, stories tumble about and fall into and out of consciousness in no particular order. It is not stream of consciousness, for there is nothing nearly as organized as a stream about it. It might better be called "splash of consciousness."

Which reminds me . . .

Laughs, Luck . . . and Lucy

I LOVE LUCY

Created by Jess Oppenheimer

This is a title of an idea for a radio and/or television program, incorporating characters named Lucy and Ricky Ricardo. He is a Latin-American orchestra leader and singer. She is his wife. They are happily married and very much in love. The only bone of contention between them is her desire to get into show business, and his equally strong desire to keep her out of it. To Lucy, who was brought up in the humdrum sphere of a moderate, well-to-do middle western, mercantile family, show business is the most glamourous field in the world. But Ricky, who was raised in show business, sees none of it's glamour, only it's deficiencies, and yearns to be an ordinary citizen, keeping regular hours and living a normal life. As show business is the only way he knows to make a living, and he makes a very good one, the closest he can get to this dream is having a wife who's out of show business and devotes herself to keeping as nearly a normal life as possible for him.

The first story concerns a TV audition for Ricky, where Pepito, the clown, due to an accident, fails to appear and Lucy takes his place for the show. Although she does a bang-up job she forgoes the chance at a career that is offered her in order to keep Ricky happy and closer to his dream of normalcy.

Baby Boom

ON JANUARY 19, 1953, Lucille Ball gave birth to two baby boys. One was born in the morning in Los Angeles and the other that night, three thousand miles away in New York City. If that isn't amazing enough in itself, try this—one of the babies was conceived eight months before it was born, but the pregnancy lasted only six weeks! I'm referring, of course, to the television baby born to Lucy and Ricky Ricardo.

Of Lucy's two sons, I've always felt a closer kinship with Little Ricky Ricardo. Although I can't claim to be his father, I feel I'm responsible for his being here.

As producer and head writer of *I Love Lucy*, I was well acquainted with the public's great fascination for all things "Lucy." But I was totally unprepared for the overwhelming reaction that met the new arrivals in the Ricardo and Arnaz households. The TV birth of Little Ricky on CBS was watched by an incredible forty-four million viewers—fifteen million more than would tune in President Eisenhower's inauguration the next day on *all three* networks. And when Lucy delivered Desiderio Alberto Arnaz y de Acha IV by Caesarean section at 8:15 on that Monday morning, the news was immediately flashed over every news service. Programs were interrupted. It was announced in schools. Seven minutes after Lucy had her baby, it was announced over the radio in Japan—and in many other countries where they had never even seen *I Love Lucy*. Somehow, they were interested.

I wasn't about to wait for news bulletins. I had arranged with Desi Arnaz to phone me at home from the hospital with progress reports. At 7:45 A.M., when Desi called to let me know that Lucy was about to go into the operating room, I asked him to leave the line open so I could be the first to hear the news.

As I sat there in the kitchen, waiting for word from Desi, I started

thinking about how far we'd come with *I Love Lucy*, and how unbelievably lucky we'd been at every step along the way. It seemed incredible
that it had only been eighteen short months since all of us had plunged
headlong into the brand new business of television. We were an eager
and innocent crew, embarking on a trip in a medium about which we
knew nothing. None of us had any inkling of the high-flying success that
lay ahead. We all were just deliriously knocking ourselves out to put the
show on the air each week. What's more, we loved the work—none of
us could wait to get to the set or to the typewriter.

Luck. There was no doubt about it. The show had been singularly
blessed with unbelievably good luck from the very moment of its concep-
tion. Somehow, the perfect group of special talents had just happened to
be available and in the right spot at precisely the right time in history
for this particular project. From the first reading of the first script, it was
apparent that the kind of material that we most easily and naturally
created was right on the button with the entire cast's sense of humor,
and they were able to perform it brilliantly with a minimum of effort.

From the initial performance of *I Love Lucy* before the cameras, there
had been magic in the air. The audience had fallen in love at first sight,
and they acted like giddy lovers, indeed. Once the spell was cast, laughing at the jokes wasn't enough for them. They soon started laughing at
the straight lines, and then at any line, as long as it came from this
particular cast. More than once I'd seen "Good morning. How are you?"
knock them right into the aisles. It was the audience's way of saying "I
love you."

Of course, the most important piece of magic was Lucy herself. Her
radiant talent, her wonderful combination of beauty and clown, her sure
touch for the human quality, which found recognition in every segment
of the viewing audience, were the sparks that gave life to the entire
series. She was truly one of a kind, and I thanked my lucky stars that our
paths had crossed when they did.

That had been in the summer of 1948, when Harry Ackerman at CBS
Radio asked me to write a script for the network's new, unsponsored radio
sitcom, *My Favorite Husband*, starring Lucille Ball. Upon accepting the
assignment I had made what turned out to be a fortuitous decision. In
My Favorite Husband Lucy played a "gay, sophisticated," socialite wife of
a bank vice president—quite the opposite of the character I had been
writing for Fanny Brice on her *Baby Snooks* radio program. Instead of
sticking to the pattern set in the previous episodes, I decided to make
Lucy's character more like Snooks—less sophisticated, more childlike
and impulsive—taking Lucy and the show in a new direction, with

broad, slapstick comedy. Lucy took to her new role like a fish to water. Harry signed me as the show's head writer, producer, and director, and we were well on our way to *I Love Lucy*.

Had Harry called me at any other time during the previous five years, I would have had to say no because of my writing chores on the *Baby Snooks* program. But a salary dispute between Fanny and the network had unexpectedly forced *Baby Snooks* off the air just a few months before. So, as luck would have it, I was available when Harry's call came.

Even Lucy's unexpected pregnancy at the end of our first television season had been a stroke of luck, although at the time it had seemed to spell the end of the series. I had learned of Lucy's impending motherhood just as we were about to begin rehearsals for one of the last shows of the season. Desi had entered the soundstage and, without saying a word, he had come over, put his arm around my shoulder, and walked me off the set and over to my office so we could be alone. I could see from his expression that whatever the news, it could only be bad.

Swallowing hard, Desi said, "We just came from the doctor. Lucy's going to have a baby." Pleased as he and Lucy were about having another child, both of them were certain that it meant that *I Love Lucy* would have to go off the air. The cardinal rule of those who controlled the new medium of television was not to present anything that might offend anyone. The CBS censor had a list of words that could never be uttered on the air, and "pregnant" was one of them. Of course, today we can not only say the word "pregnant" on TV, but also make graphic reference to all the various organs, equipment, and procedures that contribute to that condition—or lack of it. It's hard to imagine that simply putting a pregnant woman on television could ever have been considered daring. But in the early 1950s, the very thought of a TV show dealing with as real an idea as having a baby was simply unheard of. To Lucy and Desi, it looked as though they would have to quit TV just as they had reached the top.

As the show's head writer and producer, I was the one who had to decide how to save *I Love Lucy*.

"What can we do, Jess?" Desi asked. "How long will we have to be off the air?"

Without thinking twice, I grabbed his hand and shook it. "Congratulations," I said. "This is wonderful! This is just what we need to give us excitement in our second season. Lucy Ricardo will have a baby, too!"

Desi was incredulous. "We can't do that on television!" he declared. "The network and the sponsor will never let us get away with it."

"Sure they will, if we present it properly," I told him. "What better

In "Lucy Hires an English Tutor," we had Lucy arrange for an elocution expert (Hans Conried, *center*) to teach the Ricardos and the Mertzes correct English, so that her baby would be raised in the proper vocal environment.

thing is there for married couples in the audience to identify with than having a baby?"

Desi finally agreed that it was worth a try, and ran off to tell Lucy the news that she was going to have *two* babies. But as soon as the door closed behind him, I started wondering if I shouldn't have thought twice before making that decision. The responsibility of doing a series of shows on such a delicate theme, in such an intimate medium, with a star who was actually pregnant, was staggering. And maybe Desi was right about the sponsor and the network. After all, they had already made it clear to us that the Ricardos, though married, were not even allowed to share a double bed!

I quickly called a conference with my cowriters, Madelyn Pugh and Bob Carroll, Jr. The three of us sat in my office for hours, discussing every angle of the problem. We finally decided that although it had never been

Lucy with my son, Gregg, and daughter, Jo,
on the set of *I Love Lucy*.

done before, we were prepared to tackle it. We felt certain that we could extract all the inherent humor from the situation while staying well within the bounds of good taste.

And now, eight months later, I was satisfied that we had succeeded in doing just that.

As I sat there still holding the phone, a sobering thought suddenly hit me. Television, still in its own infancy, was about to give birth to its first baby, and *I* was responsible not only for its being born, but also for the way in which it would be brought up. Of course, I was not altogether

without experience on this score—my own two young children, asleep
upstairs, were proof of that—but unlike what went on in the Oppenheimer household, the decisions that I made about the upbringing of Little
Ricky Ricardo would be seen and judged by tens of millions of people
every week.

As the minutes ticked by, my thoughts reached back to my own
childhood in San Francisco, a chapter in my life that had laid the first
solid brick on the road to *I Love Lucy*. Of one thing I was sure—the
childhood that I would write for Little Ricky would be very different
from mine.

Look at It This Way . . .

I AM FIRMLY CONVINCED that having some kind of serious maladjustment in childhood that gives you an offbeat slant on life is one of the most important prerequisites for a comedy writer. If you are completely integrated, well-adjusted and happy—if you accept the commonplace as commonplace—then there's simply nothing funny in it. On the other hand, I can tell you, based on my own experience, that if you can't quite conform, if you don't feel exactly the way everyone else feels, then everything that other people do can take on a sort of ridiculousness.

Equipped with the requisite offbeat point of view, a comedy writer can find humor even in the unlikeliest of situations. My favorite example involved Lester White, a veteran comedy writer for Bob Hope and others, who died of cancer a few years ago at Cedars-Sinai Hospital in Los Angeles. After lengthy treatment, Lester's doctor finally visited him in his room one day and gave him the grim prognosis: the doctor could not predict how long Lester had to live—he could go at any moment.

"I'm sorry Les," the doctor concluded. "All we can do is try to make you as comfortable as possible for your remaining time."

After the doctor left, as Lester sat in his room contemplating his fate, a nurse entered to take his vital signs. This particular nurse happened to be extremely heavy; she must have weighed at least three hundred pounds. Lester just stared at her as she moved around the room, busying herself with taking his temperature, checking his blood pressure, refilling his pitcher of ice water, and fluffing his pillow. Her chores done, she stood at the foot of the bed and addressed Lester. "Is there anything else I can do for you, Mr. White?"

Lester looked at the enormously fat nurse standing before him and said, "For God's sake—*don't sing.*"

Another comedy writer with his own point of view is Milt Josefsberg, who wrote for Jack Benny and many other comedy greats. During writing sessions Milt would sometimes pace back and forth to get his thoughts together. In one session Milt got so wrapped up in his thinking and pacing that he paced right out the door and disappeared. The rest of us continued working. After several minutes, Milt suddenly walked back in and announced excitedly, "Hey, I had a great idea while you guys were out of the room!"

Growing up in San Francisco in the 1920s, my own particular "point of view" was decidedly offbeat: I always saw *two* of everything, and the positions of the two images were constantly changing in relation to each other. What's worse, it wasn't until I was almost thirty years old that I discovered I had double vision. Or perhaps I should say that I discovered that other people had *single* vision. I had never seen third dimension— never perceived depth, and my equilibrium was practically nonexistent. But I struggled through life on the assumption that other people saw things exactly the same way I did.

On Tuesday evenings my sister Janice and I were expected to dry the dishes after supper. When I held a dish in one hand and wiped it with a dish towel in a circular motion, the whole room spun and shifted in a confusing, then dizzying, then sickening manner. I quickly became physically ill, and it showed. My mother asked me if I was sick. When I told her I was, she instructed me to lie down for a while. A few minutes later my sister realized that she was still doing the dishes by herself, while I was lolling around on the sofa. She demanded that my mother check to see if I was still sick. Of course, by this time I was feeling much better, and I told her so. This resulted in my being marched back to the kitchen and the whirling dish towel, where I quickly got sick again. I soon learned that the thing to do was to tell my mother I was still sick, even though I wasn't. It was much more comfortable that way, even though my sister branded me a malingerer. To me, lying had become a matter of survival.

I found it impossible to look anyone in the eye. When I was talking to someone, my eyes would be darting around the room, stopping for a moment, but only for a moment, on the person's eyes, then off around the landscape again. That was all my eye muscles would allow without the pain becoming so intense that tears would flow. I was well aware that I was not looking at the person I was talking to, and that he probably thought I was shifty-eyed (which I was), and most likely dishonest. This self-consciousness would in turn often result in a mental block, causing me acute embarrassment because of my seeming stupidity.

Unfortunately, my mother's sole test for honesty was "Look me in the

Mother took my sister, Janice, and me to a San Francisco
photographer's studio for this family portrait in 1914.

eye and tell me that." I, of course, either could not look her in the eye,
or, if I forced myself to, the pain would cause tears to stream down my
cheeks and she would take *that* as an admission of guilt. Other children
soon caught on to the fact that I was unable to appear anything but
guilty, and they gleefully blamed all their misdeeds on me. I think I can
safely say I held the record in my neighborhood for receiving undeserved
punishment.

I always knew I had some kind of physical problem—I just didn't
know what it was. My parents did their best to help. They took me to
doctors—eye doctors and general doctors and internists—because of my

getting nauseated so easily. After the examination the doctor would invariably pat me on the head and say I was a good strong boy with nothing organic the matter with me, and that I should get more sun and not worry so much. Even the eye doctors. One of my eyes, they would tell me, tested 20/20 and the other, even better, 20/10. And that would be that.

My double vision made it almost impossible for me to do the things that were second nature to the other kids, such as riding a bicycle. After a long period of time trying, I managed to ride, but only if I was moving rapidly and in a straight line. And I was never able to master one little maneuver that all the other fellows at school handled with consummate ease—riding a bike between the uprights of a basketball backboard. The uprights were almost four feet apart, but nine times out of ten I ran into one of them instead of going through. To me, there appeared to be four uprights instead of two, which made *three* possible passageways, all constantly moving in relation to one another, and I had no ability to choose the right one, or even to get one to stand still.

Baseball was no different. When a hit came to me in the outfield (I could never play the infield, and the other kids let me play outfield only when no other player could be found), it started from the bat, then appeared to become *two* balls, and at this point I had to look away. Somehow I developed an uncanny ability to judge a baseball's trajectory without looking at it, so I could go to the place where it would land. When the ball came down, I was always right there—and always missed it.

Because of my vision problem and the emotional disturbances it caused me, practically every social instinct I had as a child was wrong. My actions and reactions just didn't fit into the pattern of behavior that everyone else seemed to have programmed into him from birth. Like a flight of birds suddenly swerving this way and diving that without upsetting formation, the neighborhood kids all seemed to know, God knows how, what to do and when to do it. They were truly members of a group. Not I. I could as well have been from Mars!

They didn't like me. They didn't want me around. And they told me so without hesitation. For fun, they used to tie my hands and feet and leave me, accompanied by several cats and dogs, lying in a dark, dusty coal bin for the afternoon. From their point of view, I had it coming to me. I was a self-centered, unsharing little brat. I was defensive and sarcastic. I was also bright. I delighted in telling others they were wrong and then proving it. Knowing from experience that I would need ammunition for future arguments, I carefully inventoried all the weak points of everyone I knew, and worked them into carefully worded phrases calculated to inflict the most pain.

For my part, I just couldn't understand why the kids didn't want to be around a sweet, wonderful person like me. Only because of my ability to make the other kids laugh was I eventually able to regain some contact with them.

Why I didn't become a bitter misanthrope, institutionalized for acting out my problem in some socially unacceptable manner, I'll never know. Instead of humor, I could just as easily have turned toward violence or crime to get even with society. Except for one fortunate fact: I was a resolute coward.

If I had been equipped to compete physically—if I could have bullied someone or beaten someone up—it might have been a different story. But I was unable to fight anyone and win. For openers, in a fight I always faced odds (at least visually) of two against one, and I was so hopelessly befuddled trying to make some sense out of the kaleidoscopic visual confusion that I might just as well have had my hands tied behind my back. What's worse, I had a total inability to keep gazing at one spot while things moved across it. When I got in a fight I would watch the other boy's fists. God help me if he swung and missed, for as his one fist went by, my head would turn with it, and I would soon feel his other one. This was often the last thing I felt (or saw) for some time afterward.

I worked at improving my relationships with others by studying their behavior to find out what was acceptable to the group. Then when I later found myself in a familiar situation, I would have to overpower my instinctive reaction (which was usually bitter and antisocial), and instead I would literally "act out" what I had learned by watching others. This allowed me to survive, but it had another effect as well—it made me a more than casual observer of human behavior, something that would pay off later in my writing career.

Then one day I made a monumental discovery. I had the ability to make the other kids laugh! So I began to play the fool, and they accepted me on that basis. Before long I developed the habit of taking *everything* that was said or done and seeing if I could somehow use it to get a laugh. Little by little, with increasing skill, my every waking moment saw my brain taking in everything I heard or read and testing it for comedy content: turning each phrase first this way and then that to see if any other meanings or relationships would reveal themselves, reversing the first letters of the words, reversing the order of the words, and examining it to see if I could play back on it in any possible manner. Even as a young boy I became quite adept at this, and I was usually rewarded with surprise and some degree of admiration by my schoolmates, those "normal" listeners to whom words and their meanings were simply ways to express an idea and who did not—and indeed had no reason to—look at any other relationships between them.

But I still had a lesson to learn in connection with my newfound avenue to social success, and in the thrill of succeeding where there had always been failure I almost destroyed myself before I learned it. I am speaking, of course, of restraint, for if nothing scores like success, nothing bores like excess. A seeker after humorous relationships can easily come up with something, some play on words, every few seconds. The first few attempts may bring laughs. Keeping up the same rate of effort will find those laughs turning to tolerant groans, acknowledging that the effort is recognized, but the quality is not the best. To survive, the would-be humorist must be sensitive to the fine line between the amused groan and the snarling growl. Without such sensitivity, he will be forever doomed to wooing, amusing, and finally repelling group after group for life.

In show business parlance, this is called "not knowing how to get off." I'm reminded of a piano recital I once attended. One little girl was doing fine until she approached the end of her piece, when, instead of going into the last phrase of the music, her fingers took her from the end of the next-to-last phrase back to the beginning of that same phrase. She played at tempo and hit the notes correctly, but she couldn't keep from repeating that next-to-last phrase over and over again. Finally, she cried in anguish to her mother, who was seated in the first row, "Mommy! I don't know how to stop!" and ran crying off the stage.

The memory of all the groups I must have alienated with all of my "off the cuff" remarks has mercifully dimmed over the years, but I do recall a turning point. On this particular occasion I was not my usual "trying to be funny" self for the very good reason that I was coming down with yellow jaundice (hepatitis, as it is called in modern times). I sat glumly without opening my mouth for most of the evening, only speaking once, when an opportunity fell on my ears that was so golden I couldn't let it go by, even in my misery. It was hilariously received. People recalled it and remarked on it later that evening, and I was complimented on it for weeks, both by those who were there and those who had been told of it. The remark itself has long since left me, but not the lesson. I had made *one* humorous remark all evening and was considered a wit. That had never happened before. On the many previous evenings during

which I had made *many* humorous remarks, along with a good number of
not so humorous ones, the best compliment that had come my way was
"Oh, for Christ's sake, Jess—Shut up!"

I've analyzed this "staying on too long and trying too hard" syndrome
many times and with great sympathy over the years: great sympathy not
for the audience, which is being subjected to a barrage of increasingly
inferior material, but for the poor soul who is sinking into a quicksand of
his own making. His one aim is to be considered funny. Once he has
passed the point of no return, where he begins to get on people's nerves
instead of entertaining them, it is imperative to his frail ego that he not
leave them that way. He must score once more. He has to leave them
laughing. He is desperate, and humor was never born of desperation.

I take that back. If you can point out your own desperation and get
the audience on your side, you have a chance. I recall a *Tonight Show* on
which George Gobel was the guest star. Johnny Carson was just about to
bring him on—in fact, he had already introduced him—when Bob
Hope, who was recording across the hall, wandered onstage unexpectedly.
Hope stayed on, chatting with Carson for half an hour or so. Carson then
explained that he wanted to introduce Gobel, who had been waiting all
this time. At the end of the introduction Dean Martin, who was also
rehearsing that night, came on instead of Gobel. Again a half hour of
banter between Hope, Martin, and Carson, at which point Carson insisted on bringing Gobel on, pointing out to the others that, after all,
Gobel was the star he had booked that night.

Gobel came on, and from the minute he set foot onstage, everything
went against him. His timing was off. His lines didn't go over. The only
funny thing that emerged was that he couldn't be funny. But he won the
audience over completely and saved the day when, after one of his jokes
bombed, he turned to Carson and said, "Did you ever feel like the whole
world was a tuxedo and you were a pair of brown shoes?"

Of course, Gobel was a professional who knew from experience that
he could gain favor by pointing out his failure, a position the failing
amateur wouldn't think of taking.

When I was a producer at NBC, I once produced a special live program
plugging the upcoming season, on which Gobel was one of the guest
stars. As I stood in the wings, I saw Gobel walk up to Bob Cummings,
who was waiting to make an entrance. After the two of them watched
the action on the monitor for a few seconds, Gobel pulled out a bottle
and offered Cummings a drink. Cummings told Gobel, "No thanks. I'm
on next."

"Do you mean to tell me," Gobel asked with alarm, "that you go out there *alone?*"

•   •   •

I was terribly competitive in school. This only added to my misery, because I was a rotten student. Because of my eyes, I had an awful time trying to concentrate on my studies for any length of time. I couldn't read the material, so I developed all sorts of tricks to get the information I needed from other students who, I knew, had studied well and had it down pat. I would approach one of them and engage him in conversation about the subject we were studying, deliberately taking a false position and holding adamantly to it. In trying to convince me that I was wrong, he would give me most of the information I needed.

In class, whenever the teacher would pose a problem for us, I was always the first one to shout out the wrong answer. It wasn't that I was dumb; I understood *how* to do it, but I was just so eager to get there first that I'd always make some silly little mistake.

My mother, who thought I was the brightest, most wonderful boy in the world, always said that the only problem was my lack of "stick-to-itiveness." And apparently my teachers agreed with her. When I was in the third grade, Professor Lewis Terman of Stanford University, who developed the Stanford-Binet IQ test, was beginning his landmark long-term study of "gifted" children. He asked all of the third grade teachers at our school to send their brightest students to be interviewed for the study. They were looking for children with IQs over 140. The girl who was sent from my class didn't qualify, so they asked for the next brightest candidate, and my teacher chose me. I found out years later that I barely squeaked by with a score of 141.

The discovery that I had a high IQ didn't do me any good at all. It just meant that my mother now expected even more from me—and I was deficient already as far as she was concerned. And it added to my own frustration. If I was so bright, I wondered, then why couldn't I get along better with people?

I used to talk to Professor Terman about my problems and he had the same reaction that all the other doctors had. He'd listen to me, and when it wasn't anything he could put together out of the textbooks he just advised me to wait it out and not to worry so much.

But as I progressed through school, things just got worse. I did so badly at Lowell High, the academic high school in San Francisco, that my mother became concerned that I wasn't going to be able to graduate.

Now, my mother was determined that I should attend college, so she decided to do something about it.

There was a private school for boys in San Francisco at the time, called Bates School. (In a most unfortunate juxtaposition of words, the headmaster's stationery read "Headmaster—Bates School," which always killed me.) My mother had heard that Bates School *guaranteed* that every boy enrolled there would graduate with passing grades. So she made an appointment for an interview.

After she was shown into the headmaster's office and introductions were made, she got down to business. "I want my son to graduate," she told him. "I want him to go to college. How much would it cost to come here?" To her surprise, he replied, "Well, it depends. Which college would he want to go to?"

"What do you mean?"

"Well, if you want me to guarantee him grades that will get him into San Mateo Junior College, that will be one thing. But grades that would get him into an Ivy League college would cost quite a bit more."

After consulting the family education budget, my mother chose a middle ground, and came to an agreement with the headmaster regarding my college aspirations. Sure enough, one year later I somehow managed to graduate from Bates School, with grades just good enough to get me into the University of San Francisco.

•   •   •

In the middle of my first year at the University of San Francisco, I asked Professor Terman to help me transfer to Stanford. The professor wrote a letter to the admissions committee, informing them that I was in his "gifted children" study (the "Termites," as we were called), and that my academic work so far didn't really represent my grade-getting abilities. This did the trick, and I transferred to Stanford at the beginning of my sophomore year.

When I got to Stanford, I tried to write for the Stanford newspaper, the Stanford magazine, and every other organization that involved any writing, but none of them would have me. I majored in social sciences, taking such classes as psychology, German, American history, and economics. But I still couldn't concentrate on my studies. Sometimes I couldn't even concentrate on where I was walking. One spring afternoon during my junior year, daydreaming as I crossed the campus, I walked into the street without even realizing it. I was hit (or I should say bumped) by a car, which, fortunately, was going only two or three miles an hour at the time. Upon impact, which caused me to stumble, the driver slammed on the brakes, stopped, and got out to inquire if I was all right. As I picked myself up and assured him that I was uninjured, I realized that I was addressing President Herbert Hoover! The former president had returned to his alma mater after his defeat by FDR the previous November. It was without a doubt my most memorable experience at Stanford.

•   •   •

During my high school years I had a friend named Mort Werner. A blond dynamo with a large assortment of talents, he would later become programming chief at NBC-TV, but in high school his main interest was music. He sang and played the piano, but he was also good at business and things like radio repair. While in high school he had his own radio repair shop, a real store on Clement Street from which he had an income that would have supported a man with a family. By the time I was at Stanford Mort was a professional performer, singing and accompanying himself on the piano on radio station KFRC in San Francisco.

I was an avid radio fan, especially of comedy and variety programs, but I had never actually been inside a broadcasting studio. Listening at home, each time I heard the mellifluous tones of KFRC's announcer informing the world that he was speaking from "K-F-R-C, San Francisco," I visualized him in the most posh, luxurious, tasteful surroundings imaginable. At the beginning of one summer vacation Mort invited me to come down to KFRC and visit him. I eagerly accepted his invitation. Finally I would be able to get behind the scenes and experience the glamour of the station itself.

Entering the Don Lee Cadillac Building, which housed a car dealership as its main function and the radio studios as kind of an afterthought, I asked the telephone operator where I could find Mort. She told me to go to the second floor and she would call ahead. The second floor housed the radio station. Posh it wasn't. A high-class garage, yes. I could see a raised platform with about one hundred folding chairs in front of it. There was a carpet under this small section, but beyond it the bare concrete floor stretched a hundred feet or so to the wall, through which a series of floor-to-ceiling windows looked down onto busy Van Ness Avenue.

Mort appeared, and I asked him where the studio was. He waved his hand in an expansive gesture. "This is it," he said. "That platform is where we do the *Blue Monday Jamboree.*" *Blue Monday Jamboree* was the station's biggest hit, a two-hour musical comedy variety show that aired coast-to-coast every Monday night after the news. I was one of its biggest fans.

Unfortunately for me it was a Saturday and rehearsals for *Blue Monday Jamboree* did not take place until the day of the show. But Harrison Holliway, the show's creator and emcee, happened to be there, and I had the great thrill of being introduced to him. Then Mort showed me around the rest of the studios—a series of drab rooms of varying sizes, ranging from little more than a closet for the news announcer to a quite sizable studio for broadcasts with a large cast. Each studio had a control booth, which could be seen through a plate glass window in the wall.

There was only one program, a dramatic half hour, originating at the station that afternoon, and we arrived at the largest studio just in time to watch the last couple of minutes of the dress rehearsal. It didn't make much sense out of context. As we opened the door to the control room I heard a tremendous, crunching, tearing, ripping crash, like the biggest auto accident that had ever happened. Then the music rose to a finish, there was a commercial and end credits, and everyone got up and left. Mort explained that they would come back in an hour or so to do the show on the air. I asked him if he could introduce me to some of the actors when they came back, but Mort told me that he had to leave in just a few minutes. I was afraid I wouldn't get to see any shows being done, but he assured me that if I wanted to, I could sit quietly in a corner of the studio and watch.

Before he left, Mort showed me around the studio we were in. Everyone connected with the program was either in his dressing room making final preparations for the show, or across the street getting a drink, which, for many, was their way of making final preparations. I was most fascinated when we got to the corner of the studio from which the sound effects man had worked his magic. I hit a thunder sheet, opened and closed a door, and raised and lowered a board with twenty or thirty little wood blocks hanging down from it, which sounded like an army walking by. Mort even let me play around with the cueing device for playing the sound effects that come on phonograph records. A lever, which gently lowers the needle, was securely locked in place directly over the spot on the record where the needle was to be placed down. Even if the turntable were bumped, the needle would not budge. The sound effects man would hold the record stationary on the revolving turntable and use the lever to lower the needle onto the desired track a few seconds before the cue was to be heard. Then, at precisely the correct moment, he would release the record, which would start to spin and play the sound effect.

Mort showed me the record that was on the turntable. According to the label, it had quite a few effects recorded on it. One side was a graduated series of crashes ranging from the "Auto Off Cliff" effect that we had just heard, all the way down to "Auto Into Wall, 5mph." I took the record off the turntable and looked at the flip-side label. This side had a series of sounds made by different means of transportation at various speeds, from "Motorcycles and Autos" to "Airplanes and Steamboats." After looking at the magical disc for a few seconds more, I put it back on the turntable.

Mort tucked me into a safe corner of the studio and left. I should have called home and left word that I would be late for dinner, but I was afraid to leave my spot for fear I would not be allowed back again. So I spent most of the next hour trying to figure out the best way to get around my mother, who I knew would probably have the police and National Guard out looking for me by the time I got home.

A few minutes before airtime the cast, orchestra, and technicians began sauntering in. At the appointed hour, the program took the air. I was fascinated. The melodramatic story moved inexorably toward its climax. The hero was a father who was intent on killing himself. He wanted his insurance money to pay for an operation that would restore his blind daughter's sight. Speeding toward a hairpin turn high on a mountain, he was hysterically calling out his speed—seventy—eighty—ninety miles an hour. The violins were screeching out *agitato*. Suddenly, the most awful thought struck numbness to my bones. When the sound man came back to do the show, he had no way of knowing anyone had disturbed his equipment. Suppose he had the sound effects record cued to "Auto Off Cliff" when he left, and assumed it was still that way when he returned? I hadn't even paid attention to which side was up when I replaced it. "Oh my God," I thought, "When the time comes for the crash, what if he lowers the needle, and all we hear is a steamship whistle?"

My heart, already pounding in response to the show's building drama, was now trying to hammer its way out of my chest in expectation of the shambles that might follow when he lowered the needle. There would be no way to recover from it, no way to explain it away or even to play it late. The crash, I knew from the dress rehearsal, was the very last moment of the show, followed only by music and credits!

I considered making my way over to the sound effects man and asking him if he had double-checked the record, but by then it was too late. The music was already two octaves higher than when it had started. The whole scene, on mike and off, built in dramatic intensity until, suddenly, the music cut out, the actor gave a throat-tearing scream, and after a delay long enough to make the audience appreciate the height of the cliff, the sound man released the record, and we heard . . . the crash of "Auto Off Cliff"!

Good old "Auto Off Cliff"! It was like a reprieve to a prisoner on death row. I sat trembling in the studio, drenched in sweat, until long after everyone else had left. My first "behind-the-scenes" experience in radio had made an unforgettable impression on me.

Perfect Timing

I REMEMBER MY FIRST RADIO. It was a crystal set my father bought for me in 1921, when I was seven years old. The tiny set, mounted on a board, had a little universal joint with a handle on it, which was used to manipulate a fine wire called a cat's whisker. Touching the end of the cat's whisker to different points on the crystal miraculously tuned in different stations. The crystal, which looked like a little craggy rock, yielded one local station when the cat's whisker caressed the bottom of one of its little valleys, and a different one when it rested halfway up the side of a hill, a quarter of an inch away. My biggest thrill was the unexpected moment when a spot that had consistently brought in nothing from repeated contacts suddenly delivered a station from some exotic, far distant place, such as Lodi or Watsonville, California, more than a hundred miles away. That may not sound like much to today's sophisticated audience, but to me it was breathtaking. Columbus's excitement upon sighting a landfall of the New World was as nothing compared to the thrill I got from tuning in an unknown station.

I listened to Ernie Jones and Billy Hare—the "Happiness Boys"—and Charlie Hamp at the piano. I had permanently bright red ears from the pressure of the earphones, which were made more for utility than for comfort. If the loudspeaker had not been invented there would have been an entire generation of Americans with cauliflower ears caused by those cruel little head clamps that talked. But I happily bore it with gritted teeth and throbbing lobes, spending the entire time the station was on the air—perhaps two hours a day in those days—seated at the torture rack.

I can still remember how I cried and carried on during the election campaign of 1924, just before my eleventh birthday. Vacuum tubes had been invented by then, and radios were being manufactured on a large scale. I had bought myself a one-tube set, still with earphones. When my father learned that for the first time in history the politicians were to broadcast their speeches, he commandeered my radio for the duration of the campaign. It was utterly unbelievable to him that millions of voters could sit in their homes and actually hear what the candidates had to say, *in their own voices,* instead of having to read about it in the paper the next day, after it had been filtered through someone else's reactions. I was particularly upset because this was a set I had bought for myself, with my own money, and I seriously questioned a justice system that would let someone else appropriate it—even my own father.

At the time I purchased the set, I was the recipient of an allowance of ten cents a week from my parents. The story of how I got enough money to buy the radio, an amount I could not have put by had I saved twice my entire allowance since the day I was born, is a tale in itself.

Every afternoon after school I went to the Julius Kahn Playground, built within the walls of the Presidio, a huge army reservation near my home in San Francisco. My mission was to learn to play tennis, a game at which I was particularly awful.

I soon found a much more exciting substitute. Each afternoon the older boys held a crap game in the woods behind the playground. I spent most of my time watching them. I was not yet ten years old, and just the sight of such high stakes (the opening bet was ten or fifteen cents) had me gasping. The ground was sandy, and every three or four rolls the dice would land so that no side was definitely up. Someone would yell "Cocked dice!" and after a short argument from a player who thought he should have won, they would have to be thrown again.

One afternoon on my way home I found a flat board about two feet square in someone's garbage can. That night, using another piece of wood, I built up walls on three sides of it, leaving the fourth side open so the dice could be thrown onto the board. My mother gave me a piece of green felt she had lying around, not bothering to ask me what I wanted it for (or this story would have ended then and there). I cemented the felt to the top surface of the bottom board, and after school the following day I carried it down to the playground. When the boys went out into the woods, I went with them. No one asked me what the board was for. In fact, no one even noticed it—or me, for that matter. The first time there was a call of "Cocked dice," I put my board down on the ground and said, "Why don't you use this to shoot on?" There were a couple of remarks such as "Hey, great," and "Thanks, kid." Then I was quickly forgotten, standing once again on the outside edge of the crowd, trying to peek under elbows, over shoulders, and between legs to see what was going on. But I didn't hear any more calls of "Cocked dice," and I felt well rewarded.

Then one of the biggest of the boys stopped playing and looked around until he found me jumping up and down trying to get a glimpse of the action. He came over to me and said, "You build the board?"

I nodded.

"Pretty good."

"Thanks."

"Why don't you hold the game?"

"Whataya mean?"

"Well, it's your board, so if a guy makes three passes he has to give you what he bet on the first pass."

"He wouldn't do that."

"Sure he would. He bets ten cents, then twenty cents, then forty cents. He's got eighty cents—he won't mind giving you a dime. Look, kid, how about I make sure they pay, and you and I split everything?"

So I entered into my first business partnership, and it was successful indeed. I was making six or seven dollars a day. I never figured out where the kids got all the money they were betting, but I could see that eventually it had to end up in my, and my partner's, pockets. It was some of this money that I later used to buy the radio. Trusting no one and unwilling to part with my rapidly growing bankroll for even a moment, I carried it with me in the pocket of my brown corduroy knickers. Paper money was much larger in those days, and soon my "roll" was so large that if I reached in my pocket and grasped it, I couldn't draw my hand out. For those few occasions when I needed to take the money out, I developed a technique of turning my pocket inside out and forcing the wad of bills out with the lining.

Life was lovely, and my little business, composed of only upside potential, was thriving. There was no way I could lose unless I gambled, and fortunately I had no desire to do that. Then, one afternoon, as I was about to leave for the playground, my mother asked me if I had change for a dollar. She was on her way downtown by streetcar. The fare was only a nickel each way, but sometimes the conductors got huffy when you asked them to change a bill. I carried what change I had in the same pocket as my "wad," so I had to remove that first.

More than sixty years have passed, but I haven't forgotten even one detail of the look on my mother's face when she saw my pocket give birth to a roll of bills that would have supported our family for six months.

That's me in the center, with the white shirt and tie.
The other kids might not have liked me, but I was the
only one in the fourth grade making $30 a week holding a
floating crap game after school.

Her reaction was awesome to behold. She didn't know what horrible crime I had committed, but bank robbery was the least of what she suspected. She hollered. She cried. She fell into a chair as though someone had poleaxed her. She was a failure. I was a failure. Wait until my father found out. Where had she gone wrong? I must give it back immediately.

This went on and on until she tired out enough for me to explain where the money came from and how it would be impossible to give it back, because it had come in, a nickel and a dime at a time, from an awful lot of different people. When she had relaxed to a frenzy, she made me swear I would never go near that crap game again. Even though I immediately promised, she lectured me for another hour and then hustled me off to the bank to open a savings account.

Things turned out very differently that afternoon for my playground "clients." While my mother and I were at the bank, the police raided the game. The entire group was hauled down to the station, booked, and locked up, to be released only to the custody of their parents.

My father, at my mother's insistence, gave me a severe talking-to about the dangers of gambling when he got home that evening. But in spite of his stern expression and the seriousness of his lengthy lecture, I could see in his eyes that there was a certain aspect of this episode of which he was rather proud.

My father died in an accident when I was sixteen. I don't remember much about him, except that he was an easygoing man, and he loved to laugh. I do remember wrestling with him, especially when I was finally able to pin him for the first time. And I recall an argument he and my mother once had about an employee of his, the store manager, who was, if not stealing, then at least indulging in some questionable accounting practices. My mother insisted—and she had an insist that would fell an ox—that he be fired. But my father said "Look. He runs the store better than I can. I make more with him pocketing the money than I would if I fired him and ran it myself." That was one of the few arguments between my mother and father where my mother didn't emerge victorious—he almost always gave in to her eventually.

The most memorable argument my parents ever had was in 1929, when I was fifteen years old. The stock market was soaring to unheard-of heights. The shopkeepers of San Francisco were making so much money in the market that they would spend the day at their brokers' offices, contentedly accepting the delightful fact of their skyrocketing net worth as the tape pecked it out, and a corps of young men, chalk and eraser in hand, transcribed each new, higher figure onto a large blackboard. Precious little business was being conducted in the stores. My father was deeply worried about this. He would collar anyone who would listen and keep repeating that the bubble was going to burst, that it had to end someplace.

Then, one evening, the person who came home from work was a far different man from the fun-loving dad we knew. Instead of the usual roughhousing as my sister and I flew to greet him, followed by his demanding a rundown of everything interesting that happened that day in school and out, he gave us an absentminded hug, went into the living room, sat in a corner in his favorite chair, in his favorite position, and did nothing. He wouldn't talk to anyone. He just sat. My mother was at him over and over again. "What is it, Jimmy? Did something happen? What happened? Are you sick? You can certainly tell your family. Maybe we can help. What is it, what happened?" To all of this, my father's only response was, "Nothing happened. Nothing's the matter. I'm just thinking."

But my mother was part bulldog. When she wanted to know something, she usually got her way. On the second day of this drama, she struck paydirt. Suddenly, my father blurted out the reason for his personal torture. He had, he announced to the family, sold *all* his stocks.

"What in heaven's name did you do a stupid thing like that for?" my mother demanded to know, in a scream the likes of which had not been heard in San Francisco since the appearance of my dice game bankroll.

"I didn't see how it could go on. Things just aren't worth what people are paying for them."

She stormed into the other room and got the evening paper. "What did you sell Pacific Lighting for?"

He told her. It had gone up five and a half points in the interim. She bellowed at him. "That's more than eleven hundred dollars you threw down the drain! Are you crazy, Jimmy?! How about Standard Gas and Electric?" Eight hundred dollars. "Union Carbide?" Twelve hundred dollars. And so it went, down their list of holdings, with my mother announcing each loss, her anger building along with the dollar totals. She called him every kind of a fool, and by this point it didn't take much to convince him that she was right. He cried. It shocked me. He burst out in tears, admitted his stupidity, and promised to buy all his stocks back the next morning. But he still had to suffer through the night. I could hear them in their bedroom, with Mom hacking and yacking away at him.

The next morning my father ate a hurried breakfast and left, eager to be out of the house before Mom could let in to him once again. Stopping only briefly to open his store on Market Street, he walked quickly over to his stockbroker's office, eager to atone for his stupidity of two days before. When he arrived at the brokerage house, the crowd watching the changing prices as they were posted on the huge blackboard was even bigger than usual. He pushed his way through them to the desk of his broker. He had a list of the stocks he wanted to buy. He handed it to the broker.

The broker looked at the list, then at my father. "This is no time for a joke, Jimmy," the broker said, shaking his head. "You've got a ghoulish sense of humor."

Then, for the first time, he began to sense something different that day in the spirit of the crowded room. It was quiet. The loud braggadocio of people getting richer by the minute was gone. Ashen, drawn faces gaped unbelievingly as new and ever lower prices were posted as fast as the boys with their chalk sticks could scribble them on the big blackboards. It was Wednesday, October 23, the day that the stock market felt the first tremors of the Great Stock Market Crash that would hit with full fury the following Monday. Although it was still morning in San Francisco, it was already afternoon in New York, and the tidal wave of sell orders had begun. My father's stocks were already selling for prices far below what he had sold them for. The three-hour time difference had saved us from ruin.

He called home and told Mom what had happened. She didn't give him any credit, never agreed that selling the stocks had been a good move. She told him to thank God he had had such a lucky break. I never forgave him for not letting her have it, but he didn't have a vindictive bone in his body. If I were he, I would have called her up and told her I had bought back the stocks, just as she ordered, and we had lost everything. I think a few hours of letting her sweat that one out before telling her the happy ending would have been just. But no, he let her off the hook. That's just the way my father was.

His store was the largest luggage store in San Francisco. Its sign, OPPENHEIMER THE TRUNK MAN, was a landmark on Market Street, the city's great thoroughfare, stretching across the entire first floor of the flatiron-shaped Phelan Building, which still stands at the corner of Market and O'Farrell. A 1910 San Francisco publication had this description:

OPPENHEIMER, THE TRUNK MAN

This firm has the finest display in the city at its place of business at 791– 793 Market Street. They carry everything in Trunks, Suit Cases, Leather Goods, Ladies' Hand Bags, etc., doing a wholesale and retail business. No matter what you want, they can supply you with it at prices that are right. We are pleased to call our people's attention to this firm, and bespeak for them a liberal patronage by all who appreciate courteous treatment and honest business methods. Their repair department is a feature of their business. If it's a good trunk, the chances are that it will have been bought at Oppenheimer's.

My father: James Oppenheimer, The Trunk Man.

My father had gone into the luggage business quite by accident at the time of the Great San Francisco Earthquake of 1906. The morning after the earthquake hit, he was told by the authorities to evacuate his room by that afternoon, as the fire was approaching. He needed a suitcase to carry his belongings, so he hurried down Fillmore Street to a luggage shop he frequently passed.

When he got there, the owner of the shop was beside himself. The man's house had been ruined. He was scared to death and wanted to get his family as far away from San Francisco as he could as quickly as possible. He was standing in front of his shop, just locking the door, when my father arrived. The shopowner had taken three suitcases, all he could carry, and was simply going to abandon the rest. My father convinced him that it would be better to sell the store lease and his entire inventory for ten cents on the dollar than to abandon it. They made a deal then and there. The owner left, and my father reopened the doors of the shop to a steady stream of luggage-hungry evacuees. He sold out the entire stock in just a few hours.

How he met my mother I don't know. Perhaps they met while he was hawking suitcases in the park. She told me stories about the quake, and about how her family was evacuated and spent the night in the park, surrounded by all the belongings they could carry. She stayed awake all night that night waving flies away from her sleeping father's open mouth.

Both of my parents were Jewish. In 1908, while my father was courting my mother, he had an eye operation and went blind in both eyes as a result. In his desperation, he began trying different religions. Less than a year later, during his Christian Science period, he suddenly regained the sight in both his eyes for no discernible reason. As a result, my sister and I were brought up in Christian Science. So I really didn't know much about being Jewish, except that my mother always instructed me that if anyone asked me my religion, I was to say "I'm Jewish, and proud of it." This got me a lot of bloody noses.

Before we go on, there are some things you should know about my mother.

In the beginning, there was Mother. And what a mother I had. A slight, less-than-plain-looking woman, life started dealing her off the bottom of the deck from the moment in her sixth year when her sister was born. My mother's looks were slightly above unattractive. My aunt was beautiful. My mother was talentless. My aunt was loaded with talent —dripping with outstanding ability in art, and excelling in all the social graces.

There rightfully should be a redistribution of talents each time a new child appears in a family. When a second child is born there will be, at best, a period when the newborn completely usurps the kingdom over which the first child has reigned supreme during its entire, if short, lifetime. But when time and size bring them into more even competition, the first child who finds he can't compete on looks, talent, or personality is indeed in trouble. And that my mother was, for this unevenness in genetic fortune between the two sisters was acted out for the rest of their lives.

My mother had one glorious chance to escape in her late teens, when she and a young man fell madly in love. He asked her to marry him. She agreed, and they approached my grandparents with trepidation—well warranted, as the prospective groom was not Jewish. Permission to wed was summarily refused, and my mother was devastated. When I say devastated, I don't mean a little shaken up, on the order of the San Francisco earthquake. That little tremor didn't compare to the depth of her despair, which increased a thousandfold within days when, as she was in the midst of laying plans to defy her parents and seize her happiness, her man was killed in an accident, taking with him my mother's dream of a glorious, golden life. This was the final blow, the coup de grace. It convinced her that the world was out to get her, and that if she wanted to survive she had better get it first.

The one area in which Mother was given a fair break was intelligence. No matter that she turned into an intellectual snob—at least that requires some intellect. She knew Latin backwards and forwards, and every rule of grammar. She delighted in correcting anyone who made an error in grammar (not a "grammatical error," she was wont to point out, for if it was "grammatical," it couldn't be in error). Her academic record was straight A until her second year at the University of California, when maintaining it became too much for her, and she suffered a breakdown. She was a perfectionist—anything but A was unthinkable, and this concentration on the grade, rather than on the learning, pushed her past her breaking point. She would sometimes take weeks to write a letter; she corrected it, polished it, nailed down the meaning of this phrase in fewer words, captured the exact nuance of that one with carefully chosen adjectives. She was the personification of whoever it was who said, "I'm sorry to send you such a long letter. I didn't have time to write a short one."

Her perfectionism, like her preoccupation with grades, did not arise so much from the pleasure of expressing herself exactly as from the expectation of being complimented on her ability by the recipient.

She was a stickler for honesty. She expected it and demanded it from the family. There was only one honesty to her—no gradations, no compromises. The absolute truth was the truth; everything else was a lie. Consequently, she never learned the art of the white lie, and I often suspected it was a purposeful omission, because it gave her the opportunity to say things under the protection of candor that under any other circumstances would have netted her a punch in the mouth. Woe be to the friend who ingenuously asked what my mother thought of a newly purchased gown or hat. She was given one last chance to retreat. Nothing if not fair, Mother always asked, "Do you really want to know?" Naturally, there was but one answer: "Of course." Whap! She got the full candid treatment. Nothing existed with which my Mom could not find fault.

We once wrote an *I Love Lucy* entitled "Lucy Tells the Truth," in which Ricky bets Lucy a hundred dollars that she can't go for twenty-four hours without fibbing. The next day, at her friend Caroline's apartment, Lucy is asked her opinion of Caroline's new Chinese Modern furniture. Sworn to tell the absolute truth, Lucy calmly informs Caroline that her furniture looks "like a bad dream you'd have after eating too much Chinese food." That was Mother, in spades.

Each time she left the house, she felt that every salesperson in every store in town, every waitress in every restaurant, was somehow alerted. "Mrs. Oppenheimer is going out," the message went, "let's get her!" It was war.

A perfect illustration of my mother's attitude toward the rest of the world is an incident that occurred after I was grown, when my wife and I took Mom out to dinner at one of our favorite restaurants. We had just been served our entrée when I noticed Mother looking around, as though trying to attract the attention of a waitress.

"What do you want, Ma?" I asked.

"Nothing. Do you see the waitress?"

"What's wrong?"

"It's nothing. These string beans are cold, that's all."

"Okay, let me handle it."

She was hurt. "Why do you always do that? Don't you think I know how to be tactful? The beans are cold. I want to ask her to bring me some warm ones. Does that take the secretary of state to handle?"

"No, it's just that—"

"Well, I'll take care of it, thank—Oh, there she is. Miss?"

The waitress came to the table. "Yes, ma'am?"

My mother held out the dish of beans. "I wouldn't serve these to a dog!"

At the time that this happened, I was writing the *Baby Snooks* radio program for Fanny Brice, the legendary comedienne and singing star so brilliantly portrayed by Barbra Streisand in *Funny Girl.* Less than two weeks after the episode at the restaurant, I found myself doing a last-minute script rewrite, which took me all night. At three o'clock in the morning I was practically done—the only thing that I needed was some funny dialogue for Snooks's mother in the restaurant scene. It suddenly hit me that my mother's line about the dish of beans would be perfect.

I put it out of my mind and tried to think of something else. Good as it was, I just couldn't humiliate my mother that way. But at 5 A.M., after two more hours trying in vain to think of an alternative, I finally gave up, exhausted, and put in my mother's line. Of course, everybody thought it was hilarious, and when we did the show the audience gave it a big laugh.

I didn't sleep a wink that night. How could I face my mother? She would feel that I had made a fool of her. My only chance was if she had somehow missed the show, but I didn't hold out much hope of that—she always listened to my shows, and she always gave me a full critique the next day. Sure enough, the next morning, while I was having breakfast, the telephone rang. It was my mother. I asked her if she had heard last night's show.

"Yes, I did," she answered. "And I want to ask you something about it."

I began to sweat. I could feel it coming.

"What's that, Ma?"

"You know in the last scene, the line that Snooks's mother said that got such a big laugh?"

"Yes," I said, my stomach tightening.

"Tell me something. Are there really people like that?"

Radio Days

FROM THE MOMENT I first set foot inside a radio studio, I was hooked. The fact that it wasn't the posh setting I had always imagined did nothing to diminish its glamour as far as I was concerned. Radio was magic, and this was where the magic was made. After that first day when Mort Werner introduced me to KFRC, I used every spare moment I had to hang around the station—much to the detriment of my studies at Stanford.

Harrison Holliway, whom I had met on my first trip to the station, was KFRC's general manager. But the man who was really in charge was a gentleman by the name of Sylvester L. "Pat" Weaver, Jr., the innovative broadcasting pioneer who later, as head of NBC-TV, created both the *Today* show (with Mort as producer) and the *Tonight* show. I had no official position at the station, but after a while Weaver, Holliway, and everyone else got used to seeing me there and didn't challenge me. I was as helpful as I could be, running errands and doing favors for people. I had about as much contact with actual radio as the janitor, but I felt so "inside," so "professional," that I could hardly stand it. Occasionally I was allowed to do something exciting and creative, like being a part of crowd noises, which consisted of muttering "Hubba hubba hubba." I recall a moment during one of my first crowd appearances—before I gained expertise at hubba hubba-ing—when I was so carried away with the thought of little me actually acting that I missed the director's cut-off cue. The sound effects door closed, leaving the crowd—that is, all the crowd but me—on the outside. My solo "hubba hubba" dropped into the love scene taking place inside. But these "acting" opportunities were few and far between. Mostly I just got to hang around.

The kind of folks who peopled radio in its early, relatively unorganized days were the sort of nervy, brash, crazy, loveable characters immortalized in newspaper stories such as Hecht and MacArthur's *The Front Page*.

Most of them had a wild sense of humor, along with a prodigious appetite for alcohol. But none was more memorable, at least to me, than one Arnold MacGuire. Arnold was a writer, actor, newscaster—he could do anything that needed to be done around the studio, as well as a lot of things that were better left undone. Drunk or sober, his greatest kick was making faces or holding up signs to actors while they were on the air, attempting to break them up. When Mac walked in the door of a studio that was on the air, all the actors turned away from him with the precision of a marine drill team. When he was sober, he had a deadly ability to make actors laugh when they shouldn't. When he was loaded, his attacks were much more brutal and primitive, but just as effective.

He always seemed to be working on Christmas Day. Or perhaps it's just that I remember some things that happened on various Christmases. He might walk in one studio door and out the other while a newscast was going on, singing Christmas carols at the top of his voice, leaving whoever was on mike at the time to explain or to try to ignore it. The ones who were able to explain it, and perhaps make a joke in the process, got off easy. They were people who could roll with the situation. The ignorers didn't really ignore it. They just didn't say anything about it out loud. But Arnold MacGuire well knew the inner turmoil they were going through. A couple of minutes after one of Arnold's stunts, their tongues would invariably cease to take orders from their brains, while Arnold, listening delightedly in another room, would rock with glee at their verbal goofs.

On more than one occasion, Arnold walked through the studio during the course of a broadcast wearing nothing but a hat. Some of the world's most misplaced guffaws came in the middle of religious programs visited by Arnold MacGuire in the buff on Christmas Day.

Mac was also responsible for one of radio's most unintelligible moments. It wasn't Christmas, but New Year's Day. He was set to read the morning news, but he had been out making the evening's news, and he had come directly to the studio without a moment's rest or recuperation. He was many sheets to the wind but assumed an air of ultrasophistication and exaggerated control in an attempt to hide his intoxicated condition. He sat in the studio and read the copy he was going to deliver, dutifully looking up the hard-to-pronounce foreign names and places in the newscasters' reference books. Suddenly, with only forty-five seconds to go until airtime, he became violently ill. He had no choice but to dash for the men's room, hoping he could empty his stomach and get back to the mike in time.

Off he ran to the privy, where he fell to his knees on the tile floor and delivered his goods in record time. He sped back to the studio, coming to a brake-screeching, cartoon-type halt at the microphone, with just enough time to compose himself, pick up his script with exaggerated aplomb, and look over at the engineer, who raised his hand, finger extended, and lowered it to point at Mac.

Those who had the privilege of hearing the beginning of that newscast will never know what words Mac's brain instructed his mouth to articulate. What came out is difficult to describe. It was definitely human, yet it had a strange, moist, muffled quality, as though the words, if words they were, were riding in a bubble making its way to the top of a container of bottled water.

What had happened was that along with his undigested stomach contents, Mac had unknowingly deposited his full set of dentures into the toilet bowl. The harder he tried to articulate meticulously, the more slobbery the sound came out. It sounded like a man whose lips have suddenly turned into noodles. The engineer grabbed the first person he saw, who happened to be Harry the janitor, and had him read the rest of the news. Phrasing and pronunciation suffered a bit, but at least one could recognize the words.

Another time, for a period of about three weeks, Mac drove everyone crazy with a story he insisted on telling over and over and over again. He carried it to the point where one or two people had angry words with him, and one actor actually threatened to punch him in the nose if he told it once more. The story they were thoroughly sick of was about a man walking through a nudist camp with a flatiron tied to his private parts. When asked why, he answered, "We're having an erection contest tomorrow, and that's my handicap."

Just as suddenly as it started, Mac's campaign of telling this story mysteriously ceased. Then, on one of the shows he was writing, the actors ran into an acute case of delayed-script-itis. In those days it was not unusual for a program to begin broadcasting while the finishing pages were still being written and fed to the mimeo machine. The pages would be rushed in and silently passed around to the actors as they became available. But on this particular show it got so bad that an actor would almost literally be handed the next page as he finished reading the last sentence of the preceding one. There was no time to look ahead and see what was coming. It was a young actress named Bea Benaderet, playing a helpless old lady about to be evicted from her home, who read a line addressed to one of the muscle men who was evicting her.

"Why do you have that flatiron tied to your wrist?"

The completely unsuspecting evictor, an actor who was hired for the day and didn't know the joke, was, to put it mildly, startled at the response to his next line:

"We're having an ejection contest tomorrow, and that's my handicap."

A bomb dropped into the studio could not have drawn more reaction from the previously sensitized actors, musicians, and technicians in the know. Some were rolling around on the floor, holding their sides. Others were draped hopelessly over the piano, or clinging to the microphone stands as their knees gave way beneath them. Everyone was unsuccessfully trying to hold back hysterical laughter. The director, through laughter-teared eyes, was frantically throwing cues to this person and that—to the sound effects man, to the orchestra leader, to anyone whose eye he could catch—in a vain attempt to restore order. Finally, the orchestra played. That is, the piano, violins, and drums. Wind instrument players could produce nothing but meaningless squeaks as they tried to play through their laughter.

You would think that Mac would have been fired for such a stunt, but such was the attitude in those early days of radio that he stayed on.

Mac was responsible for writing the connecting banter for the emcee as he introduced the various acts of the *Blue Monday Jamboree*. One of the acts, which was on the show every week, was an old vaudeville couple who called themselves Doakes and Doakes. Their routine consisted of the two of them singing a song, in harmony, entitled "Don't Go in the Lion's Cage Tonight Mother Darling, the Lions Are Ferocious, and They Bite." It wasn't much of a song, but it was only designed to be a framework that allowed them to tell jokes. After every few bars, the music would stop, they would tell a joke, and the music would start again.

Every week MacGuire admonished each act to get its material in early. Most of them didn't respond, partly because they hadn't finished writing it yet, and partly because they knew from experience that Mac, when he needed a joke for the emcee, was not above lifting one from an act that had already been turned in. Doakes and Doakes, however, always turned in their material at least a week in advance. And every week, as Mac would get stuck writing the show, he would use one of their jokes in the script, and then another, until he had used them all.

Each week Doakes and Doakes would sit there during the show, smiling and waiting their turn, until they heard one of their jokes being told. They would exchange alarmed looks, he would take out a pencil, she would hold out their script, and he would scratch out the joke which was just used. The scene repeated itself again and again until, by the time Doakes and Doakes were introduced—usually with a joke from their own routine—there was nothing left for them to do but go up to the mike and sing the song.

Every time the music stopped, they would frantically signal it to continue. People wrote in, saying that Doakes and Doakes were pretty good singers, but why in the world didn't they learn another song? As far as I know, they kept doing that forlorn routine, stripped of everything but its musical skeleton, until the *Blue Monday Jamboree* was no more.

●   ●   ●

During the year I hung around KFRC, the station came of age. Don Lee had another station, KHJ, in Los Angeles, as well as a few other stations around the state, and they formed a network of sorts. The Don Lee–Columbia Network, so called because it comprised all of the Columbia Broadcasting System's affiliates on the West Coast, even fed a few programs to CBS for coast-to-coast broadcast.

CBS and NBC—the "biggies"—had long since gotten very precise in their timing, "pulling the plug" if a program was not off the air within five seconds of its scheduled time. The Don Lee stations, on the other hand, would broadcast a program ahead of time, on time, or behind time, depending on when the previous program finished. If the preceding show took too long, then the next one would start two, or four, or even seven minutes late. If it was too short, the next one was free to start if it was ready. If not, the audience would be treated to twenty-five or thirty choruses of the outgoing show's theme, during which time the orchestra leader would amuse himself by modulating to a different key for each chorus and changing the rhythm, playing it as a fox trot, then a waltz, then a tango, and so on, until the director signaled that the next program had taken over.

There were some wonderful, small, enjoyable moments that started as inside jokes and were later discovered by the listening audience. One of them was the brainchild of Claude Sweeten, the station's orchestra leader in San Francisco. An afternoon show called *The Happy-Go-Lucky Hour,* with Al and Cal Pearce, alternated its originating station, starting the first half hour in San Francisco and switching to the Los Angeles station, KHJ, for the second half hour one week, and then reversing the procedure the following week. At the end of the first half hour the orchestra would play the theme. The orchestra leader at the other station could hear this through earphones. Because the key and tempo were set, it was no problem for him to get his orchestra playing simultaneously with the one in the other studio. When they were in perfect sync, the engineer switched from one city to the other. A listener could not tell when the engineer faded one city's orchestra out and the other in.

One afternoon Claude was feeling mischievous. Instead of playing the theme in the usual manner, he played it as a waltz. The other leader, in Los Angeles, was nonplussed, but managed to get the message across to his musicians in time to match the San Francisco music within the span of one chorus. Of course, the following week, when it was L.A.'s turn to feed it to San Francisco, he repaid the compliment, challenging Sweeten and company by playing the theme as a beguine.

A feud had begun, and one of the best parts of the show for many weeks was listening to how many choruses it would take the receiving orchestra to match the music being fed to them. They threw every known musical variation at each other: changes of key, changes of tempo, tangos, waltzes, fox-trots, beguines, Bach-type fugues, Beethoven-type symphonies, you name it. The challenge reached new heights when the decision was made to have the engineer fade from one to the other at the end of the first chorus, whether the other orchestra had matched it or not.

There were great celebrations when the San Francisco orchestra stumped the musicians in Los Angeles, causing them to come on the air in complete musical confusion. The partying was especially fun for hangers-on like me, who had no responsibility and therefore didn't have the pressure of worrying about what would happen if the on-the-air switchover was a fiasco. I had no way of knowing that one day, as a TV producer, I would be faced with responsibility for my own intercity network broadcast switchover, and that it would give me one of the biggest scares of my professional career.

The occasion was the eleventh annual Emmy Awards broadcast, in 1959. I was the program's executive producer, and we had decided to broadcast live from *three* locations: the Moulin Rouge in Hollywood, the Ziegfeld Theatre in New York, and the Grand Ballroom of the Mayflower Hotel in Washington, D.C. (where the news programming awards would be presented). *Father Knows Best* star Robert Young, in Hollywood, was the primary host for the evening, but we also had hosts and presenters in each city.

If, say, a presenter in Hollywood announced the name of an award winner who was in New York, we simply switched to the camera in the Ziegfeld Theatre, where the honoree would come to the stage and receive the award. This system worked without a hitch all evening—until the time came for presentation of the final Emmy. Jack Benny, in Hollywood, had just finished presenting the Trustees' Award to Bob Hope. As Hope and Benny walked into the wings, we cut to New York. Standing on the stage of the Ziegfeld Theatre, Ed Sullivan read the nominees for the "Most Outstanding Single Program of the Year," and tore open the envelope. "And the winner is," Sullivan announced, " 'An Evening With Fred Astaire'!"

We quickly cut from New York to a shot of Fred Astaire in the audience at the Moulin Rouge in Hollywood. Jack Benny was to give Astaire his Emmy, the ninth award won by him that evening. The camera stayed on Fred as he rose from his seat, smiled at the people around him, and started down the aisle. In the control room, we suddenly realized that there was no one on the stage! Jack Benny was nowhere to be found. So far, the home audience knew nothing of this, because we kept the camera tight on Astaire. But it would only be a matter of seconds before both he and the camera would reach the empty podium. Astaire, seeing that there was nothing but a bare stage to greet him, looked around in puzzlement as he walked down the aisle.

In the control room all hell had broken loose. Everyone (including me) was shouting orders left and right, trying frantically to find Jack Benny or to get word to someone else to get onstage, pronto.

In his seat at the back of the theater, Robert Young also noticed Jack's absence. He started walking down the left-hand aisle toward the stage just in case he needed to fill in as a presenter. But Young had no way of knowing if Benny was about to make his entrance, and the last thing he wanted to do was to come on the stage and get in the way just as Benny reappeared.

From our vantage point, we watched helplessly as Astaire climbed the steps at the right-hand side of the stage. When he got to the top of the steps and saw that there was still nobody at the podium, he hesitated again. Robert Young, realizing that it was now or never, tore down to the front of the theater and dashed up the steps on the opposite side of the stage. As the audience at home watched the smiling Astaire approach the empty podium from stage left, Young sprinted to the podium from stage right.

Arriving just moments ahead of Astaire, Young grabbed the Emmy and dramatically tossed it into the air with his right hand, catching it in his outstretched left hand just as Astaire, with the camera following him, arrived at center stage to accept the proffered statuette. The millions of viewers at home thought Young had been standing there with the Emmy in his hand the entire time, waiting for Astaire. But the theater audience, who knew better, went absolutely wild.

Amid the thunderous applause, Astaire whispered to Young, "For a second I didn't think you were going to make it!" Up in the control room we breathed a huge, collective sigh of relief. Thinking back to my days at KFRC, and the butchered switchovers from San Francisco to Los Angeles, I finally understood why Claude Sweeten's antics had always made the station manager so nervous.

But back in 1934, in San Francisco, all I knew was that listening to the other orchestra try to get up to tempo in one chorus was great fun. So when Don Lee gave the word that the sloppy orchestra switchovers were childish and had to be stopped, I thought he was simply being a killjoy.

The truth, however, was that radio itself was growing up, and just as in life, childish amusements that are acceptable from children are no longer tolerated from young adults. Word came down from above, in the form of a memo from Don Lee himself, that all programs on the Don Lee stations would henceforth take the air precisely on time, and relinquish it within ten seconds of schedule. If they didn't sign off on time, the engineer had instructions to "pull the plug" and cut them off.

At about this time, Harrison Holliway added a new department to the *Blue Monday Jamboree*: "Interviews with Interesting People." On one unforgettable night the interviewee was a man who had been hired to make a parachute jump over San Francisco. He was describing the experience, telling Holliway of the prearranged signal between him and the pilot of the open cockpit plane. It was agreed between them that when they neared the right spot the pilot would waggle the wings twice, at which time the jumper would get up in position to leap. When they arrived at precisely the exact spot, he would waggle the wings once, and the man would jump. Well, this fellow was explaining how he felt the wings waggle twice and he got up on the edge of the rear cockpit, ready to jump, but when he looked down, he couldn't see San Francisco. He couldn't see anything. It was a pea soup fog. As he was trying to figure out what to do, he felt the wings waggle once. He decided not to jump, he said, and climbed back down.

Then he felt remorseful. After all, he was hired to do the job and should go through with it. So he climbed back up on the edge again. This time he started to wonder how the pilot knew where they were if he couldn't see any landmarks to go by, so back down he climbed. Then, he related, as the studio audience and multitudes of people within radio

Harrison Holliway, KFRC's station manager and creator
and emcee of *Blue Monday Jamboree*.

earshot hung spellbound on his every word, he had another change of heart. He decided the pilot *must* know what he was doing. The pilot was experienced, and certainly wouldn't tell anyone to jump if it was danger-ous. So he climbed up again, and was fighting a mental battle: "Should I jump? Yes. But we're no longer over the right spot. Jump anyway. Well . . ."

That's as far as he got. Time had run out, and Mr. Lee, true to his memo, pulled the plug for the first time. Another program came on the air, and the audience was left hanging: Did he or didn't he jump?

The switchboard lit up like Mount St. Helens in full volcanic eruption. It seemed that no one within range of a telephone was willing to go to sleep that night without knowing whether this fellow had jumped or not. Those who were more frugal wrote letters. All week long extra postmen had to be assigned to handle the unbelievable volume of angry and inquisitive mail. It was one of the first times people in radio felt the impact and power of the mass communication medium. Special announcements had to be made on the air that the jumper would return the following week to finish his story. Of course, it wasn't lost on the front office that this was priceless publicity. The radio people were beginning to realize the strength of this young giant they had on their hands.

The program had a record audience the following Monday, when the jumper returned and revealed that he had indeed jumped. The "Interesting People" segment continued as a regular feature for a long time, but none of the interviews approached the impact of the parachute jumper until one seemingly ordinary Monday, when the guest was an engineer from the railroad.

On the day of the program, at the afternoon rehearsal, Holliway was running through the interview with the engineer, who had just mentioned that the pattern of the train whistles was actually a code with which engineers communicated between themselves.

"What is the difference between the various whistles?" Holliway asked.

"They all mean different things," the engineer replied, and went on to say that one long and two shorts mean one thing, two longs and two shorts mean another, three shorts have yet a different meaning, and so on.

"What is your favorite whistle?"

"That's easy. It's a private whistle; just between me and my wife. Long, short, long, short, long, long. I blow that when I'm about four miles out. My wife hears it and starts preparing dinner. She knows exactly how long it takes me to get home after I blow the whistle, and when I walk in the door a piping hot meal has just been set on the table."

"Hold it. Hold it." Holliway was upset, stopping the rehearsal. "This is too sterile. We should be hearing these whistles," he called to the director. "He should be blowing them for us."

Holliway grew more and more excited by his new thought. He turned to the engineer. "You must actually blow them for us. How can we arrange that?"

The engineer offered that there usually were extra whistles in the shop being repaired. He suggested calling the railroad to see if they had one they could send to the studio. He did, and they had one; but they said it wouldn't work unless the building had compressed air they could tie into. Holliway assured them there was plenty of air power. He was ecstatic, like a kid waiting for a new toy. They promised they'd get it there as fast as they could, and for the rest of the afternoon Holliway paced nervously up and down, tensely watching the street for the delivery truck.

No one bothered to ask the obvious question: If this fellow's wife could hear the whistle when he blew it from four miles away, then when it was blown in a closed, window-walled room with several hundred folks sitting within thirty feet of it, wasn't it going to be rather loud?

It took longer than anyone expected, and Holliway was nearly out of his mind when finally, at about six o'clock, a tremendous truck and trailer pulled up in front of the building. It was about half a block long, and it was carrying the whistle, which appeared to me at the time to be roughly as long as the Washington Monument, and as big around as the Stockton Street Tunnel. Everyone was shocked. Somehow, when a whistle like that is mounted on a huge railroad engine, everything is in proper proportion. But when put next to ordinary objects and people, it becomes awesome—almost unearthly.

Holliway, however, was delighted. A second, smaller truck, which followed the first, unloaded twenty or thirty laborers. Like Lilliputians trying to maneuver a trussed Gulliver, they managed to inch the whistle off the truck, snake it into the building, and worm it slowly up the stairs and into the studio. It was so heavy and bulky that airtime was approaching by the time they wrestled, tugged, and levered it into position. Its top cleared the ceiling by less than six inches.

The whistle cord was set so the engineer could reach up and pull it while he stood at the microphone. By the time the workmen finally tightened down the connection to the compressed air pipe, there was no time to test anything. The audience was already filling all those folding chairs, and in the background, through the windows that formed the entire wall, the heavy evening traffic on Van Ness Avenue was crawling by, unaware of this impending wedding of realism and technology.

The program took the air and everything went along fine, until it was time for the fateful interview. The railroad engineer and Holliway took their places. It was only a mildly interesting spot until Holliway asked him what the different whistles meant. He began to describe them, as per the original script, but Holliway stopped him and said, "But it's silly to talk about them, when we can actually hear them with our own ears. The railroad has been good enough to send us this spare whistle. The first one, you said, was one long and two shorts?"

"That's correct," the engineer said, and while Holliway beamed at him with creative anticipation, he pulled the cord.

The entire wall of windows shattered and blew out onto Van Ness Avenue. The performers on the stage were scattered like rag dolls. The audience, sitting in their folding chairs facing the stage, slid backwards across the floor as a unit, expressions of bemused interest still on their faces, riding their moving seats until they came to rest against the wall of now glassless windows. The sound blew out the transmitter, and the station was off the air for two weeks. Mr. Lee, I understand, was hit with something like fifty-eight suits for broken eardrums. It was one of the more memorable moments of early radio.

The Passports

AT THE END of spring quarter of my junior year at Stanford University, I came home to a family conference called by my mother to consider our immediate future. She informed us that, with my sister graduating in June from the University of California, this was a critical time in our lives. She pointed out objectively that I was not exactly setting the world on fire with my grades, and that in any event the degree in social sciences that I was pursuing would have no practical value in enabling me to earn a living, as an engineering or law degree would have.

We had a certain amount of money to spend, she explained, some of which would be needed to pay for the remainder of my college education. Or, she continued, if I wanted to forego my last year at Stanford, the three of us could take an extended trip around the world.

It was a now-or-never situation, as my sister would undoubtedly be working or married by the time I graduated. The decision was left to me, and after giving it careful consideration (for about three seconds) I opted for the trip. I felt that I would learn more that would help a writing career by traveling around the world than by continuing my studies. As it turned out, I was right.

A few days later my mother and I went downtown to the passport office. The interview was uneventful, until the passport clerk came to the subject of my father.

"Is your husband living?" he asked her.

"No. He died four years ago," my mother calmly replied.

"Where was he born?"

"Germany."

"Was he a naturalized U.S. citizen?"

"Yes."

"What year?"

"I don't know exactly. I believe it was 1893."

"And when were you married?"

"In 1910."

At this, the clerk excused himself so he could check the naturalization files. He was gone for almost fifteen minutes. When he returned, he had a strangely serious expression on his face.

"I've checked all the naturalization records for this office from 1890 through 1900. There is no record of any James Oppenheimer."

My mother, for once, sat speechless, a shocked expression on her face. The interviewer continued.

"Passports for your children will not be a problem, but I'm afraid that unless you can prove that your husband was a naturalized citizen, I can't give you a passport, Mrs. Oppenheimer."

"Why not?" my mother demanded indignantly. "I'm an American citizen. I was born right here in San Francisco!"

"Yes, I understand that," he explained. "But you said that you and your husband married in 1910. Under the immigration laws in effect at that time, when you married James Oppenheimer you took on his citizenship. Unless you can prove that James Oppenheimer was a naturalized citizen when you married him, you are a citizen of Germany and are subject to deportation."

A sense of panic swept over us. Was he really saying that my mother, a San Francisco–born Jewish woman of fifty-three, was going to be deported to Hitler's Germany? There had to be some way out.

My mother spoke first. "How can we prove that he was a naturalized citizen, if you just checked the records and there's no James Oppenheimer there?"

"These records are only for persons naturalized in the city and county of San Francisco," the interviewer explained. "Is it possible that he was naturalized somewhere else?"

"Yes, of course it's *possible*," my mother answered angrily. "But isn't there some central file in Washington that can be consulted? I wouldn't know where to begin looking."

He seemed genuinely sympathetic. "I'm sorry. All records are kept locally. You have to know the city where a person was naturalized in order to obtain his citizenship records."

And that was that. We hurried to the Western Union office down the street, both of us mentally composing a list of every city that my father had ever mentioned. I sent telegrams to more than a dozen immigration offices, and then we returned home to await the replies.

One by one the offices wired back over the next few days: "NO JAMES OPPENHEIMER NATURALIZED IN THIS OFFICE." We all became more and more panicky. Finally, almost a week later, we received the telegram we had been waiting for. "JAMES OPPENHEIMER ADMITTED AS A U.S. CITIZEN IN THIS OFFICE OCTOBER 20, 1893." My father had become a citizen not in San Francisco, as we had assumed, but in Sacramento. The disaster was averted.

Ironically, this terrifying episode was the inspiration for an episode of *I Love Lucy* more than twenty years later. The show was called "The Passports," and concerned Lucy's attempt to get a passport for a trip to Europe. The show opened in the Ricardo apartment, with Ricky and Lucy talking about going to the passport office. Lucy had just told Ricky, Fred, and Ethel that she had wired the Jamestown Hall of Records to send her a copy of her birth certificate, when the telephone rang.

RICKY. *(Into phone)* Hello . . . *(He listens a minute.)* Oh—well, just a minute, please. *(To Lucy.)* Honey, it's a collect call for you from the Jamestown Hall of Records.

LUCY. Oh, it must be about my birth certificate. *(She takes the phone from him. Into phone.)* Hello. . . . Yes, I'll take the call. *(Pause.)* But there must be some mistake. My maiden name was Lucille McGillicuddy and I was born in Jamestown . . . *(another pause)* . . . well, I'm *positive* . . . *(another pause)* . . . well, I don't understand . . . oh, well, you *misunderstood* me! Yes, you're looking under the wrong year. I was born in nineteen— *(She looks around and sees that Ethel is eagerly leaning forward, listening to what she says. Lucy covers the mouthpiece with her hand.)* *(Muffled)* Nineteen —*(She tries repeating the number muffled, two more times, but he obviously can't hear her.)* Look, you know the year you just mentioned—well, it's three more years than that! . . . No, not backwards—*forwards*. . . . *(Ethel gives a sign of "oh drats.")* Yes, I'll hang on. . . . *(She turns to the group.)* They were looking under the wrong year.

ETHEL. *(Disarmingly.)* Really? What year were they looking under?

LUCY. Nineteen—Oh, no you don't!!! *(Into phone)* Yes . . . but there must be some mistake. . . . Well, I . . . all right, thank you. *(She hangs up.)* How do you like that!

RICKY. What's the matter, honey?

LUCY. They can't find my birth certificate. There's no record.

ETHEL. Oh, there *must* be.

LUCY. Well, there isn't. If I'd known Jamestown was going to be that careless, I'd have been born somewhere else!

RICKY. But honey, you need your birth certificate if you want to get a passport.

LUCY. But what do you want me to do? They never heard of me!
FRED. *(Teasing her.)* Maybe you were never born!
LUCY. I was too! *(She starts to cry.)*
ETHEL. Fred . . .
FRED. I was only kidding her.
RICKY. Of course you were born.
LUCY. *(Crying.)* Well, you know it—and I know it, but as far as James-town is concerned, the stork just dropped me and didn't tell anybody!

The rest of the episode concerned Lucy's unsuccessful attempts to obtain an acceptable substitute for a birth certificate—affidavits from two people who had known Lucy since birth. In the end, it turned out that Lucy was actually born not in Jamestown, as she had thought, but in *West* Jamestown.

· · ·

At the time I left Stanford my entire writing career consisted of winning a "Why I Love California" essay contest in the third grade. We were due to leave on our trip in the fall, and during that summer I wrote a piece that I hoped the *Blue Monday Jamboree* would use. The routine was based on an old joke about a man who went to a butcher shop and asked for a pound of "kidleys." The butcher couldn't figure out what he wanted until the customer pointed to a display of kidneys. "Oh," the butcher said, "You want *kidneys.*"

"Of course," the man replied. "I said kidleys, diddle I?"

I chose to call my character, who couldn't pronounce his N's, "Justan Niddlewitz," which came out of his mouth as "just a little wits." The routine ran a couple of pages, during which I explored every possibility of substituting *L* for *N*. The finish came when he told about what he had for dinner, and, pulling a banana out of his pocket, asked, "Wal a balala?"

I worked it over until I felt I had it polished and edited as well as possible. Then I took off for KFRC. It was Monday; they would be in rehearsal for the *Blue Monday Jamboree.* Arriving at the station, I waited through a dress rehearsal, then, as Harrison Holliway left the stand, I handed him the pages and asked him if he thought he might use it. To my delight, he scanned it then and there and said it looked pretty funny to him. He called to everyone to sit down and listen to a routine, and handed it to Bob Bence, the announcer, to read with him. Bob Bence was a wonderful man who later became a good friend of mine, and he had a great voice. But a comedian he wasn't. The cast sat stony faced through the entire presentation. I didn't see anything funny about it either. When it was over, Holliway handed me back the script. "Sorry, kid," he said. "I thought it had something."

"Well, he read it all wrong," I said.

"Think you could do any better?"

"Of course I could."

I figured that if Bence heard me say the lines, he would understand and be able to do them himself. So Holliway told everybody to sit down again, and I went up to the microphone with him and read the part. To his surprise, and mine, every line got a laugh. I looked around for Bob Bence, but before I could locate him I heard Holliway's voice saying to me, "Okay, kid, be here at six o'clock. You're on tonight."

This was something I hadn't imagined in my wildest dreams. Writing material for someone else to read was one thing, but performing was quite another. Up to that time my entire acting career consisted of a solo hubba hubba when I missed the crowd scene cutoff cue. I was not a performer, but I knew that if I said I couldn't do it, that would be the end of the skit. So I said nothing. I was shaking like a leaf as I paced up and down going over and over the material. I called home and told my mother to listen. I went across the street to the bar and asked one of the musicians to order a drink for me. I wasn't a drinker, but it was what people in the movies did when they were nervous. It didn't do me any good. Just as I finished it, I realized that I didn't have the banana I needed for the show. I ran down the street until I found a grocery store, and bought a banana. It was a little on the ripe side, but all I had to do was pull it out of my pocket.

After what seemed like a month or so of anxious pacing backstage, the time finally came for the cast to take their places. I sat there, living a dream—or a nightmare. Finally, I heard the words of my introduction. I walked up to the microphone with legs that would barely support me, and waited for Holliway to begin. Incomprehensibly, the first line out of his mouth was one that occurred halfway down the page. I realized, and confirmed it with a quick glance at his eyes, that Holliway had had more than one too many before beginning the program. I was horrified, but it turned out to be the best thing that could have happened to me. I had to lead him back up to the beginning of the routine and still make some sort of sense. This demanded all my attention, and I didn't have time to worry about my nerves.

We finally got on track, and I became vaguely conscious that every line was getting a roar from the audience. That was when I really got nervous. I was holding my script with both hands, but this didn't keep it from shaking so badly that I could barely read the jumping letters. What's worse, the rattling paper was making quite a racket. I decided to let go of the script with my right hand and use that hand to hold my left wrist steady. It helped. At long last, we arrived at the "Wal a balala?" line. I reached into my pocket and delivered the line as I pulled the banana—but it wouldn't budge! It had worked its way crosswise in my pocket, and was stuck. I desperately but vainly tried to free it, finally exerting so much force that I broke the banana peel. My hand came out of my pocket holding a glob of mashed banana pulp. The laugh easily topped anything that had happened before.

The acts on the show, as they finished their routines, came offstage into a lounge area to wait until they went back for their final bows. Everyone congratulated me on being such a big hit on my debut. I accepted their kudos with what I thought was grace, and sauntered over to the refreshment table to pour myself a cup of coffee. Still shaking, I nonchalantly poured coffee on the table, the floor, down my pants leg, and over my other hand, which was holding the cup. Out of a total of about two quarts, I got maybe ten drops into the cup.

After we had taken our bows and the actors had all left I called home to see if my family had heard my smash debut, expecting a reception at least equal to the one afforded Lindy on his return to New York. My mother answered the phone.

"Well?" I asked, "Did you hear it?"

"Which one were you?"

"Justan Niddlewitz."

"Was that you? It didn't sound like you."

And that was it. Like "Bring home a bottle of milk." She didn't seem to realize what a momentous occasion it was. As for me, I felt that I had not only arrived, but that I was set for life. I relived my great performance again and again during a sleepless night.

The next day proved how wrong my mother was not to take my new career seriously. I got my first-ever professional check. For writing and performing a smash hit routine on a national coast-to-coast radio program, I received the magnificent sum of seven dollars and fifty cents, less seventy-five cents commission to the Thomas Lee Artists' Bureau (Tommy was Don Lee's son).

The thrill of leaving on our trip around the world was dampened considerably when Harrison Holliway asked me to do the character on a weekly basis. I was heartbroken, but I had to tell him that we were leaving in five days. The continuation of the great career that had begun that Monday would have to wait until my return.

· · ·

Just a few words about our trip, which lasted for six interesting and delightful months. The cost, for the three of us, was just under five thousand dollars. In 1934 the only way to cross an ocean was by ship, and the seas were dotted with hundreds of vessels carrying their passengers and cargo from one end of the world to the other. Many lines provided ships to service the large and profitable business of transporting people and things from place to place. The Dollar Line, the President Line, Matson, Canadian Pacific, British and Orient, and North German Lloyd were just a few of the many companies, each of which had as many as a ship a week visiting any given port.

The wonderful part of all this was that there was a reciprocal arrangement under which you could purchase a ticket around the world and it would be honored on any steamship you decided to use for any segment of the trip. You could get off whichever ship you happened to be on when it reached Singapore, for example, and stay for as long as you wished. When Singapore got dull, you went to the travel agent and asked what ships were due in. He would give you a choice of three or four that would be in within a day or so, and you booked passage on one of them to the next place you wished to disembark, thus making your way around the world in as many stops as you wished, each lasting as long as your pleasure demanded.

Another fascinating aspect was that every foreign country was indeed *foreign,* because airplanes and television had not yet saturated the world with Westernism. Each one was excitingly different. The native dress was colorful and distinctive. The architecture was unique to that place and those people. The inhabitants spoke a foreign tongue, and there were very few who communicated in English.

Of course, although this was exciting, it could be frustrating. I remember that when we got to Tokyo I bought myself a Japanese-English dictionary and went down to see the Ginza, the main shopping street, foolishly thinking that the book would enable me to do the haggling for myself. At the first store, I consulted my dictionary and said, *"Honkeshi,"* which means handkerchief. The salesgirl dutifully showed me a handkerchief. So far, so good, I thought to myself. Consulting my dictionary once more, I said *"Ikura desuka?"* which means "How much?" The girl immediately blossomed out in a flow of Japanese that I couldn't make head or tail of, and of course we had to get an interpreter and do the whole thing over.

We took eight different ships, ranging from the *Empress of Japan*, the huge liner that carried us across the Pacific, to a Dutch ship whose chief claim to fame was the length of its name, which started at the bow and ran almost to the fantail. It was the *Johan van Oldenbarneveldt*, and contained four hundred or so Dutch citizens leaving the colonies and returning to their homeland for a sabbatical year. Out of the entire passenger list, only ten of us spoke English. Before the few days we were together had passed, we all knew the stories the others had to offer and were pretty sick of them. But there were quite a few attractive non-English-speaking young girls among the passengers, and there was music and dancing. Even with the limited experience of my twenty-one years, I was amazed at the depth of the relationship that can be entered into without the participants sharing a common spoken language.

The smallest ship that we sailed on was a Japanese vessel named the *Choon Marie*, which took us across the inland sea from Kobe to Moji. It was only 2,500 tons, about the size of a ferry boat on San Francisco Bay. It was the typhoon season, and the night before our scheduled noon departure on the *Choon Marie* we had gone out on the town in Kobe. We got home early because a typhoon was expected by midnight. I sat up waiting for it, but when the sky was still clear at 12:30 A.M., I went to sleep.

At 6:30 in the morning I was practically knocked out of bed when all of the windows blasted open at once, as the typhoon struck with gale-force winds and a torrent of rain. I got sopped closing the windows. Peering out through the rain-pelted glass, I saw a fence blow over on top of a car that was parked in front of our hotel. Across the street a tree was pulled out by its roots and toppled over. Another car was parked at the corner, and I watched with fascination as one fender detached itself from the rest of the car and came floating through the air with reckless abandon until it crashed into a telephone pole.

The Oriental Hotel, where we were staying, was right at the waterfront, and the powerful wind was blowing out to sea, holding back the tide. Then at 7:15 the wind suddenly veered in the other direction and the tide came in with a fury. All the streets were flooded to a depth of two feet. The hotel grill was flooded as well, and at the docks the water was three feet higher than the surface of the wharf. The storm smashed in steel doors and soaked everything in the warehouses.

The *Choon Marie* was supposed to sail at noon, but we were told that it would be postponed because of the typhoon. However, by 11:30 the typhoon had subsided and we were assured once again that it would leave at twelve, as originally scheduled. We were rushed aboard one minute before noon. The *Choon Marie* sailed promptly, four and one-half *hours* later.

Despite the physical attraction of a city, its architecture, and the colorful dress of the people, we found time and again that human relationships—knowing someone who lived there—was what really counted. Again and again, a personal contact raised a place from travelogue to trip highlight. This was the case in Singapore.

In 1934 Singapore was a hot and sleepy English outpost. After we had seen the Raffles Hotel (of which it has been said that if you sit on the front porch long enough, everyone you know will pass by), we took a tour of the town, went to the zoo, and, after two days, had just about had it. I had noticed posters stuck on telephone poles announcing some fights. Tickets were available at Frankel's Department Store. I went to buy tickets and entered a one-story building. No one was evident, so I called "Hello." A voice came from my left. "Over here."

Walking in the general direction of the sound, I made my way down aisles and around displays until I came to a sort of clearing. In the middle of it, seated at a desk, was a most unusual-looking gentleman. He had graying hair, a pleasant, round kind of face, and from about the level of his ears he seemed to spread out in all directions. He was heavy. His chest formed a table straight out from his chin. In his mouth, he held a cigarette. The very tip of the cigarette was just touched by the tip of a pyramid of ashes formed by many cigarettes he had smoked earlier that day. You had the feeling that once he settled in a comfortable position, he never moved.

I asked him how much fight tickets were. He asked me what my name was. I told him.

I asked him how much fight tickets were. He asked me where I came from. I told him.

I asked him how much fight tickets were. He asked me who I was traveling with. I told him.

I asked him how much fight tickets were. He told me to go back to the hotel and tell my mother that his wife would be by to pick us up at five o'clock. We would be having dinner with them.

At five o'clock sharp a huge, open limousine, driven by a liveried chauffeur, pulled up in front of our hotel. In the back were two women, one of a size to make a balanced pair with Mr. Frankel, the other a young, extremely attractive girl about my age, whom Mrs. Frankel introduced as her daughter.

Both Mrs. Frankel and her daughter were as warm, open, and friendly as a pair of puppies. We were driven to their home, which was a huge mansion with more servants than rooms, and we found at dinner that they had invited a handsome young British officer from the military establishment stationed there, as a date for my sister. After dinner, we went to the fights.

We changed our plans and stayed in Singapore, encouraged to do so by the Frankels, much longer than we had anticipated. They insisted that we dine with them and be their guests at different functions every night. And every night they had a different British officer for my sister. We could feel how isolated they felt, and how interested they were in talking to people from the "outside."

Singapore was transformed for us from a sleepy little nothing town to one of the highlights of our trip. We kept in touch with the Frankels for many years, but lost track of them during the war, after the Japanese invasion. I will always remember Mr. Frankel as a true character. No matter where we went, theater, opera, or fights, he would be asleep within minutes of sitting down and awake at the sound of the final applause, clapping louder than anyone else and remarking what a good production it had been.

One afternoon I was in Mr. Frankel's bedroom, waiting for him to finish getting dressed so we could go to the theater. Frankel was sitting, barefoot, on the end of his bed, buttoning his shirt. He was extemporizing on the difficulties that many expatriates have in adjusting when they return to the U.S. after living in the Far East for any length of time.

"The problem, you see, is that most Americans here become far too dependent upon their servants to do everything for them while they are living here, and without realizing it they become incapable of doing anything for themselves."

"That's where I'm different," he continued, adjusting his collar. "I won't have any trouble if I ever go back, because I've made a point of remaining completely self-reliant while I've been here in Singapore."

At this point Frankel stopped talking, raised his hands in the air, and clapped them together twice. A servant appeared in the bedroom doorway.

"Hand me my socks," he commanded the servant, gesturing at the pair sitting on the bed next to him.

Handcuffs and Other Mishaps

AFTER BEING ABROAD for six months, my mother, my sister, and I returned to San Francisco the following January. I went to the radio station at my very first opportunity, my mind filled with uproarious ideas for the resumption of Justan Niddlewits. Mort Werner broke the bad news to me. Two weeks after I had left on the trip, Eddie Cantor had introduced a character on his nationwide program who was identical to Justan—a fellow who pronounced the letter *N* as *L*. He had made ten or twelve appearances, and then was dropped. So much for the continuation of my career. I was certain that one of Cantor's writers had heard me on the *Jamboree* and had stolen the idea. At first I wanted to sue and carry it to the Supreme Court, but I eventually realized that there was nothing I could do about it.

I soon became involved in various activities at the San Francisco Jewish Community Center, which was only a few blocks away from our apartment building. My original reason for joining the Center was simple —I was interested in a girl who spent a lot of time there. But soon after I joined I became involved with the Center's little theater group, the Community Center Players. I knew there was something special about the Players when I first attended the rehearsal for one of their plays. It was an extremely ambitious and complex production for such a small group, especially because all of them were also holding down full-time jobs. But it was their enthusiasm and dedication—their willingness to stay up all night if necessary to rehearse, paint flats, or build sets—that made me anxious to meet the director who had evidently inspired such fervor in his cast and crew. His name, I was told, was Ralph Freud. And if the people who worked with him were to be believed, he should have been listed just above God on the list of all-time greats.

Determined to meet the great Mr. Freud, I decided to try out for a part in the Center's next production. To my great surprise, I not only got to meet him at the tryout, but I also got the part!

Ralph and I hit it off right away. I was especially fascinated by his stories about his early life. He told me that his mother had been working in a London fish market when she met and married Ralph's father, a touring American magician known as "Hillier the Great." She became part of the act, and Ralph was literally born on the road and slept in a trunk. Some years later, Hillier suddenly and unexpectedly deserted them and returned to the United States. His abandoned wife had picked up enough magic by this time to allow her to continue the act, with Ralph assisting as he could. Eventually she remarried, and the family emigrated to the United States and settled in Detroit, where Ralph worked with the famous Jessie Bonstell Players.

One day, when he was about sixteen, Ralph opened the paper and saw an ad for a local theater. "On Stage—Hillier the Great!" That afternoon he went to the theater and sat in the aisle seat of the front row. At one point in the act, as Ralph well knew, Hillier would ask for a volunteer from the audience. No sooner were the words out of his mouth, than Ralph volunteered and climbed up on the stage. His father shook his hand and, for the audience's benefit, asked if they had ever met. Ralph just smiled noncommittally. Hillier then instructed him to test the legitimacy of some knots he was tying on a rope around a large box into which Hillier's assistant had climbed. When the assistant magically appeared walking down the aisle, Hillier asked Ralph to attest to the fact that the knots were untampered with. Ralph did so, Hillier thanked him, shook his hand again, and ushered him back to his seat. When the show was over, Ralph went home. Hillier the Great had no idea that his assistant that day had been the son he had abandoned in England.

Ralph told me that he considered it to be a kind of punishment for his father. Even though Hillier knew nothing of it, Ralph knew, and that was enough.

Ralph's wife, Mayfair, was a dead ringer for Wallis Simpson, whose romance with King Edward of England was the news of the day. The resemblance was so close that people followed her around, gesturing and whispering to each other. Mayfair, a talented actress, was quite amused by it all and did nothing to dispel the illusion, playing the part of the never-to-be Queen of England to the hilt.

Ralph's knowledge, as with many self-educated people who learned for the love of learning, was boundless. If you needed to know any literary reference, any dramatic reference, any scientific know-how, chemical formula, or mechanical expertise, you had only to ask Ralph. Despite the fact that his formal education never went beyond grammar school, Ralph would, in later years, earn a full professorship at UCLA, where he was selected to establish the Theater Arts Department. The Ralph Freud Playhouse on the UCLA campus is a well-deserved memorial.

After a few weeks of acting, making sets, painting scenery, rehearsing, and engaging in all the other great activities a little theater group shares, I was invited by Ralph to dine with him and Mayfair. In addition to his many other talents, Ralph was a gourmet chef. For dinner that evening, he had prepared roast duck with oyster stuffing. I won't say I can still taste it, but I distinctly recall being astounded that anything could taste that good and not be illegal. The three of us got along famously, and, after polishing off everything edible within a radius of twenty feet, we retired to the living room. Ralph and Mayfair sat on the sofa. I sank into an overstuffed chair.

The next sensation I had was of opening my eyes. To my great chagrin, I realized that I must have fallen asleep. My watch showed a little past eleven. Horrified, I began to wonder how I could apologize for this lack of manners, but a glance at the sofa proved I was home free. Ralph and Mayfair were both sound asleep. We were so relaxed with each other and so full of wonderful food that we had all dropped off immediately when we came in contact with the overstuffed furniture. When my stirring woke them, we all laughed and decided that it was a good omen—a perfect way to start a long, close friendship. And it turned out to be just that.

It wasn't long before I became Ralph's most dedicated disciple. As we approached opening night of the play for which I had auditioned, I threw myself into the rehearsals with increasing zeal. Amazingly, due to some unavoidable cast changes in the course of rehearsals, I ended up playing the leading role. What's more, on opening night I got the biggest laugh of the play!

This would have been terrific—except that the play was supposed to be a tense drama. It was the very first moment of the very first scene. Although we had rehearsed the play many times, we had never presented it in front of an audience. The opening curtain rose on a darkened living room set. It was night. The room was empty. Directly upstage, behind a sofa, was a pair of French doors, through which the audience could see a night sky. I was crouched down out of sight just outside the doors. The script called for me, while staying out of sight, to slowly open one of the doors, crawl through, slowly close it behind me, and, after a moment's pause, pop my head up from behind the sofa. This move was designed to startle and frighten the audience, at which point I would stand to reveal myself in full figure.

The mood must have been perfect, for when my head popped into view, a lady in the audience screamed. The scream scared me so much that I immediately ducked down again. After about a five-minute laugh, we managed to continue. We struggled all evening to recapture the mood, but the audience would have none of it.

During my tenure with the Community Center Players, we had many wonderful, hilarious experiences, which provided me with a rich source of situation comedy routines later in my career. I'll never forget the opening night of a three-act play, the title of which escapes me. Somehow, even during rehearsals, no one noticed that the script had a fatal flaw. There was a group of lines in the first scene of the first act that was almost identical to a group of lines in the last scene of the third act. You can guess what happened. On opening night, with a full house, the curtain came up and the play started. No more than five minutes into the first act, we hit that fatal group of lines and unknowingly segued into the last scene of the third act. When the curtain attendant heard the last lines of the play, he dutifully dropped the curtain. We didn't know what hit us. The audience must have thought it strange indeed that the play was so short, had no story, and ended before several of the characters on the stage had been introduced. Ralph, when he got control of his laughter, came out in front of the curtain and explained what had happened, and we started over again.

Another play we did was *Judgment Day*, in which I, wearing a monk's cape, made my entrance into the courtroom by making a dramatic leap from the window. When I leaped, the cape caught on a couple of nails on the window frame, and I leaped right in, followed by the entire courtroom wall, which fell over on the jury. We did the rest of the scene with the jury holding the wall up.

One of my most notable performances was in a play called *The Bat*, in which I played the hero. In the last act I was revealed as a detective, and I was supposed to pull out a pair of handcuffs, snap them on the villain's wrists, turn him over to a policeman to lead away, and proceed to carry on a torrid love scene with the leading lady, during which there were two full stage crosses. To add to the realism, we had borrowed a pair of real police handcuffs from the cop on the beat. I had them tucked into my trousers. When the fateful moment arrived, I revealed who I was, informed the other fellow that he was under arrest, snapped one of the

The Bat. That's me, seated at center stage, and the great Ralph Freud standing at the far left, with the rest of the cast. Using real police handcuffs didn't work out exactly as planned.

cuffs on his wrist, and went to put the other on him. Some strange force was holding it back. The handcuff had somehow gotten locked around one of the belt loops on my trousers. The two of us, captive and captor, stood there vainly trying to get it off, pulling, tugging, trying to break the loop, but to no avail. After several minutes of this, Ralph stuck his head in through what was supposed to be a third-story attic window and growled, "Get on with the play!"

What followed was probably one of the strangest love scenes ever played. The only way that the leading lady and I knew to play the scene

Judgment Day. When I leaped in from the window, my monk's cape caught on some nails and the entire courtroom wall fell over.

was the way that we had rehearsed it, but now here was this third party with his left hand attached to my trousers. If I crossed the stage, he crossed the stage. He did everything in his power to appear natural— ignoring us, looking around as though he were at a museum or about to measure the room for curtains. But when I took the leading lady in my arms, he was virtually between us. At the same time, the actor who played the policeman didn't know what to do, because he had always made his exit early in the scene, with the criminal in tow. He couldn't figure out a way to get offstage gracefully, so he stayed onstage, hoping he wouldn't interfere with the action. Unfortunately, because he had always exited with the prisoner, he had never watched the rest of the scene being played. He inevitably managed to be standing just where we wanted to go. He spent the entire scene leaping out of our way.

The scene was unbearably funny to the audience, particularly because we rose to the occasion, remembering all the good schooling and discipline Ralph had instilled in us, and played the scene exactly as rehearsed, ignoring with intense seriousness this human appendage we dragged through the love scene with us, to say nothing of the uniformed jumping jack. Our discipline under fire, Ralph told us later, had made him proud of us.

Of course, embarrassing foul-ups in front of a packed house are a fact of life in live theater. My favorite such moment occurred years later, when it was my good fortune to be in the audience for the Los Angeles Civic Light Opera Company's presentation of Frank Loesser's *The Most Happy Fella,* starring Robert Weede, the opera star, as the owner of the ranch, with Art Lund as Joey, the ranch foreman. Weede and Lund had been doing this play together for more than a year on Broadway before taking it on the road.

There is a scene in the first act of the show in which Joey tells the boss that he is restless and will soon be giving up his job and moving along. He says that he knows the signs when he gets this yearning to move on, that he can feel it in the breeze, he can hear it in the sound of the train whistle at night, etc. The owner of the ranch is seated on a little backless bench at the front of the stage, and Joey stands behind him. At one point, Joey puts one foot up on the bench.

On this particular night, Lund, like every good male actor, had undoubtedly checked the fly on his trousers just before stepping onstage. The fly was closed. What he didn't realize was that the zipper was broken and coming apart behind the pull. Lund was holding his hat in his hand, and as the scene progressed and he shifted his weight this way and that, his fly would open and close. Since he was wearing white shorts, the effect was something like flashing a light at the audience. Laughs that didn't belong began to ripple through the house, and neither man knew why. Weede, I could see, was angry. The veins began to stand out on his forehead, and his nostrils flared. He obviously thought Lund was mugging from behind him.

Finally, Lund put his foot up on the bench. The fly opened really wide, and an explosive, gargantuan laugh acknowledged it. Without knowing any more than he did before, his instincts took over. He whipped his hat over to cover his fly. This simply increased the volume of the laugh. When he put his hand behind his hat and did a braille appraisal of the situation, his eyes opened wider than the fly. The laughter took another quantum jump in volume. Now Lund turned his back on the audience, who could see him pulling and tugging and desperately trying to get it closed. Memories of my own handcuff experience rushed through my mind as I hung helplessly over the side of my seat, gasping for breath. Nothing helped Mr. Lund. At long last, he sucked in his breath, folded his trousers over the fly, pulled his belt tight, turned to the audience, and said, "It's busted. There's nothing I can do about it." This got him a huge round of applause. Weede, out of the side of his mouth, hissed, "Say your next line of dialogue!"

But Lund was nothing if not theater-wise. One could actually see him thinking, "If I don't calm them down—shame them into being quiet— the whole performance is liable to be lost." He stood there, quietly looking at the audience, implicitly saying, "I will not continue until you are quiet." Little by little the laughter subsided, until there were just a few titters here and there. But Lund wouldn't tolerate even that. People around the titterers shushed them, until finally he had the audience of several thousand people completely and absolutely silent.

Lund had been playing this scene almost every night for more than a year, and his lines were almost second nature to him. So you can't blame him for not considering his next line of dialogue out of context before delivering it to the hushed audience:

"Every night I feel it in the breeze."

The audience couldn't believe their ears. The ensuing laugh spread across the theater like a tidal wave, instantly engulfing the entire house in a deafening, high-pitched roar. Lund, momentarily dumbfounded by the response, broke into a broad grin. It took a good ten minutes before the audience, completely spent, quieted down enough for the play to go on.

Not all of my dramatic efforts in Jewish Community Center productions resulted in unintended humor. Nevertheless, I found out soon enough that I just wasn't cut out to be an actor. I was much too self-conscious. As a matter of fact, on one occasion Ralph and I were in a play called *The Bachelor's Baby* and my self-consciousness almost got Ralph a broken nose. We were performing the play in the greenroom, where the audience was right in the same room with us and on the same level. I was sitting next to Ralph, and my mother was in the audience, not too far away. After each line I would look at her and she'd just silently shake her head, as if to tell me, "It's no good." This started to bother me so much that I finally blew it completely, forgetting where I was in the script.

Ralph's next cue for me was simply a laugh, and then my next line was "What are you laughing at?" So Ralph started to laugh, but I didn't deliver my next line. And I somehow got the idea, because I was embarrassed about my performance, that he was laughing at my embarrassment, and the more he wanted to give me the cue the louder he laughed and the angrier I got. I was just about to belt him right in the nose when the cue girl finally called out my next line. After that we decided that I was probably a much better writer than actor.

I decided to try my hand at writing comedy material for a nightclub act. There was an act called the "Three Radio Rogues" playing at a nightclub called the Bal Tabarin in San Francisco. A friend of mine who worked as a busboy at the club told them I was a clever young writer. They asked me to come down, see the act, and write some material for them. If they liked it, they said, they would pay me.

I went to the club, asked for them, and introduced myself. I fully expected to hang around backstage or at the rear of the club and listen to the act. But they would have none of that. They had reserved a ringside table for me. I was so acutely self-conscious, alone at a table so close that the spotlight lit me as well as them, that I really missed the first half of the act. At least I couldn't recall it afterward. But it was a good act, in which they did impersonations of various personalities and told jokes and gags, both as themselves and as the celebrities.

Shortly after I sat down, the waitress came over for my order. I felt I should order something, but I was not at all sure how much the cover charge was, and whether the money I had in my pocket—about four dollars—would be enough to pay for it. So I ordered a cup of coffee. I should have ordered champagne, for when I asked for the check I was told that it had been taken care of. This made me feel tremendously important, and I vowed that I would write material the Radio Rogues would love.

I spent the next four days dreaming up and writing down gags that I thought would be right for the act. Finally, feeling that I had a respectable output for them to look at, I called and made an appointment to see them at the club. There was only half an hour before they had to go on, but they took the material and excused themselves, saying they wanted to go over it in private, which I could understand.

About twenty minutes later they came out and told me that my stuff showed a lot of talent, but there were only three jokes that they could use. At their going rate of three dollars and fifty cents a joke, they owed me ten fifty. In a moment of rash generosity, the spokesman gave me eleven dollars and told me to forget the change. To me it was like being given a hundred-thousand-dollar contract. A top act, one that played all the best clubs, was actually going to use some of my material! I went down and listened to their act, or, more precisely, listened to my three jokes—for that was all I really heard—many times before they left town.

It didn't occur to me at the time, but when the Radio Rogues paid me for those three jokes they didn't return the other twenty pages of material. I guess I figured that because they couldn't use them, they had thrown them away.

Years later, when I was producing Edgar Bergen's radio program in Hollywood, who should be on it but one of the Radio Rogues! He didn't recognize me when I greeted him, but when I mentioned my name and the circumstances, he remembered immediately. Their act, he told me, had broken up some years before. Evidently he didn't remember *all* the circumstances, for during a break he took me aside. "Kid," he said, "I knew way back then you were going to make it. That material was sensational."

"As I recall, you only used three jokes," I reminded him.

He looked at me like I was crazy. "Are you kidding? We used everything you gave us. That stuff kept us going for months!"

. . .

During my days with the Community Center Players, I was also working at various jobs. The Golden Gate Bridge was under construction at the time, and the first job I got was spinning cable on the bridge—an extremely hazardous job that paid well, but for which I was particularly unsuited, given my double vision and my nonexistent equilibrium. Fortunately, when I told my mother of my good fortune at landing the cable-spinning job, she insisted that I call them back immediately and tell them I was unavailable. I argued the point, but to no avail. If not for her stubbornness, I have no doubt I would have ended up at the bottom of San Francisco Bay.

The first position that I actually took was working for a relative who was a wholesale fur dealer. I wasn't interested in furs, and I wasn't interested in business. But I had to do something to earn a living, and so I was stuck. I was paid the minimum wage of sixteen dollars a week. Most of the time my boss had me cleaning up, delivering furs to various stores, or taking inventory, in the hope that I would learn fur values by observation. What I discovered was that the most important thing was the label—the name of the store from which the fur was purchased. My presence in the office during lunch hour, when some retail store might call and want a coat sent over immediately, justified my salary. The boss taught me a little about the procedure, and I got so I didn't make a complete fool of myself. One lunch hour I received a call from one of the most prestigious stores in the city, noted for its luxurious fur department.

"We have a customer," the voice from the store told me, "who is willing to pay fifteen hundred dollars for a mink coat. Do you have one you can bill to me for eight hundred dollars?"

I didn't, but I told him I would check and get right back to him. I then called another wholesale furrier, as I had been taught to do, and asked "Do you have a mink coat that you can bill to me for five hundred dollars?" Whether he had it or not, he said he did. For all I know, he called still another dealer, who billed the coat to him for two hundred fifty dollars. In any event, he brought me the coat, I took it to the prestigious firm, they sewed their label into it, and the customer left, satisfied with her new mink coat. She should have worn it inside out with the label exposed if she wanted the real value to show.

That experience reminded me of the story about the little boy who asked his father, part owner of a hardware store, to tell him what "ethics" meant. The father replied, "Son, let me explain it by telling you a story."

"Let's say I'm down at the hardware store, working the cash register, and a customer walks in, buys something for seventy-five cents, hands me a bill to pay for it, and I give her a quarter change, and she takes it and walks away."

"She's almost out the front door when suddenly I notice that I'm holding a *ten* dollar bill. When I took the money from her, I thought it was a one dollar bill, which is why I only gave her a quarter change. She obviously thought so, too. And she's just about to leave the store, without any idea that she's been unintentionally shortchanged."

"Now, this is where 'ethics' comes in," the father continued, raising his finger to emphasize the point. "I have an important decision to make. Should I tell my partner?"

While not quite the same as shortchanging, there was something about the whole fur pricing and relabeling procedure that seemed almost obscene to me, and I knew in a very short time that I didn't have the right mental attitude to succeed in that business. Curiously, my employer came to the same conclusion shortly before I did.

Following my brief stay in the fur business, the whole routine of "Do you know anyone who might have a job for Jess?" "What can he do?" "Well, he's very bright," began again, and this time a family friend got me placed as a life insurance salesman for the New England Mutual Life Insurance Company. They told me I would have a drawing account of $25 per week, which meant I could get that much each week, and they would deduct it from future commissions. After a trial period of two months, during which I drew $200 and generated commissions totaling $19, the insurance company agreed with the fur dealer about my talents.

During my tenure as an insurance salesman, I usually ate lunch with several friends who were also working nearby. I recall many lunchtime sessions when we would eat and then sit for fifteen or twenty minutes in a parked car and watch the parade of people walking up Grant Avenue. We would play a game in which we took turns trying to crack each other up by ad-libbing a humorous personal history of the next person to turn the corner from Geary Street and walk toward us.

Another subject would invariably come up during these sessions. We spoke about our futures, our ambitions, and our expectations, and the same question surfaced every time: "If you were assured of making fifty dollars a week for the rest of your life, and you could never make more, but you would never make less, would you take it?" Without exception, every one of my friends said yes, they would take it in a minute. They pointed out that with an income of fifty dollars a week a person could get married, buy a house, live comfortably, and put his children through college. For some reason, I could never see myself settling for that. I don't know what prompted it, but I had dreams of making it big.

· · ·

Shortly after we returned from our world trip, my sister Janice moved to Washington, D.C., where she got a job as a social service worker. In January 1936 my mother went to Washington to visit Janice for a few months. The day my mother left I quit my job and went into writing full-time. Ralph Freud let me share his office, and got me writing jobs here and there. The jobs varied, ranging from dramatic epilogues for a women's club convention to dramatization of the year's progress for the board of directors of a large company.

I wrote a one-act play, my first, and it was produced by the Community Center Players. It was a "strike play"; this was the era of Clifford Odets's *Waiting For Lefty* and Irwin Shaw's *Bury the Dead*. The Community Center Players put on a good production, and the kids acted it out beautifully. It hadn't taken me long to write it. I had just written one line following the other simply because it seemed to be the next line to put down. I hadn't thought it out—it was sort of an instinctive drama. But I was taken aback when, after the performance, one after another of the adults who had been in the audience came up to talk to me about all the symbolism and premises that they had read into it. I took credit for these things, of course, but it was a great revelation to me that all of this was being read into this work, which, as far as I was concerned, was just a matter of putting down each line as it came into my head.

After all the favorable comments about my play, people started asking me for advice about writing, and I willingly gave it to them. I didn't realize what a swelled head I was getting. Ralph Freud did. He took me aside one day and gave me the devil. He called me lazy and ridiculed the idea of my calling myself a writer. "Here you have only written a single one-act play and you call yourself a writer," he said. "I know people who have written *fifty* three-act plays, and they don't dare to call themselves writers! What have you done, that you are so proud of? You should write at least three three-act plays this summer. They might be good or bad. That doesn't matter. Only one thing matters. Work. The very same qualities that make for success in any other business apply in this one. Aptitude and conscientious perseverance. A businessman is just as much an artist in making deals as you are in writing a play. It is a knack, a bent of the mind, a gift. You have to have it in the first place, but it takes lots and lots of practice and work to perfect it. Now scram. I am not going to talk to you again till you get a three-act play finished and show it to me."

I was devastated. I worshiped this man, and I knew he was right. It was the best thing that could have happened to me, a good stiff jab to my pride. It snapped me out of it, and I soon disciplined myself to write at least four or five hours a day. Before long I had finished that first three-act play that Ralph had demanded. And I wrote another one-act play which won a contest and was presented over a local Oakland radio station for Kay Jewelers. The prize was proudly announced over the air as a twenty-five dollar gold wristwatch. But the real thrill for me was to hear living, human radio actors reading my lines and the vibrant voice of the announcer proclaiming to the world (or, rather, that small portion of it listening to that particular station that afternoon) that I had written it.

I tried sending some jokes to Burns and Allen, with predictable results. "Dear Mr. Oppenheimer," the polite reply from their secretary said. "We wish to thank you for your interest in submitting your jokes to us. However, we are returning them herewith inasmuch as we have two writers under contract who write all of our material and therefore, we are not in a position to accept any outside scripts, etc."

It was the first in a long line of rejection letters that I would receive over the years. For some reason, I've held onto all of them, amassing quite a collection. If I had to pick my favorites, they would be several letters that I received in the late 1950s, when I was working at NBC-TV. These particular rejections came not from producers or performers, but from other writers.

I was developing a new, limited-run dramatic series for NBC, called *The Ten Commandments*. Basing each show on a different commandment had its limitations, of course. As I told *Daily Variety* at the time, "If we get a thirteen-week deal, we'll have to make up some."

Each of the ten shows in the series was to be written by a noted author or playwright. The pilot episode, a stirring drama starring Arthur Kennedy and Anne Francis, was written by Ben Hecht. But some of my attempts to persuade other literary giants to lend their talents to the project were not quite as successful.

For instance, when I wrote to John Steinbeck, saying that I hoped that I would be able to "goose" him into working on the series, I received the following response:

Dear Mr. Oppenheimer:

The goose, so far, hasn't worked. I'm so busy on a piece of my own work that I'm afraid it would take a guided missile to goose me into your project at this time.

Anyway, I loved being goosed. Thanks again.

Yours very sincerely,
John Steinbeck

Edna Ferber, author of the immortal *Show Boat*, wrote this reply to my agent Ray Stark's letter requesting her participation in the series:

Dear Mr. Stark:

It is pleasant to know that you and Mr. Oppenheimer thought of me in connection with the contemplated Ten Commandments television series.

I don't quite know why I sit here trying to write a novel, with my face snarled over the typewriter day after day, week after week, month after month, when I could be jazzing up the Ten Commandments. But there it is, and here I am working in Connecticut.

My thanks to you, and to Mr. Oppenheimer just the same. Sorry. I can't be one of the ten writers.

Sincerely,
Edna Ferber

Upon receiving this, I immediately wrote back to Miss Ferber:

Dear Miss Ferber:

As Ray Stark told you, I was very interested in securing your services as one of the writers on my Ten Commandments television series. All that, however, has changed.

The mere fact that you could refer to the job as "jazzing up" one of the Commandments made my mind up. You simply must jazz one up for me. There are no ifs, ands or buts. I can wait as long as necessary. The project

December 1, 1956

Mr. Jess Oppenheimer
National Broadcasting Company, Inc.
Sunset and Vine
Los Angeles 28, California

Dear Mr. Oppenheimer:

    The goose, so far, hasn't worked. I'm so busy
on a piece of my own work that I'm afraid it would take
a guided missile to goose me into your project at this
time.

    Anyway, I loved being goosed. Thanks again.

                Yours very sincerely,

                John Steinbeck

JS/c

West Cornwall
Connecticut
December 20, 1956

Mr. Jess Oppenheimer
National Broadcasting Co., Inc.
Sunset and Vine
Los Angeles 28, California

Dear Mr. Oppenheimer:

    I have tackled most of the Commandments in real life and
bruised some of them rather badly. I don't covet anybody's wife, but
I steal. I am afraid this project, while noble and fascinating, is
not for me. I can't think of any colleague either. Thanks for thinking of me, however, and a Merry Christmas to you and Moses and the
others.

                Cordially yours,

                JAMES THURBER

JT/ek

Letters from John Steinbeck and James Thurber.

will take a year, anyway. I'll save one of the Commandments for you. Or I'll let you write an Eleventh or Twelfth—anything you say. There has to be some way we can work together on this project.

Please?

Sincerely,
Jess Oppenheimer

The following letter came by return mail:

Dear Mr. Oppenheimer:

Miss Ferber is out of the city for a short time. I spoke to her about your letter, among others (via telephone). She asks me to say that you have probably confused her with some other correspondent in the matter of your proposed Ten Commandments television series.

The term "jazzing up" one of the Commandments was not used by her in her letter.

She asked me to thank you again for thinking of her in connection with the program. She definitely will not be able to take part in it.

Sincerely,
J. B. Garden

Somewhat perplexed, I pulled out the letter I had received from Miss Ferber and read it again, just to make sure. I had not been imagining things—there it was in black and white. I put a copy of the letter in an envelope and sent it to her. A few days later, I received a reply, this time from Edna Ferber herself:

Dear Mr. Oppenheimer:

I am so glad to have the copy of the letter containing the "jazzing up" term as applied to your proposed Ten Commandments television series. But I am horrified, too. It was good of you to take the trouble to send it.

Here is the background of the letter, so far as I am able to reconstruct it:

I have a secretary who is intelligent and reasonably efficient, but she is given to improvisation. A frustrated writer, probably. On occasions other than this I have been embarrassed by statements in letters which I have not dictated or read. When, as in this case, I am intent on a long and somewhat difficult piece of work, I sometimes give her merely the gist of what a letter should contain. I suppose I said to Garden, "Look, please thank Mr. Stark and say that I'm busy with a longish job. Here I am sitting all day with my face in the typewriter. I don't want to jazz up the Ten

Letter from Edna Ferber.

Commandments." I don't even recall having used such a term. But if I did, it certainly wasn't meant to be used in a letter to Mr. Stark or to you.

How rude it must have seemed to you and to Mr. Stark. After this I'm going to read the letters I sign. There probably are lots of people who haven't been as thoughtful as you about confronting me with the fruits of Garden's pungent pen.

My best wishes to you for the success of the series.

Sincerely,
Edna Ferber

Of all the letters I received declining participation in the *Ten Commandments* series, my favorite is this one, which I received on Christmas Eve from James Thurber:

Dear Mr. Oppenheimer:

I have tackled most of the Commandments in real life and bruised some of them rather badly. I don't covet anybody's wife, but I steal. I am afraid this project, while noble and fascinating, is not for me. I can't think of any colleague either. Thanks for thinking of me, however, and a Merry Christmas to you and Moses and the others.

Cordially yours,
Thurber

Going Hollywood

IN THE SUMMER OF 1936 I went downtown to the Golden Gate Theater to see the stage presentation of *A Day at the Races*. Before turning it into a movie, the Marx Brothers were taking it around the country as a live stage production in order to work out the kinks in the script and to perfect their timing. After the show I went to the stage entrance, hoping to get a look at the Marx Brothers in person. I arrived at the stage door at the same time as a rather large family, apparently friends of Groucho's. The doorman, who had their name on a list, waved them through. I suddenly realized that the doorman thought that I was part of the family and was waving me through with them. I hastily accepted his invitation.

Once backstage, I stayed away from the family in order not to be pointed out as an impostor. I got into a conversation with a lovely and friendly young lady who was also just standing around. She turned out to be Chico Marx's daughter, Maxine, and when the Marx Brothers left the theater to go out to dinner in Chinatown, she invited me to join them.

Dinner, of course, was a million laughs. What more could a young man who wanted to earn his living in comedy ask for than dinner with the Marx Brothers? I can remember nothing that was said or done during the meal—just a gorgeous rosy glow of euphoria—but I will never forget the scene when Groucho went to the cashier to pay the check.

The cashier was a wizened old Chinese gentleman of many years and little humor. I recall his tiny eyes, the few strands of long hair that made up his beard, and the metal-rimmed glasses over which he peered. Groucho handed him the check. The old man picked up an abacus and rattled the beads back and forth expertly.

"Thirty-eight dollar, seventy-fi cents," he announced.

Groucho gave him a look of shocked surprise. He snatched the abacus out of the old man's hand, picked up the check, rattled the beads around

like he was playing a tambourine in a Salvation Army band, and threw
the check and abacus back on the counter.

"Twenty-fi dollar, sixty-fi cents," replied Groucho.

With great composure, as though he had been politely asked to please
check the accuracy of his arithmetic, the old man picked up the abacus
and the check, redid his calculations, and came up with the same answer:
"Thirty-eight dollar, seventy-fi cents."

Groucho grabbed them back, did his bit with the abacus again, and
gave the old man a *different* amount than he had the first time. Now it
was the old man's turn again. There ensued a seemingly endless series of
such confrontations, with Groucho ending up with a different number
each time, and the old gentleman always politely and patiently refiguring
and arriving unswervingly at his original total.

Groucho's figures ranged from a low of $8.10 to a high of $47.95. The
watching crowd was hysterical—some of them rolling on the floor and
others leaning against the wall for support and sliding down to the floor
when their legs would no longer hold them—but the cashier's expression
was as unchanging as his abacus total.

Even after Groucho finally paid him the correct amount and the
maitre d' told the cashier who Groucho was, the old man remained
indifferent. He had never heard of Groucho Marx, and he couldn't have
cared less.

•   •   •

At about this time, radio production was beginning to concentrate in
the three big centers: New York, Hollywood, and Chicago. San Francisco, which had bred a number of popular programs, had lost them, and
was facing an exodus of talent, most of which was taking the short hop
down to L.A. Several of my actor and announcer friends had made
successful transplants, so one day I announced to my surprised family
that I wished to pull up stakes, go to Hollywood, and be a writer.

My mother was against it. With my father gone and my sister living in
Washington, D.C., Mom was afraid to lose me. My uncle, a staid businessman and patriarch of the family both before and after my father died,
dismissed the idea with a snort. "All he wants to do," he admonished my
mother, "is go down there to be with all those show girls."

It looked as though I was destined to remain where so many people
were losing their hearts to little cable cars, while I was dying to get out
and couldn't. Then one evening, during a rehearsal break, I was venting
my spleen to some of my fellow Centerites about the unfairness of life in

general (and mine in particular). I didn't know that Ralph Freud was also listening until the next day, when he called me into his office. We had a long talk about what a big move I was contemplating, the odds against my succeeding, how serious I was about a career, and related subjects. Finally, Ralph explained that he had been testing my determination. He told me that in his opinion I had talent, and that if I wanted him to, he would be glad to meet with my family and see if he couldn't get them to budge somehow.

The crucial meeting came. My family cited chapter and verse to Ralph about my history, my lack of "stick-to-itiveness," the fact that I had always been bright, but not particularly responsible, and on down the list of my faults, which was lengthy indeed. My friend Ralph was masterful. "I grant you all these things," he said, "and I can only tell you that I know hundreds of successful people in show business and other creative arts who have just such shortcomings. They also have this other, elusive, imaginative, innovative faculty called talent. I think Jess has talent, and that with a modicum of lucky breaks he can be successful. Why don't we work out a test run? You allow him to go down to Hollywood for a few months and try to establish himself as a writer. If he hasn't made it within that time, he will come back, get a nice, respectable nine-to-five job, and never say a word about it again."

All the family members looked at each other. It was hard to rebut a proposition that was so fair. Certainly a short period out of such an unproductive life at such an early age couldn't hurt anything. And I had a small inheritance from one of my father's uncles, so it wasn't going to cost anyone anything. Anyone but me, that is.

My family agreed that I could buy myself a second-hand car and go to Hollywood in search of my fortune. I would be given only six months to prove myself. If, within that time, I had not earned, through writing, a minimum of five hundred dollars, I would come back with my tail between my legs and begin serving a life sentence in San Francisco. Ralph had done more than his part. Now it was up to me.

I can still see the used 1927 Packard convertible I chose to carry me to my Armageddon. It cost me two hundred dollars of my legacy.

My Packard was creamy yellow, with blue stripes. I vividly recall my drive down to L.A. in it. I was completely euphoric, and spent much of the trip singing at the top of my lungs (a condition that reads better than it sounds, as I have a tendency to sing one song in many keys). I vowed that none of the success or monetary reward I was sure to win would persuade me ever to sell this car.

Anyone interested could have tracked me from my home in San Francisco all the way to the heart of Hollywood by the trail of oil that dripped out of the Packard's ancient and overworked crankcase. It was, after all, ten years old—but to me, it was like a brand new 1937 Pierce Arrow.

It was early afternoon when I arrived in L.A., after a nine-hour drive, which had begun before dawn, 450 miles to the north. I immediately headed for the world-famous corner of Hollywood and Vine. As I drove up to the intersection and stopped at a traffic light, I could see a large building on the corner with a vertical sign that said "Equitable Building of Hollywood." On the corner to my left, throngs of shoppers were streaming in and out of the Broadway Hollywood department store. To my right stood a large drug store, and on the opposite corner I saw the striped awnings of the Coco Tree Restaurant. One of the big red cars of the Pacific Electric Railway rumbled by on its way down Hollywood Boulevard, powered by a maze of electrical cables strung overhead. I decided to park and experience this magical location a little more fully.

Standing on the corner, watching the crowds and feeling that history was in some way being wrought, I noticed the large clock that hung from the corner of the Equitable Building. It was two-thirty. I realized that it had been a long time since I had eaten. I decided to try the drug store, which advertised a soda fountain. I went in, sat down on a stool, picked up a menu and looked it over. Then a most prophetic thing happened. While waiting to place my order, I glanced at the people around me. Looking to my right, I discovered that I had sat, or fate had seated me, next to one of the only two or three people I knew in Hollywood. His name was Ed Max, a talented actor and sometime writer who had left San Francisco just a few months before. Following a general greeting and exchange of some news, Ed asked me what I was doing in L.A. I told him I wanted to become a writer.

"I hear that Young and Rubicam needs comedy writers for the *Packard Hour*," he announced.

"What's a Young and Rubicam?" I asked him, showing my provincialism. Young and Rubicam was at that time, and still is, one of the largest advertising agencies in the world. Ed patiently explained that fact to me, and informed me that Y&R, as it was known, had just opened a Hollywood office in the Equitable Building, directly across the street.

It may sound odd in light of today's distribution of responsibility in the making of shows, but in those days the networks were simply facilities suppliers. They rented their studios and broadcasting equipment to the programs, which were owned by the sponsors and produced entirely by the advertising agencies. Under this arrangement, of course, a sponsor could move its program to any network it wished, and into whichever time spot it could bargain for. More than infrequently, a network would have an entire evening of programs destroyed because a sponsor of a hit show decided to move it to another network. This situation changed a few years later when William Paley, the head of CBS, decided he did not want to have that Sword of Damocles hanging over his head anymore. So he went out and bought both the *Amos 'n' Andy* and *Jack Benny* programs. This led to the networks slowly taking over ownership and production of the shows, with the advertising agencies having less and less to say about production.

But on that day in October 1936, the agencies were in complete control, and I had just finished lunch with the man fate had chosen to point me in the right direction. I paid my check, crossed the street, consulted the directory, and proceeded onward and upward to the Young and Rubicam suite on the sixth floor. Within a year or so, Y&R's radio department would occupy two entire floors of the Equitable Building, but at that time it consisted of a small waiting room in which a secretary sat behind a little desk, with two doors, one on either side of her, each, presumably, leading to an office. Two men were standing in the waiting room in deep conversation. As I approached the secretary I could see the name "Mr. Harrington" on one door and "Mr. Stauffer" on the other. "Miss Sides" was the name on the secretary's desk.

"What can I do for you?" Miss Sides asked warmly. She was tall, willowy, and had long, dark hair.

"I want to be a comedy writer. What do I have to do?"

She gave me a friendly laugh. "The man for you to see is Tom Everett. But he won't be back until after six. Why don't you come back and talk to him then?"

"Okay, I will."

I was turning to go, when my ear caught something that one of the two men in the waiting room had said. He had mentioned Tom Everett, a name that had had no meaning to me only three minutes before, but that had become all-important since my brief conversation with the secretary. Pretending to study the framed advertisements displayed on the waiting room walls, I listened intently to what these two gentlemen had to say about this name which had suddenly been inserted into my life. And they told me plenty.

One of them was complaining to the other that Everett had asked him to write a sketch for *The Fred Astaire Packard Hour,* and then, when he submitted it, Everett turned it down. Indignantly, he repeated exactly what Everett had said he wanted in the sketch—the length, the subject matter, the situation. The other man related the same story, reciting what Everett had told him he wanted, and griping because he, too, had been turned down. Between them, they told me precisely what Everett was looking for. I decided to dash home and see if I couldn't knock it out in time to bring it with me when I came back at six o'clock to see him.

I closed the door to Y&R behind me, on my way to home and typewriter. It suddenly struck me—a typewriter I had; a home, I didn't have. At least not within 450 miles.

I drove east on Sunset Boulevard, looking for apartments to rent. About ten blocks away, just before reaching Western Avenue, I saw a large "For Rent" sign on a newly built apartment building with six furnished units. The posted price was $37.50 a month, which sounded reasonable. I stopped the car, went in, and paid the first month's rent on the spot to a startled landlady. She had never before rented an apartment without the tenant looking at it first.

She let me into my apartment. I took the key, pushed her out of the room, unpacked my typewriter from the car, and prayed that Everett wouldn't come back until six-thirty. If so, I felt that I could knock out a draft of the material he wanted—not polished, but close enough to show that there was something there.

It was six-twenty when I entered the Y&R waiting room again. Miss Sides greeted me with a smile. Tom Everett came in five minutes later. He seemed in an awful rush. (I found out later that he always seemed in an awful rush.) But Miss Sides, bless her heart, took firm command. "This gentleman is a comedy writer," she said. "I took the liberty of making an appointment for you to see him."

Mr. Everett had a little office I hadn't noticed, off the waiting room. We went in and sat down. He had no sooner asked me what my name was than the door opened and a middle-aged man stuck his head through. I was awestruck. This man was one of the giants in the humor field. He wrote an extremely popular syndicated daily newspaper column under his initials, M.G.B., did radio shows, pictures, everything.

"Everett," he boomed, "I've got to see you."

I could see how much of Everett's attention I would get if he interviewed me while this big name waited fuming outside. I got up, walked over to him, and handed him the envelope containing my sketch. "Mr. Everett," I said, "I'm a writer, not a talker. Why don't you talk to him, read this at your leisure, and let me know if you're interested."

"Thanks, kid," he said. This was not an unusual appellation for me, as my face was so cherubically innocent and unlined at this stage in my life that I was usually taken for under eighteen.

The following day I made arrangements for gas, electricity, and a telephone, which I was assured would be installed as soon as possible, but not before another day or two had passed. I got acquainted with my one-bedroom apartment and spent a lot of time imagining that Everett was desperately trying to call me and would have to give someone else the job because he couldn't locate me. Of course, if he was in such dire need of me, all he had to do was to get in a car and come to the address on the letter. But I didn't think of that. It would have saved me a lot of anguish while I was sweating out his response.

On the second morning after my aborted interview, at eleven o'clock, the phone man showed up. At five minutes to twelve, he was finished. I spent from then until one o'clock pacing up and down trying to decide whether I should call up Y&R and give them my new phone number in case they wanted to get in touch with me. I finally figured out just how to put it in a way that wouldn't make me appear too anxious, and I had the phone in my hand, when I heard the mailman outside. My ears must have been pretty good in those days, made even more sensitive by excited anticipation, because when I went down to the apartment's mailbox the mailman was still two houses away. I waited patiently while he put the mail in the various apartments' boxes. He had a couple of letters held out. He looked at the name on the letters, then at the name on the mailbox, and started to put the letters in my box. I said "I'll take those. They're for me."

"Oppenheimer?"

"That's right. I've just been here a couple of days."

He kind of snorted, handed me the letters, and went on his way. The first envelope bore my mother's distinctive handwriting. She was good for a letter every day, I knew, and had written the first one immediately on learning my address. The other envelope said "Young and Rubicam" in the upper left hand corner. I sat down and looked at it. My adrenaline was flowing, and my heart was pounding. I was afraid to open it. My first instinct was to tear it open immediately. Then I realized that it might be, and most probably was, one of those polite "Thank you for thinking of us, but your material does not fit in with our present plans," letters which every writer has gotten. Eventually, though, I knew it would have to be opened.

It was about two o'clock when I ripped off the flap. Forty-five minutes later, I worked up the courage to take the letter out of the envelope.

"Dear Mr. Oppenheimer," it said, "Please call me. I want to talk to you about a staff writing job on the *Packard Hour*." It was signed by Tom Everett. I could have died at that moment and considered mine to be a life well spent.

I called Everett, but he was out. Miss Sides said she was sure he could see me at about four-thirty. Needless to say, I was waiting in the reception area when he returned.

"Well, I read your stuff, and I liked it," he said as he showed me into his office. "Curiously enough, what you wrote was right in line with a show we're preparing."

"Well, that's a coincidence," I said with a straight face. "Maybe it's a good omen."

"Let's hope so. Where have you been working?"

"San Francisco. KFRC, KYA, KJBS, KGO, KPO." I suddenly realized that I had named every radio station in San Francisco, whether I had worked there or not. As I finished each station, it seemed better to name another station than just to leave a deadly pause. He seemed to take it as a matter of course.

"Uh—I'd like you to join our staff, writing the *Packard Hour* with Fred Astaire. What's your salary?"

I had no idea in the world how much to ask for, and I certainly couldn't tell him that my total lifetime earnings to date from radio were seven dollars and fifty cents.

"Uh—How much time is involved?"

"It's a full-time job. What do you have to have?"

"Hmm. Well, what does staff normally pay?"

"We're flexible."

"I see."

I couldn't see any way to prolong the conversation, and I wasn't about to name a figure, so I just sat there. He must have realized he wasn't going to get any numbers out of me, and broke the silence. "How does one twenty-five sound?"

I sat for a moment, ostensibly making up my mind, but actually trying to smooth the quiver out of my voice. I used as few words as possible. "Okay."

"Fine, welcome aboard. When can you start?"

"Is now too soon?" is what I wanted to say, but I agreed to begin the following morning at nine o'clock. Everett explained that I would meet the rest of the staff, get an assignment, and later in the day attend a rehearsal. Then he took me around the office and introduced me to Joe

Suddenly I had a job working in nighttime radio in
Hollywood, writing for Fred Astaire!

Stauffer, a plump, amiable, easy laugher, who welcomed me warmly. Tom
Harrington was the other agency VIP. Harrington was the top man in
the office. He was achingly slender, weighing perhaps a hundred pounds.
He radiated a kind of frailty, which was accentuated by the softness of
his voice. As someone once said about Irving Berlin, "You had to hug
him to hear him." I was later to learn that that soft voice got results like
a clap of thunder.

Mr. Stauffer seemed genuinely interested in the new staff member
and asked me about my background. He mentioned that he had been
transferred from New York six months before, so when he asked about

my experience, I repeated my trick of listing the names of every station in San Francisco. Just as an oft repeated story loses impact, the number of stations didn't seem impressive enough this time around, so I went back over the list, rearranging the call letters as I went, and ending up with about three times as many stations as San Francisco had. I was full of the heady wine of landing a job and hobnobbing with the boss. As I said good-bye, Miss Sides was by the door. She congratulated me and noted the fact that Mr. Stauffer had seemed taken with me. I replied that I liked him, too. "It's so good to have his smiling face back here in the office," she said. "For the past two months he's been in San Francisco."

Back in my apartment, I sat down to write a letter home, bearing the glad tidings. I was ecstatic. I was working in nighttime radio in Hollywood, and I was the happiest twenty-three-year-old alive! I got to the part about the salary being a hundred and twenty-five dollars and realized that Everett hadn't told me whether it was per month or per week. But it didn't matter. At one hundred twenty-five dollars per month, I would have the required five hundred dollars in just four months—two months ahead of schedule.

I had to wait for my first paycheck to arrive before I knew my salary. It was one hundred twenty-five dollars per week.

Dancing on the Air

THE MORNING AFTER I was hired, I met the other fellows on the *Packard Hour* staff. To my great surprise, one of them was KFRC's staff writer and sound effects man, Austin Peterson, who had come to L.A. a few weeks before to try his luck as a writer in Hollywood. An even greater coincidence, we discovered after we had greeted each other, was that we had both rented an apartment in the same building. And Pete—as his friends called him—was not the only other KFRC veteran at Y&R. Supervising all of Young and Rubicam's radio programs from New York was none other than Pat Weaver, KFRC's former director of news and programming. Weaver had left KFRC for the East Coast a year or so earlier to try to break into network radio at CBS and had discovered, as I had, that the real action was not at the networks but at advertising agencies like Y&R.

There was one other writer on the staff besides Pete, a gag man named Eddie Moran. He was a most amazing person with a warm, outgoing personality—the archetypical stand-up comic type. Eddie's personality overwhelmed you to the point that his looks disappeared. His confidence, warmth, openness, and general demeanor made you oblivious to the fact that his nose occupied three-quarters of his face. I remember thinking to myself once that Eddie would be quite handsome if it weren't for his looks.

Eddie Moran was on the staff with me for two years, but I could not even venture a guess as to whether he was a good writer. What he was was the master of the art of double-talk. His mouth would put out words, and they would be good English words, each one having a meaning, and he would laugh it up and put in inflections, and dramatize an exit and an entrance, and pantomime a piece of business. When he was finished, everyone was hysterical. But somehow that sketch never got written. It couldn't, because the whole harangue didn't make a damn bit of sense.

Shortly after I was hired, I was sitting in the office one day, trying desperately to get an idea, when in came Eddie and told me he was going to give me a break. He explained that he had been assigned to write a sketch, and that he already had a great sketch idea all worked out, dialogue and everything, but he had to get to the race track, and didn't have time to put it on paper. He was willing to tell it to me and let me get full credit for it, just for writing it down. I said okay, and he proceeded to tell me a sketch that was really brilliant. He had me laughing hysterically, falling down, savoring the kudos I would get for turning this gem in. I thanked him and he left for the track.

I put a piece of paper in the typewriter. Nothing happened. I couldn't quite remember how the sketch started. Slowly I realized that I couldn't quite remember the middle, either, or the end. I had been introduced to Eddie Moran, the hard way. I was still without any ideas for my own assignment. What's worse, now I had also committed to write the sketch that had been assigned to Eddie—and I was starting from scratch on that one, too.

Fortunately, inspiration finally hit me, and I completed Eddie's assignment, in addition to my own. The sketch turned out to be pretty good, although bearing no resemblance to whatever Eddie had double-talked to me. I even got some compliments on it. I later discovered that Eddie was going around telling people, "I gave the kid a break. I laid the whole thing out for him."

One evening after rehearsal, Eddie and I were sitting in Nickodell's Melrose Grotto when an acquaintance of his, quite drunk, happened to notice Eddie as he staggered by our booth. He made a U-turn, which almost took him to the far wall, and found his way back to us. He sat and looked Eddie squarely in the eyes for almost a full minute. He obviously had some terrible tale to tell, a story he couldn't bring himself to articulate, it was so horrible. Finally, Eddie saw that we would be there until closing if he didn't do something. "What's new, Horace?" he said.

"What's new?" Horace bellowed. "What's new? I'll tell you what's new. Mildred is leaving me. After all these years. I'm going to kill myself!"

"Now just a minute, Horace. I'm not going to let you kill yourself until you hear a story I'm going to tell you. After that, you can do what you want. Okay?"

Horace seriously agreed. For the next fifteen minutes, Eddie Moran spun out a succession of nonwords, unrelated inflections, dazzling dynamics, and sympathetic facial expressions that smacked of silent-picture acting. I had a terrible time keeping from laughing. I would drop silver-

I stood on a chair to get a better view of the festivities at Young and Rubicam's 1936 Christmas Party. Austin Peterson is in the doorway, partially hidden by Harry von Zell. Among the others pictured are True Boardman, far left, Mildred Heredeen, seated at left, Carroll O'Meara in front of the window, Tom Harrington, just to the right of Carroll, with a raised drink, Jack van Nostrand, in front of my left shoulder, and Nat Wolfe, standing at far right.

•   •   •

ware, so I could pick it up. I even stuck a napkin in my mouth. But Horace saw none of it. His eyes were riveted on Eddie, and he was drinking in every nuance of whatever it was he thought was being said to him. Finally, Eddie signaled by his tone that his tale was through. The tears were streaming down Horace's cheeks.

"Oh my God!" he wailed. "I never thought of it like that. I never considered her side at all. I'm gonna go home and apologize," and he reeled off into the night.

•   •   •

The lifeline between Y&R's offices in Hollywood and its radio department on Madison Avenue in New York was a teletype machine. The sound of its bell would often set off a race down the hall to see what important message was being transmitted. This was, of course, long before the days when faxing messages became as easy as feeding a piece of paper into a machine. Instead, if someone gave the teletype operator in the New York office a document to send to Hollywood, he would have to retype the entire thing into the machine. As the operator struck each key, that character would appear on paper in Hollywood, at the same speed as it was typed in New York (provided that our teletype had not run out of paper).

Because of the importance of this link to the East Coast, during office hours there was always one person responsible for attending to the machine, seeing that it was supplied with paper and that any urgent messages were promptly delivered to the proper party. If a transmission began during office hours, whoever was assigned to the teletype would have to remain at the machine until the message was completed, even if that meant staying after closing.

One day, just as the offices were about to close, the fellow assigned to the teletype was telling me about the big date he had planned for that evening. Suddenly the bell on the machine rang, signaling the beginning of another message from the New York office. Line by line the message slowly came out of the machine as it was typed in New York. Soon everyone else in the office, including me, had left, but the transmission —now several pages long—continued.

An hour later the teletype was still clickety-clacking away, and the paper was still spilling out of the machine with no end in sight. The poor guy had no choice but to call his date to tell her he would be late.

Two hours later he was still waiting for the message to finish. Frustrated and furious, he called his date again, this time to cancel. Not wanting to risk losing his job, there was nothing he could do but sit helplessly, his anger growing by the minute at the world in general and at Y&R's Madison Avenue office in particular. He spent the time trying to think of ways to take his revenge. Finally, the seemingly interminable message from New York came to an end. There was a short pause, and then the machine typed: "PLEASE ACKNOWLEDGE RECEIPT OF THIS MESSAGE." This was what he had been waiting for. Seating himself at the keyboard, he typed back "MESSAGE GARBLED. PLEASE REPEAT," grabbed his coat, and walked out the door.

•　　•　　•

The *Packard Hour*, I learned after reading through some of the scripts during my first few days at work, was a variety hour starring Fred Astaire, who emceed the show, sang some songs from his movies, and tap-danced on a four-foot-square wooden floor with microphones placed around it. Tap dancing doesn't seem like the sort of thing that people would make sure they were home to listen to on the radio, but the precision of Astaire's taps and the sophistication and intricacy of his rhythms somehow conjured up the complete picture in the audience's minds. Fred Astaire was at the top of his popularity. He had just completed *Swing Time*, his sixth movie with Ginger Rogers, and was in production on his seventh, *Shall We Dance*. The other elements of the program were composer-pianist-conductor Johnny Green and his orchestra; Charlie Butterworth, a popular comedy character actor in pictures, who appeared in either a monologue or a skit; Conrad Thibault, a baritone; singers Trudy Wood and Francia White; a guest star; and a skit involving everyone.

Astaire was an utter perfectionist, sometimes spending as many as twelve hours at a time with the orchestra rehearsing dance routines that no one would ever see. The director once suggested to him that he save himself all of this rehearsal time and just let a drummer make the tap dancing sounds with a couple of drum sticks—no one in the listening audience would ever know the difference. But Astaire would have none of it. The radio audience was tuning in to hear him dance, and that was what they were going to get.

I was assigned the task of writing lead-ins. Lead-ins are something peculiar to variety shows, award shows, and such, in which an emcee has the all but impossible task of introducing a performer and getting a laugh at the same time. If the person being introduced has some relationship with the introducer, the job is much easier. For instance, Bob Hope introducing Bing Crosby could easily generate humor because of their relationship and the audience's knowledge of it. Or Jack Benny could introduce any of the regulars from his show. Benny once introduced a musical number this way: "We will now hear 'Who Knows,' from *Rosalie*, played by Phil Harris, who knows from nothing."

Writing lead-ins was a good experience for me. I had to learn economy of words and the necessity of incorporating an idea. Everyone seemed pleased with what I was doing, and life took on a wonderful routine.

Once a week, when the script was put together, the staff would all troop over to Fred Astaire's mansion in Beverly Hills to let him read it over and give us his reactions. For some reason, he always asked us to come at 6:00 P.M. Every week we would arrive on time, and Fred would settle down to going over the script and making sure he understood what was intended. He was easily amused, not a critical or suspicious personality, as many big stars are. Every week Fred would laugh and shake his head as he read the script, and say, "I don't know where you guys get these funny ideas." And every week, at about 6:45, the butler would come into the room and announce that dinner was ready. Fred would pardon himself and go to dinner. The butler would ask each of us what we would like to drink, and then he would serve it. Again, before Astaire's dinner was over, the butler would refill our drinks.

I usually ordered a martini, just to be one of the boys. So I was thoroughly useless by the time Astaire came back to finish up the last half hour or so of our conference. I always wondered why he didn't ask us to come forty-five minutes earlier, but the routine never changed during the thirty-nine weeks of the show's existence.

The first sketch I wrote, the one that got me the job, never saw the light of day. A change in plans, probably dictated by a guest star not liking the subject matter, put it on the permanent back burner. But just a few weeks later I wrote a sketch that was actually produced on the air. It featured Charlie Butterworth as the proprietor of a store. This store sold doors, exclusively, and it had door samples lining all four walls. Butterworth had been there ten years, trying to find his way out. The humor was definitely "low-brow," typical of the screwball comedies of that period. A sample:

> BUTTERWORTH. What kind of door, stranger?
> MAN. I want an oak door.
> BUTTERWORTH. How about this model? "Whispering Hinges" we call it. Made of Pine.
> MAN. I said *oak*.
> BUTTERWORTH. Sorry, wrong lumber.

After that night, after something I had written besides a lead-in hit the air, I began to feel like I belonged, like I had a proprietary interest in the show.

A few weeks later I got a letter from Jerry Herst, a good friend in San Francisco who was an aspiring song writer. He and his lyricist, Jack Sharpe, sent me a batch of songs and asked whether in my newfound sphere of influence it would be possible to show them to Fred Astaire. Of course, they pointed out, if Astaire would deign to sing one on the air, it would make a career for them. I wrote back, telling them that they had woefully overestimated my influence, which was virtually nil, but I would see what I could do.

One morning I had an opportunity, songs in hand, to explain the situation to Johnny Green, the orchestra leader. He said he would look at them, but he said it with the tone of a person who has looked at thousands of songs without ever finding one with any merit. In other words, because we both worked on the same show, he would look at them, but I shouldn't expect anything. To my great pleasure, by the time he had read the second song he was saying, "Not bad." Finally, after looking through the whole batch of about twelve songs, he said, "Okay, Jess. When I get a chance, I'll show them to Fred. If he wants to do one, we'll do it."

Several more weeks dragged by, with no word. Then, at rehearsal one day, Johnny came over to me with some news. "Fred is going to sing one of your songs next week." I thanked him and ran out to send a wire to Jerry Herst, telling him the news, and the date the show containing his song would be on.

Jerry sent me a wire a couple of days before the show, saying that he and Jack Sharpe had hocked everything they owned to pay for wires they had sent to every music publisher in the country, asking them to listen to the song. They waited with bated breath.

On the day of the show I was sitting in the studio, watching the dress rehearsal and feeling quite warm and wonderful at being able to make this happen for my pal, Jerry. Astaire had gone over the song and arrangement several times with piano only; this would be the first time he sang it with the orchestra. I was happy and excited as I listened to the introduction. Astaire walked onstage and took his place by the microphone. As he did so, a trumpeter, Andy Sechrist, rose from his seat in the band, instrument in hand, and took a position on the other side of Astaire's microphone. I noticed Astaire looking at him with a sort of "What's this all about?" expression.

The orchestra played the intro, and as Astaire began singing the melody, the trumpet began playing a countermelody. After only a few bars, the whole thing broke down.

"What seems to be the matter, Fred?" Johnny Green asked.

"I can't sing against that countermelody. You'll have to take it out."

"It's an integral part of the arrangement. I can't take it out. Impossible."

I was listening to this with an ever-enlarging ball of lead in the pit of my stomach. It didn't help anything when I heard Astaire say, "Well, we'll have to do another song. We'll get another song in here."

Through my mind flashed thoughts of poor, trusting Jerry and Jack, waiting excitedly in San Francisco with empty pockets and full expectations for their work to be performed on national network radio because of good old Jess. How could I ever face them after a debacle like this? But what could I do about it? I suddenly realized that I was on the stage. Without any personal knowledge of what was happening, I had, they later told me, yelled out, "No! No, wait!" Now, here I was, standing onstage, with every eye focused on me.

Johnny Green was saying, "I'm sorry, Jess. Maybe we could schedule it again later."

"Later" was the same as never. "No, wait," I repeated, Uh . . ." I couldn't think of a thing. But *someone* was talking. I suddenly realized it was me! "Why couldn't we," my voice was saying, "uh . . . put the trumpet player on a separate mike backstage, where he could see Johnny, but Fred couldn't hear him?"

"Fred?" Johnny Green said.

"Let's try it," said Astaire, and no sooner said than done, and the crisis was averted. They put the trumpet off where Astaire didn't even know it was playing, and mixed the output from the two mikes in the control room.

The name of the song was "So Rare." It was snapped up by a publisher who heard it on the program, and became an instant success, staying on the *Hit Parade* list for many weeks. It soon became a standard, and is still heard today.

After the program, several well-wishers who came backstage congratulated Fred on his courage in singing against a difficult countermelody on live radio.

"Well," Astaire said, with that typical, self-effacing downward look of his eyes, and with a delightful sense of humor, for he was looking at me as he continued, "if you're a musician, those things don't bother you."

As the season went on, Johnny Green and I got to be good friends. Johnny was a gifted musician and composer—he would later win an Academy Award for the score of *Easter Parade* and become musical director at MGM. I, on the other hand, knew nothing about music. But Johnny and I did have at least one thing in common—both our hairlines were starting to recede. Johnny, who at twenty-eight was five years older than I, had a good head start, but he was determined to hold back the tide as long as humanly possible. He bought every product in existence that claimed to restore hair growth, and soon he had me trying them along with him. Nothing worked, of course. But as our hair continued to fall, our desperation led us to try more and more drastic remedies: ointments, salves, creams, tonics, scrapers, vibrators, and suction devices, you name it, Johnny and I tried it. The worst of all was a "scalp agitator"—a diabolical-looking gadget with two rubber pads, which grabbed my head on either side and alternatively pulled my ears up until they were on top of my head and down until they were touching my shoulders. Fifteen minutes on this machine left my head looking and feeling like a gigantic blood blister. After that, I decided that maybe going bald wasn't so bad after all.

Just about the only thing that grew out of all of these hair growth treatments was an idea, fifteen years later, for an *I Love Lucy* episode entitled "Ricky Thinks He Is Getting Bald." Ricky, thinking his hairline is receding, resorts to all the same awful concoctions and contraptions that I had tried. By the time we did that show, my hairline had receded all the way to the back of my neck, but it no longer bothered me. When I dictated the script for the scene in the show in which Lucy uses the "scalp agitator" on Ricky, I included this personal note in the stage directions: SEE THE PRODUCER. HE ENDURED THIS PARTICULAR MACHINE AT THE START OF WHAT HAS TURNED OUT TO BE A VERY BECOMING LACK OF HAIR.

•   •   •

At the end of his thirty-nine week commitment, Astaire called it quits, and for the summer the *Packard Hour* became a music program featuring Johnny Green and his orchestra and precious little in the way of dialogue. I decided to take some of the money I'd saved and spend the summer at a dude ranch in Victorville that I'd read about, called "Gwen Behr's Yucca Loma." I had always admired cowboys in the movies, and I had the notion that living with cowboys would somehow make me more like them. Not surprisingly, it didn't quite work out that way. I soon discovered that the cowboys' best fun was to get drunk and then ride into town and pick fights with the locals. This obviously wasn't for me. But that didn't deter me from hanging around with them as much as possible. I even started using my full name—Jesse James Oppenheimer.

One evening, after I had been at the ranch a couple of months, the ranch hands and I were all squatting around a campfire, talking for more than an hour. For the first time since my arrival, I was really starting to feel like "one of the boys." Then someone suggested that we all ride into

Victorville, to a bar called the Green Spot. There were general grunts of agreement, and everyone stood up. Everyone but me, that is. I discovered to my dismay that I couldn't move my legs! A moment of panic quickly turned to embarrassment when I realized that as I was squatting there both of my legs must have fallen asleep.

One of the cowboys looked down at me and asked, "Aren't you comin', Jesse?" I told him I would take care of dousing the fire and that I'd catch up with them. Fortunately they were all too anxious to go get drunk to question my motives, and a few moments later I breathed a sigh of relief when they all jumped on their horses and rode off in the direction of town.

As soon as they were safely out of sight, I rocked myself back and forth until the weight of my upper body slowly toppled me over onto one side, and began furiously massaging both legs. It took me ten or fifteen minutes of this before I could stand up. I quickly put out the fire and jumped on my horse to follow them.

I rode the horse at a dead gallop down the straight road toward town, leaning forward in the saddle, my hair blowing in the wind. My earlier embarrassment had all but vanished—in my mind I appeared like a movie hero riding to the rescue of some maiden in distress. Unbeknownst to me (but apparently well-known to my horse), I was fast approaching a shortcut back to Yucca Loma that took off at a forty-five degree angle from the main road I was on.

Suddenly, without warning, my horse turned into the shortcut and galloped off across the field, while I kept going in a straight trajectory down the main road, horseless, still leaning forward (but without a saddle), my hair still blowing in the wind, until I found myself tumbling head over heels in the dust.

My body and ego both badly bruised, I realized that I would never be a cowboy. Walking back to the ranch in the moonlight, I made my plans to return to Hollywood to see what writing jobs were available for me at Y&R.

·   ·   ·

While I was working on the *Packard Hour*, one of the most popular radio programs on the air was the *Jell-O Program*, starring Jack Benny. General Foods, maker of Jell-O, was a big client of Young and Rubicam, and the show was broadcast on NBC from the same studio as The *Packard Hour*.

One of Benny's writers was a fellow named Al Boasberg, who was one of the greatest "wild" joke men in the country. Boasberg had been supplying Benny with jokes since his vaudeville days, and now he worked for Benny just on weekends. Bill Morrow and Ed Beloin would write the script for the program during the week, and then on Saturday afternoon, with Al Boasberg in attendance, the cast would do a reading to get everybody's reactions, after which Morrow and Beloin would do another rewrite. At each of these sessions Boasberg would always come up with three or four tremendous jokes.

Boasberg passed away in June of 1937, shortly before I left for Gwen Behr's Yucca Loma. When I returned to Hollywood from the ranch, I learned that someone at Y&R had told Jack Benny that I was a promising young comedy writer who might be right for Boasberg's job. I went and talked to Benny, and he gave me the job, at about one-hundredth of Boasberg's salary. Strangely enough, the same sketch that got me my first job on the *Packard Hour* was the clinching factor in my getting this assignment as well, but it still never made it on the air.

Benny was a great audience—and a great editor. You could give him a line that would make him fall on the floor laughing, but if it was the slightest bit out of character, as soon as he recovered he would say, "That's the funniest gag I ever heard. Too bad we can't use it."

He also had the best timing of any comedian I've ever seen, and he knew it. If you listen to any Jack Benny program, you'll notice that after practically every laugh, the next line is Benny's, even if it is only a "Hmm" or an "Oh?" No matter who had gotten the laugh, Jack was the one who determined when the audience had had long enough to react and it was time to continue.

My stint with Jack Benny was almost effortless for me because of the way we worked and the fact that the Benny character was so well-defined, as were the characters and attitudes of Phil Harris, Mary Livingstone, and all the other supporting players. Because I didn't have to show up until the cast was ready to read the script on Saturday afternoon, it was just a case of sitting around the table and thinking of things and saying them as they came into my head. There was no construction, no having to work out a premise or an idea or a basis for anything. Just whatever I could think of that was funny. It was without a doubt the easiest writing job I ever had.

Because my duties on the Jack Benny program left my weekdays free (and didn't pay enough to take care of the rent), I needed another job. Y&R assigned me to the writing staff of the Packard Motor Car Co.'s new program, a variety show called *Hollywood Mardi Gras*, hosted by

Lanny Ross, a popular tenor, and featuring comedians Walter O'Keefe and Charlie Butterworth. Don Wilson was the announcer, moonlighting (as was I) from his duties on the Jack Benny program. Each week the show featured big-name guest stars. On our first show, we had Amos 'n' Andy. A week later, our guests were Fred Allen and his wife, Portland Hoffa. Fred had been "feuding" with Jack Benny for almost a year, and it was still going strong, much to the delight of the listening audiences of both their programs. (Once, when Jack was a guest on Fred Allen's program, Jack was talking about his ad-libs, and Allen interrupted him, saying "You couldn't ad-lib a belch after a Hungarian dinner!" Jack shot back, "You wouldn't dare say that if my writers were here.") Having Fred Allen on the Packard program put me in the unusual position of being a writer for Jack Benny *and* for Fred Allen at the same time. If anything, being on both sides of the fight just added to the fun. On the Packard show, Allen wasted no time letting the audience know how he felt about Jack:

PORTLAND. Want a peanut, Mr. Wilson?

ALLEN. Don's no elephant.

WILSON. Oh! Portland doesn't mean any harm, Fred. Everybody's been kidding me about my size lately. I'm on a program Sunday night with a fellow. You know who I mean.

PORTLAND. I know! Jack Benny . . . the comedian.

ALLEN. Listen, Portland. I don't mind you mentioning names, but you don't have to go into *details*.

The following year I left both the Jack Benny program and *Hollywood Mardi Gras* when I landed a job writing for ventriloquist Edgar Bergen on the *Chase and Sanborn Hour*. At first blush, writing a radio show for a ventriloquist might seem a bit strange, but given my earlier experience at writing a radio show for a dancer, this didn't strike me as odd at all. The truth is that Bergen had created such a unique comic personality for Charlie McCarthy that millions of listeners tuned in to hear Charlie, not to hear a ventriloquist. Whether Charlie was conversing with Bergen, Don Ameche, or some guest star didn't make a bit of difference to Charlie's millions of fans.

I recall one time, back in those days before tape recorders were invented, when we wrote a sketch that ended with Bergen, Charlie McCarthy, and Mortimer Snerd joining together in three-part harmony! We were so used to writing for the three of them as distinct characters that the impossibility of this feat simply didn't occur to us. Nor did it occur to anyone who read the first two revisions of the script, including Bergen! It wasn't until rehearsal, when Bergen, with Charlie on one knee and Mortimer on the other, opened his mouth (and their mouths) to sing, that it suddenly dawned on everyone that even Bergen wasn't *that* talented.

One thing always struck me as peculiar about Bergen's relationship with Charlie McCarthy. As real as Charlie was to Bergen and everyone else, in Bergen's mind Charlie only came into existence from the moment that Charlie actually uttered his first line of dialogue. One time we were rehearsing in a big empty auditorium. A singer was performing at center stage, and an NBC vice president named John Swallow was in the audience, talking to someone.

The girl finished singing, and now it was Bergen's turn. He walked up to the microphone, took Charlie out of the suitcase, put him up by the mike in the chair, and waited for Swallow to finish talking.

After a minute or two the director pushed the talkback button and said "Go ahead Edgar, it's okay." But Bergen protested, "Oh, no. Mr. Swallow is talking." The director assured Bergen, "It's all right, Edgar. He won't mind." But Bergen just repeated "Oh, no, I couldn't."

Swallow finally stopped talking, and Bergen started his routine. At this point Bergen had spoken Charlie's first line, so in Bergen's mind Charlie was now in existence. Then, in the middle of the routine, Swallow started talking again. Charlie immediately looked out into the audience and shouted "Will you shut up out there!" Bergen, genuinely panic-stricken, said "Charlie, what's the matter with you? That's Mr. Swallow!" And Charlie answered, "I don't give a goddam *who* he is!"

At this, Bergen turned absolutely white. Then Charlie yelled at Swallow, "Keep your mouth shut or get out of here!"

Bergen could say all these things as Charlie, but to hear it scared him to death.

•   •   •

It was not unusual for radio writers to be working on several programs at the same time, and I was no exception. In addition to my regular job on the *Chase and Sanborn Hour*, I worked on a few segments of *Texaco Star Theater*, starring Adolphe Menjou. One of the shows featured Leo Gorcey and the Dead End Kids doing an adaptation of a dramatic short story I had written in San Francisco. Another program I wrote for was the *Lifebuoy Program* starring Al Jolson, where my writing chores once again included doing lead-ins. One of my favorites was this one:

JOLSON. Folks . . . I'm going to introduce a man to you now, whose name has become a legend in the theater. His magnificent acting has thrilled us, on the stage, screen, and radio. And it is a pleasure to have him here tonight. Ladies and Gentlemen . . . Mr. John Barrymore. (*Applause.*)

BARRYMORE. Thank you very much . . . and thank you, Al. That was a most gracious introduction.

JOLSON. I hope you liked it, John.

BARRYMORE. I hope you meant it, Al.

JOLSON. Why, John, do you doubt for one minute that I didn't mean all those nice things I said about you?

BARRYMORE. Why, no Al, I . . .

JOLSON. Do you say my voice suggested a lack of sincerity?

BARRYMORE. Don't get me wrong . . . I . . .

JOLSON. I mean . . . could you really tell?

BARRYMORE. Ah . . . even if I thought you meant that, I could not say so. That is the price I must pay for my being here.

JOLSON. Ah, but John . . . how little that is.

BARRYMORE. Yes, it is little.

JOLSON. Compared to the price *I* must pay for your being here.

The piece of work that I submitted in order to get the job on the *Lifebuoy Program* was—you guessed it—the same unproduced sketch that had gotten me the jobs on the *Packard Hour* and on Jack Benny. Jolson liked it, but the program ran too long and my sketch got cut from the show. I was disappointed, but I decided that it was probably for the best. After all, if that sketch were ever actually to make it on the air, how would I get my next job?

The Eyes Have It

IN DECEMBER 1938 I signed on as head writer of a new variety show that Y&R was producing for Gulf Oil, called *The Gulf Screen Guild Show*. Each week there were different guest motion picture writers, directors, and stars, and all of their salaries for appearing on the program were turned over to the Motion Picture Relief Fund to be used for the building of a home for aged, sick, and needy motion picture workers. Because of this, we had a steady stream of the biggest names in Hollywood on the program. In just the first three weeks, our stars included George Murphy, Judy Garland, Reginald Gardiner, Ralph Morgan, Jack Benny, Joan Crawford, Ernst Lubitsch, Loretta Young, Fred Astaire, Frank Capra, Bette Davis, Robert Montgomery, Franklin Pangborn, and Basil Rathbone.

For the fourth broadcast of the *Screen Guild Show*, I learned that our guest stars would be Marlene Dietrich and Frank Morgan. At the time, Morgan was in the middle of filming *The Wizard of Oz*, in which he played the title role. I arranged to meet Dietrich for lunch at the Brown Derby so we could discuss the show.

Lunch with Marlene was a revelation. She was warm, bubbly, vivacious, and had a delightful sense of humor—precisely the opposite of her low-pitched, monotonic screen persona. This is fantastic, I thought to myself. All this time she's been playing the same character, and that's all the public knows. I'll write a sketch for her that will showcase her true personality, and it'll be a sensation!

The sketch, featuring Dietrich and Morgan, was a send-up of spy movies. I eagerly awaited the first run-through. But when Marlene spoke her first line, my heart fell. The energetic, vivacious woman I had been so thrilled to discover in the restaurant was gone. In her place was the familiar, sultry "Dietrich" character from all of her previous films.

As soon as the scene was finished, I walked over to her. "Marlene,

98

what happened? I wrote this scene as a showcase for you—to show the public the *real* you—bright, outgoing and funny."

"Believe me," she said, her voice in that familiar low whisper, "*This* is what they want."

Ironically, although Dietrich's film career was in the doldrums when she appeared on the program, she regained her popularity later that year when she costarred with Jimmy Stewart in *Destry Rides Again*—a picture that for the first time showed the moviegoing public her more human and humorous side.

Dietrich liked the sketch I had written, even if her characterization wasn't exactly what I had had in mind. Frank Morgan was quite another matter. He complained bitterly about the writing, although I was never able to pin him down on exactly what it was that he didn't like. But I spent most of the night rewriting it anyway, just to quiet him down.

The next afternoon, following the first run-through of the rewritten sketch, Dietrich remarked that she liked the original version better. Despite all the effort I had put into the rewrite, I had to agree with her. During a break Dietrich took Frank Morgan aside and demanded that he tell her what it was about the original sketch that had caused him to make such a fuss in the first place. "Oh, there was nothing really wrong with it," Morgan replied. "I've just learned over the years that if you complain about a script, the writers will go back to work on it again, and they usually improve it."

We did the original version on the air.

After starting out as strictly a variety program, the *Screen Guild Show* soon began doing dramatic presentations, changing its name to the *Screen Guild Theatre*. One director of the program had a unique method of conveying the desired "mood" to the actors—he had colored theatrical lights installed and would give his signals to the actors while the show was on the air by cueing a lighting technician (probably the only lighting technician employed in radio broadcasting), who would shine a colored spotlight on the actors according to the director's wishes. Red light meant rage, blue light meant calm, green jealousy, and so on. Our guest stars reluctantly complied with this unorthodox procedure until one evening, in the middle of the show, when the actors suddenly found themselves staring at blank pieces of paper. It seems that the final script revisions had been mimeographed in blue ink, and when the blue floodlight hit them, the ink became invisible!

•   •   •

In the spring of 1941, I joined the writing staff of *The Rudy Vallee Program*, sponsored by Sealtest on NBC. Vallee, often credited with being the originator of the radio variety show, had been one of the biggest stars on radio since 1929, when he and his Connecticut Yankees began their weekly broadcasts of the *Fleischmann Hour*. Throughout the thirties, his nasal renditions of such songs as "The Vagabond Lover" and "My Time Is Your Time" had a hypnotic effect on millions of American women, much like what Frank Sinatra would achieve a few years later.

I had met Rudy two years earlier, when he guested on the *Screen Guild Show*. Although Vallee was popular as a singer, we did quite a bit of comedy on the program, which also featured Joan Davis, John Barrymore, Maxie Rosenbloom, and many guest stars. But much as Rudy enjoyed getting laughs, he was by no means what you would call a comedian. He did a decent job with the gag lines we gave him, but he never seemed to grasp what it was that made them funny. At the run-throughs he was always one beat late laughing at each gag. And his performance remained exactly the same from the first rehearsal until airtime.

I remember we once wrote a long sketch that ended with Rudy delivering a great punch line. It was met with uproarious laughter from the studio audience. Rudy enjoyed it immensely. In the middle of the following week's show, Rudy suddenly turned to the audience and ad-libbed the same punch line that had gotten such a reaction the week before—this time by itself, without any of the preceding material. The audience just stared at him. Rudy later told me he just couldn't understand why *last* week's audience thought the line was so much funnier.

By the time I joined Rudy Vallee's program, my salary had risen to five hundred dollars a week. Although I had long before set my sights higher than the guaranteed-for-life fifty dollars a week that my chums would have settled for, I still had trouble believing that I was making this much money for doing what I most wanted to do. In fact, my agent had to forbid my answering a producer when he asked me my salary, because I could not say it without giggling. The conditioning of years of San Francisco values never bridged the gap to fanciful movieland.

•   •   •

After the Japanese attacked Pearl Harbor, I joined the Coast Guard. I was given the rank of chief petty officer and assigned to the Wilmington Patrol Base in Los Angeles. I did practically no traveling during my four years in the Coast Guard. In fact, when I received my discharge, and my wife's sister gave a welcome home party for me in Liemert Park, a Los

Some of the guys I served with in the Coast Guard. *Left to right, top row:*
Dick Quine, Jack Dempsey, Dick Stabile, and Cesar Romero.

Angeles suburb, I had to go farther to get to my own welcome home party than I had ever traveled while in the service.

At Wilmington I was assigned to serve as yeoman to Lieutenant Rudy Vallee. I was in charge of interviewing all of the men who came back from overseas and dramatizing their exploits on a radio show that I put on, called *Together We Serve*. It was basically a recruiting show for the Waves and Spars (the women's auxiliaries of the Navy and the Coast Guard). Rudy Vallee and Mary Astor were the costars.

In addition to *Together We Serve*, I wrote recruiting shows for the Eleventh Naval District Coast Guard Band, of which Rudy was bandmaster. The band consisted of enlisted men who had previously been professional musicians in such famous bands as those of Paul Whiteman, Tommy Dorsey, Jimmy Dorsey, Jimmy Grier, Raymond Scott, Woody Herman, Freddy Martin, Ted Lewis, Fred Waring, and many others. It was a talented group, to say the least. The harpist was Robert Maxwell, who had been with Toscanini and the NBC Symphony. Jimmy Grier did the orchestrations and arrangements. The piano player was Eliot Daniel, who had been hired away from Freddy Martin by Rudy years earlier, when he got his first radio show. Like me, Eliot had been working on the Sealtest program when the war began, and both of us signed up for Rudy's Coast Guard unit shortly after he was selected to serve as bandmaster.

It was at the Wilmington Patrol Base that I finally discovered my double vision. I had been given what I considered a detestable assignment. I had to collate one thousand copies of a thirty-page script. They had given me a thousand page ones, a thousand page twos, etc., and I had to arrange them into one thousand scripts running from page one to page thirty. I knew this process would make me sick to my stomach, though I didn't connect this with my eyes at all. I would have to do a few pages and rest until my nausea went away, then do a few more pages and rest, and so on. I waited until nighttime so I could use the mess hall, with its long tables.

Walking along with a stack of page ones in my hand, I placed them one at a time on the table. As I had predicted, within a few minutes I was so sick that I had to stop and sit down. While I was resting, a thought occurred to me. The trouble seemed to come when I took a page from the stack and followed it to the table with my eyes. Great confusion followed, with the room spinning by. I wondered to myself, could I avoid the problem by keeping my eye on the page that was already down, picking up the next sheet, and putting it in place without ever looking away from the sheet on the table? I tried it. It worked! The job took most of the night, but I didn't get sick again. I decided I had a problem with my eyes.

The following morning, as I stood in the men's room, shaving, I pondered the events of the night before. Standing at the next sink was an acrobat named Rand Hall. I figured that Rand must have excellent eyes to be an acrobat. So I said, "Rand, look over the sink on the opposite side there. You see that sign that says PLEASE BE SURE TO TURN OFF THE FAUCET?"

Rand nodded.

"Do me a favor," I continued. "Look back this way, then turn as quickly as you can and look at the sign." He did.

"How long did it take the signs to come together?" I asked.

Rand gave me a look I won't forget. "There's only one sign."

"I know there's really only one," I assured him, "but when you turn quickly like that, and they separate, how long does it take them to come together? It takes a couple of seconds with me."

"I only see one sign. It never separates."

He managed to convince me that he only saw one sign at *all* times and under *all* conditions. This was shocking news to me—a supposedly intelligent, grown man. It was the first time in my life that I realized that other people see things "all in one." I was delighted that I had found this defect in myself (I assumed that it could be corrected), but furious with myself at the same time. How could I have missed it all these years? How was it possible that I never suspected, never complained, never spoke of it before?

I suddenly remembered a story I had heard, of a doctor who asked a difficult-to-diagnose patient to describe a typical day in his life. The patient said, "Well, I get up about seven, eat breakfast, wash, dress, throw up, take the subway to the office . . ."

"Wait a minute," the doctor said. "You mean you throw up every morning?"

And the patient answered, "Yes . . . doesn't everyone?"

I guess each of us tends to think that all people see and feel things the same way we do. Having nothing to compare it with, I had always assumed my vision was normal.

I began to think back now to all the clues that should have sounded warning bells. There were millions of them. For instance, I had a terrible time telling whether an officer was a commander, lieutenant commander, or captain. The gold stripes on their sleeves ran together and moved in relation to each other, so counting them was an impossibility. I had quickly learned to address every officer as "Captain." If he really was a captain, I was right. If he wasn't, I had complimented him.

I thought back to the many nights I had worked on radio scripts at Y&R until five or six in the morning and then driven home on the winding road to my apartment in the Hollywood Hills. I literally had to hold my hand over my left eye as I drove up the hill because the eye hurt so much. I always thought I was simply overtired. After all, as soon as I had a good night's sleep, it didn't hurt any more.

That morning I visited the infirmary at the Coast Guard base. They had no facilities for treating my vision problems, but they gave me permission to see a civilian doctor. I went that afternoon. The doctor checked my eyes and told me I had an extreme horizontal muscle imbalance. He also told me I had never seen third dimension—I had never perceived depth in three-dimensional space. I gave him a terrific argument on this. After all, I told him, I had passed the boy scout test for judgment of distance. But of course he was right. I had been judging distance based on a set of factors that had nothing to do with depth perception. Had the target been isolated in space, I would have had no way to even approach a guess.

The doctor gave me a set of exercises and told me to do them religiously, at the same time categorically stating that I wouldn't, that no patient in his experience had ever kept them up long enough and relentlessly enough to achieve a real cure. In his experience a slight improvement resulted in so much more comfort that the patient figured he was normal and discontinued the exercises.

I began orthoptic exercises that very day, and I am still doing them today, decades later. My eyes are still improving. I begin to see what the doctor meant when he said I wouldn't keep it up. But after crossing a thousand exciting horizons, each of which I thought must be the ultimate, I realize there are many more ahead.

When, with the help of these exercises, I first experienced 3-D, a most distinct memory flashed into my mind. It was an incident during my college days at Stanford, when a group of us had decided to drive down to Los Angeles for the Stanford-USC football game. We spelled each other on the driving.

Please don't ask how I was able to drive. I got my driver's license in 1932, when my family got its first car. Suffice it to say that the qualifications for getting a driver's license were somewhat lax in those days. There was no vision test, no driving test, nothing. My mother had taken care of the financial arrangements at the car dealer, and the next day the car salesman showed up at our apartment building with the new car and four driver's licenses: one for my mother, one for my sister, one for myself, and even one for my father, who had been dead for two years!

In any event, when the appointed time came during the college road trip to Los Angeles, I took my turn at the wheel. At about four in the morning a terrifying thing happened. I was driving along, with everything seeming normal, when in an instant the entire scene was magically transformed. I can tell you now what it looked like in terms that you can understand; I could not have then. The whole vista suddenly took on a strange aspect. It was on one plane horizontally as far as I could see. The road was flat and stretched out and into the distance before me; the trees abruptly rose on both sides, standing in space; the hood of the car took on a shape and stood up from the road. I could see all these things at once, and it was a most terrifying and weirdly uncomfortable feeling. It was like a fairy wonderland where everything appears unreal. I didn't like it at all. I had to shake my head roughly several times before the scene reverted back to what (to me, then) was its natural appearance. I said nothing of it to anyone. I was afraid I might be losing my mind.

Ironically, long before I discovered my eye problem, I had always been fascinated with 3-D viewers—"stereoscopes," as they were called. I had even talked with others about the remarkable effect they provided. But I only spoke to my fellow viewers in generalities: "How wonderful they make things look," I would remark. "Isn't that an interesting effect?"

It was semantics. The other people were thinking (Oh, why didn't they say it? I might have caught on!) that the stereoscope was wonderful because it made things look *just like the real world,* while *my* interest came from the fact that it made things look weird, unnatural, and most *un*lifelike.

In the weeks following that first visit to the eye doctor, I learned that the real world *does* consist of planes and corners; that people and things *do* stand out vertically and have contours, just as when you look through a 3-D viewer. I'm certain my wife, Estelle, whom I met a month or so later, never wants to hear me say again that I thought all women were flat until I got stereoscopic vision, and then I married the first one I saw.

A few days after I began my eye exercises, I got a message one morning that Rudy Vallee wanted to see me. As I approached Rudy's quarters, part of me was thinking about our next show, while another part was still thinking about my eye problem. I knocked on his door, and, hearing no answer, opened it and went in. Rudy was nowhere to be seen, but I heard the shower running in the bathroom. A second later I heard his voice call, "Is that you, Jess? I'll be right with you."

I stood waiting for him, looking at a photograph on the wall. I realized that I was seeing double, as usual. With great concentration I forced my eyes to make the two images of the photo merge into one. I was still relishing this small achievement when Rudy appeared, a towel wrapped around his waist. "Good morning, Jess. How are you?" he asked, drying his hair with another towel. I didn't answer. I had suddenly become preoccupied with my eyes again. To me, Rudy seemed to have *four* nipples on his chest, instead of two. But this time, no matter how hard I tried to fuse the two images, things just got worse. Finally, by crossing my eyes, I managed to see only two nipples, but they were lined up *vertically* instead of horizontally! And what's worse, Rudy now had two heads! Defeated, I finally gave up. Rudy followed this strange series of expressions on my face and asked me what was wrong. I told him briefly about my newly discovered eye problem, about my double vision, about the exercises that I had begun the previous week, and about the difficulty I was having at the moment. He listened calmly and then spoke.

"I guess I should tell you something about myself, Jess," he said. "I was born with two complete sets of nipples on my chest."

•   •   •

After Wilmington I was assigned to public relations and given an office in the Taft Building on the corner of Hollywood and Vine, directly across the street from where I got my first job at Young and Rubicam. The building housed so many servicemen that it was often called "Fort Taft." Just down the hall was O.W.I., the Office of War Information, run by my high school chum, Mort Werner, who had come down to Hollywood a year after I did. Mort's wife, Marty, was "G.I. Jill," broadcasting over Armed Forces Radio to the troops overseas.

Among Mort's duties at O.W.I. was purchasing popular records for the "G.I. Jill" broadcasts. Mort bought all of his records at Wallichs Music City, at Sunset and Vine, just a few blocks away. Music City, owned by Glenn Wallichs, who not long afterward founded Capitol Records, was a unique place—much more than just a record store. With the second-floor offices of most of the music publishers on the other side of Vine Street, it was always the first store in the country to get the latest recordings. A disc jockey named Ira Cook used to broadcast his radio show from Music City's front window. It also housed a complete recording studio, and all of the big bands and recording artists came to Music City either to cut discs, or for autographing sessions, or to appear as guests on Ira Cook's record program. Nat King Cole used to come in, and songwriters like Sammy Cahn and Johnny Mercer would pass the time there. The store's jingle, "It's Music City, Sunset and Vine" (sung to the tune of "Rock-a-bye Baby"), was recorded by everybody from Frank Sinatra to Jerry Lewis and became a familiar refrain to Los Angeles radio audiences for many years.

The manager of Music City's Pop Record Department was a pretty brunette named Estelle Weiss, whom Mort had gotten to know pretty well during his many visits to the store. After a little prodding, Mort finally got me to go along with him to Music City to meet Estelle. I was wearing my chief petty officer's uniform, the cap of which concealed my fast-disappearing hairline. Estelle didn't seem too impressed with me. I thought she was lovely.

A couple of weeks later, I got up the nerve to go back to the store by myself and ask her out on a date. Estelle told me that because so many servicemen were coming in all day and night, the ladies who worked at Music City had made a pact not to go out with anybody that they met in the store. Luckily, she made an exception in my case. Four years later, on August 5, 1947, we were married, with Mort serving as my best man. By that time I was almost thirty-four, and I wanted to have kids right away, but Es, who was only twenty-four, wanted to wait awhile. We compromised and waited exactly four months.

• • •

After "Fort Taft" I was transferred to Columbia Pictures Studios, where the motion picture *Tars and Spars* was being made, and I worked on that for about a year and a half. My outfit included Dick Quine, a young actor who would later become a prominent motion picture director (*Bell, Book and Candle, The World of Suzie Wong, Strangers When We Meet*). The comedian of the troupe was an unknown seaman first class by the name of Sid Caesar. Sid and the others had been out doing a stage presentation of *Tars and Spars* to whip up recruiting for the Coast Guard.

While I was stationed at Columbia Studios, I was able to play golf at least one afternoon a week at Griffith Park. I'd had a fascination with the game of golf ever since I was thirteen, when my Uncle Joe let me caddy for him at the Merced Country Club in San Francisco. When I was fifteen my friend Charlie Silverstein took me out to a public golf course and taught me to play. We used to play at the Lincoln Park and Harding courses, out by Sea Cliff. I remember the first tee on one of

I'm not sure who took this photo of Es and me, moments after we arrived in Honolulu
for our honeymoon in 1947. Es still has the hat.

them had a sheer drop on the left down to the sea. If you missed, your
ball went right into the Pacific Ocean. There must have been ten thousand golf balls down there in the water.

The Griffith Park course wasn't nearly as hazardous. Our usual three-
some from Columbia Pictures consisted of Morris Stoloff, musical director at Columbia, Freddie Karger, a musician at the studio, and me. One
day Morris brought along Jule Styne, who was writing the songs for *Tars
and Spars* with Sammy Cahn. On the fifth green, Freddie couldn't find
his favorite putter in his golf bag. But on the sixth green, Freddie noticed
that the putter that Jule was using looked exactly like the one he had lost.
"That's a nice looking putter," Freddie remarked. "Where did you get it?"
Jule looked up from his ball. "This putter? It was a gift. Why? Is it yours?"

One isn't always given such an opening. I can remember another day at Griffith Park when I was using one of a dozen golf balls that I had received as a gift, with my name printed on them. On the third tee I sliced the ball so badly that it went onto the next fairway, although I couldn't see exactly where. As I approached the area where I thought it might have landed, I saw another golfer on the fairway, preparing to take a swing. Thinking that it might be my ball, I called out to him, "Say, are you sure that's your ball you're playing?" The golfer stopped his swing, picked up his ball, looked at it closely, and then put it down again. "Yeah, this is mine," he called back. "I'm playing an Oppenheimer."

I never saw that ball again. I collapsed in such convulsive laughter that by the time I stopped and picked myself up, the golfer had already hit the ball and walked out of sight.

During my tenure at Columbia Pictures (and for a long time before and afterward) the president of the studio was Harry Cohn. Cohn was one of the most powerful and feared men in Hollywood. And he held a grudge longer than anyone in the business. Bill Frawley—*I Love Lucy*'s Fred Mertz—once told me that Cohn had started out on Tin Pan Alley as a song plugger back in 1915, when Frawley was a headliner in vaudeville. Song pluggers were always hanging around the stage doors, waiting for headliners to leave the theaters, so they could try to interest them in some new tune. But Cohn, being Cohn, didn't like to wait in the back alleys with the rest of the boys and bribed the doorman to let him in backstage. One night he knocked on the door of Frawley's dressing room at the Palace Theater, introduced himself, and tried to interest Bill in one of his songs. Frawley politely explained to Cohn that he considered his dressing room to be like his home, and he made it a point never to discuss business at home. "If you'll just wait outside with the other song pluggers," he told him, "I'll be happy to discuss the tune with you." Cohn, being Cohn, would have none of this, however, and left the theater in a huff.

Twenty years passed. One night Frawley was in his dressing room at the Broadhurst Theatre on Broadway, having just finished another evening's triumphant performance as costar of the smash hit play, *Twentieth Century*. Everyone expected Hollywood to make it into a major motion picture. Harry Cohn was by now president of Columbia Pictures, and the whole theater was abuzz with talk that Cohn was in the audience that evening.

Suddenly there was a knock on Frawley's dressing room door. Frawley opened the door. It was Harry Cohn.

"Do you remember me?" asked Cohn.

"Of course I do," replied Frawley.

"Do you remember the night I tried to interest you in a song?"

"Yes."

"Well, I've just bought this show for Columbia, and I just came backstage to tell you you're not going to be in the picture!"

One of my good friends at Columbia was Saul Chaplin, an academy award–winning composer and pianist who wrote, among other things, "Bei Mir Bist Du Schön," and "The Anniversary Song." He told me that once, when he and his wife, Ethel, were sitting at home one evening between Christmas and New Year's Eve, he received a telephone call from Harry Cohn.

"Saul," Cohn said, "Joan and I haven't heard from you yet about our New Year's Eve party. I'd like you to be there." This was a shock, to say the least, because Saul had never received an invitation to this or any other party thrown by the Cohns. He and the studio head traveled in different circles, rarely saw each other at the studio, and had never seen each other socially.

In fact, Saul and his wife had already sent out invitations for their own New Year's Eve party.

"We never received an invitation," Saul informed him.

"You didn't?!!" Cohn replied. He was upset. "It must have gotten lost in the mail. But that's not important. I assume that you and your wife are going to be there."

"Actually, Ethel and I would like to come, but we've planned our own get-together that evening and the arrangements have already been made."

"You're having a party?" Cohn asked rhetorically. He seemed surprised. "How many people have you invited?"

"About twenty."

"Well, call it off and come to my house. It's going to be spectacular."

Saul knew they couldn't go.

"I'm sorry," he said. "It's just too late to cancel our party."

Cohn made one more attempt. "I can't change your mind?"

"I'm afraid it's just impossible."

"All right, then," said Cohn, realizing that Saul's mind was made up. "By the way, what's the name of that other piano player at the studio?"

When Harry Cohn died in 1958, more than two thousand people attended his memorial services, held on Stages 12 and 14 at the studio. It was the largest crowd ever to attend a Hollywood funeral. Red Skelton, appearing on his television program later that week, commented, "Well, it only proves what they always say—give the people what they want, and they'll come out for it."

•   •   •

Just before I was transferred to Columbia Pictures, I was assigned to the Times Building, Public Relations Department. No sooner had I sat down at my desk than the sailor at the next desk introduced himself and asked me if I'd like to write for Fanny Brice in addition to my Coast Guard duties. It turned out that he was Fanny's son-in-law, an agent named Ray Stark, who would later produce such movies as *Funny Girl* and *The Way We Were*. I signed Ray as my agent and started writing Fanny Brice's radio program, *Baby Snooks*, together with Everett Freeman.

Baby Snooks starred Fanny as Snooks Higgins and Hanley Stafford as Daddy. Snooks was a wise-beyond-her-years little girl who constantly drove Daddy crazy. The show was basically an examination of the relationship between adults and children and what makes children tick. In one show, Daddy had just given Snooks a spanking:

DADDY. Snooks, I have a favor to ask of you. (*Pause.*) Snooks, your father is talking to you.
SNOOKS. I don't want you to be my father no more.
DADDY. What kind of talk is that?
SNOOKS. You hate me.
DADDY. Nonsense. I spanked you this morning because I love you.
SNOOKS. You got a funny way of showing it.
DADDY. But it's the truth. If I had hated you, do you know what I would have done?
SNOOKS. Yeah. You'd have killed me.
DADDY. No. I would have left you alone to grow up into a selfish, greedy girl who always has to have her own way. How would you like that?
SNOOKS. (*Wisely.*) I'd like it.
DADDY. Oh, what's the use. Will you at least talk to me?
SNOOKS. No. You spanked me, and I'm sore at you.
DADDY. Look, Snooks. I spanked you, in the first place, for your own good. And in the second place, you're not "*sore.*" You're angry. Do you understand?
SNOOKS. Yeah, I'm angry in the second place.
DADDY. Right. Now come over here and sit down.
SNOOKS. No.
DADDY. Why not?
SNOOKS. 'Cause I'm sore in the first place!

The great Fanny Brice as Baby Snooks.

After I had been writing the *Baby Snooks* show for about a year, the chief commandant of the Coast Guard discovered that I was moonlighting. He sent me a wire warning me that if I continued to do so, he would have to dock me my entire salary. At the time I was making more than $750 a week on the *Baby Snooks* show and something like $75 a week from the Coast Guard, so I kept right on writing for Fanny. I stayed with the *Baby Snooks* show even after I was discharged from the Coast Guard in 1946.

I was lucky to have the opportunity to work with a tremendous talent like Fanny Brice. Fanny was a great singer, an outstanding dialect comedienne, a true star in every way. Yet with all her gifts, probably her most lasting contribution was as Baby Snooks—with her amazing talent for capturing the inflections and tones of a small child.

Ironically, even though I wrote the *Baby Snooks* show for Fanny for many years, it wasn't until later, when I had my own small children, that I realized how good she really was. Fanny had kids down perfectly, with remarkable attention to detail. When my daughter, Joanne, was four years old, she acted just like Baby Snooks!

On one occasion I was watching television at home with my family when the telephone rang. It seems that there was another Jess Oppenheimer listed in the West Los Angeles telephone directory, and he happened to have a teenage daughter named Joan. Not exactly the same name as our four-year-old daughter Joanne, but close enough to cause confusion. Joanne answered the phone, listened for a while, and then we heard her tell the caller, "Just a minute. I have to ask." She turned to Es and calmly asked, "Mommy, can I go out dancing tonight?"

Another time, when my daughter had the measles, I slept at the foot of her double bed. In the middle of the night she turned over and accidentally hit me with her arm, waking both of us. I watched as Joanne, still half asleep, got up on one elbow in the darkened room to see what it was she had hit. Glancing in my direction, she said "Oh, pardon me, Mister," and then rolled over and went back to sleep.

With the advent of television, many of the big radio stars were forced to take cuts in salary. Fanny Brice, who at the time was making $5,500 a week for working one day a week on the *Baby Snooks* show, was asked to cut her salary to $3,000. She flatly refused. As a result, her show, at the time one of the most popular on radio, went off the air in May 1948. Suddenly, for the first time in years, I found myself without a job.

My Favorite Comedienne

WHEN THE SNOOKS SHOW went off the air, Es was five months pregnant with our first child. Es and I spent most of June and July buying and moving into a small house on North Bundy Drive in Brentwood and preparing for the arrival of the baby. But by midsummer I began to worry about where my next paycheck was coming from. Ray Stark had let it be known around town that I was available, but there still weren't any good prospects.

Snooks wasn't the only comedy program departing the airwaves. The hottest trend in radio at the time was the giveaway program. Fast-talking emcees would parcel out free refrigerators and other prizes to contestants who could come up with the right answers, and the public was eating it up. There seemed to be more quiz shows on the air every week. This didn't bode well for comedy writers.

I was sitting in my office one hot afternoon in August, wondering what to do next, when the telephone rang. It was Harry Ackerman, head of West Coast network programming for CBS Radio. "Jess," he began, "have you heard the new show Lucille Ball is doing for us—*My Favorite Husband*?"

I told him I hadn't heard it.

"It's only been on for a few weeks. Frank Fox and Bill Davenport have been doing most of the writing, but they've got to go back to *Ozzie and Harriet* when the hiatus is over. Would you be interested in writing a script for us?"

In the previous twelve years I had worked with practically every star in Hollywood, but for some reason I had never run into Lucille Ball. I knew who she was, of course—I had seen her in *Stage Door*, with Katharine Hepburn, and *The Big Street*, with Henry Fonda. Apart from that I knew relatively little about her. The impression I had of her was that of a wisecracking showgirl type—a far cry from the Baby Snooks character I had been writing for the past five years. But Harry had caught me in a particularly receptive mood.

"Sure," I said. "Why not?"

"That's great. Do you know Lucille?"

"I've never met her, Harry. But I'll listen to the show this week. When is it on?"

"Friday night at nine. Why don't I send you over a couple of scripts so you can get a feel for the show?"

"That would be fine. By the way, who's the sponsor?"

"We're still looking for one."

The scripts arrived the next morning. *My Favorite Husband*, I learned from reading them, was based on a book called *Mr. and Mrs. Cugat: The Record of a Happy Marriage*. It really was sort of a society show. As the announcer, Bob LeMond, explained at the beginning of one episode:

We present *My Favorite Husband*, a new series based on the delightful stories of Isobel Scott Rorick's gay, sophisticated Mr. and Mrs. Cugat, starring Lucille Ball with Richard Denning.

Ten years ago, the town's most eligible bachelor, George Cugat, married socially prominent Elizabeth Elliot. The lavish wedding kept the society columns all over the country in copy for weeks. . . .

After the honeymoon, George sold his polo pony, bought a stylish suburban home, took the first job that came along—fifth vice-president of a bank—and now the Cugats are just George and Liz, two people who live together and like it.

The idea that I came up with for a segment of *My Favorite Husband* was something of a departure from the scripts that Harry had sent me. I decided to make Liz Cugat a little bit less sophisticated, a little bit more childlike and impulsive, than the character who had appeared in the first few shows—in short, more like Baby Snooks. She would be a stage-struck schemer with an overactive imagination that got her into embarrassing situations. This would give me an excuse to engage Lucy in some broad slapstick comedy.

The story line involved Liz's scheme to get the lead in the Young Matrons League's annual theater production, over George's objections. An exchange of dialogue between George and Liz in the opening scene set the tone:

LIZ. And I'll tell you something else, George Cugat. There's going to be a famous Hollywood director in the audience and I'll make a bet with you he'll offer me a contract.

GEORGE. Oh Liz, stop it. You're talking like a child.

LIZ. Come on. We'll make a bet. How much?

GEORGE. No you don't. This is just a trick so I'll let you be in the play. Well, I have to go to the office, dear. Sorry I had to deprive you of a Hollywood career.

LIZ. Very funny. What has Betty Grable got that I haven't got? Or Lana Turner.

GEORGE. Nothing, dear. In fact, you have something they haven't got.

LIZ. *(Pleased.)* I have? What?

GEORGE. Me! Well, see you later, dear. If you want me, I'll be at the bank. *(Sound: door open and close—telephone dialing.)*

LIZ. Hello, Ann? Liz. I just spoke to George about being in the play. He put his foot down. Absolutely no. He was really definite about it. What time are we going to the tryouts? Of course I am. It's a challenge now. If I get the part think how surprised George will be on opening night. To say nothing of that Hollywood director.

Liz goes to the auditions, and to her delight the theater group's amateur director tells her that with a little practice she'll be a strong contender for the lead. Later, when Liz is in her bedroom rehearsing a love scene, George comes home unexpectedly and hears her from the hallway. When he enters the bedroom and realizes she was talking to herself, he thinks she's having a breakdown. He secretly arranges for a psychiatrist, Dr. Schweinkampf, to come over to the house to observe Liz, posing as an old college chum. Meanwhile, Liz discovers that the famous director, a local boy who made good in Hollywood, was an old college classmate of George's. When George tells Liz he's bringing an old college friend home to dinner, she assumes that their guest is really the movie director, and proceeds to "audition" for him by going into a series of virtuoso performances:

GEORGE. Well, here we are, Doctor.

SCHWEIN. One moment before we go in. Don't be nervous, Mr. Nougat.

GEORGE. That's Cugat.

SCHWEIN. It doesn't matter. Now don't worry if she seems to act normal. I can diagnose her condition by subtle little actions and movements. Don't do anything to arouse her.

GEORGE. All right. Here we go. *(Sound: door open.)*

GEORGE. *(Oversweet singsong.)* Liz. Li-i-i-zzz. Oh, there you are. Liz, I'd like you to meet an old friend of mine—Uh—Art Jones.

SCHWEIN. How do you do, Mrs. Cugat.

LIZ. (*Oversexy, almost Mae West.*) Hullooo, boys. I'm certainly glad you came up to see me.

GEORGE. Whah? Now Liz, please—

LIZ. There's a sofa over there, Mr. Jones. Why don't you get out of that hard chair and slip into something more comfortable?

GEORGE. Maybe Mr. Jones likes that chair, darling.

LIZ. (*Suddenly switching into high hysterical drama.*) Darling? Now you call me darling (*Dramatic laugh.*) But what am I when we're alone? Your slave. (*Starts crying.*) You beat me with a cane and push my poor broken body down the stairs. Oh, I don't care for myself, but you pushed the children after me!

GEORGE. The children? I did not.

LIZ. Then where are they? (*Breaking down.*) Oh, I can't stand it, putting on this sham in front of your friends (*Fading.*) I'm leaving, leaving this life of hypocrisy. (*Hysterical.*) Leaving, do you hear? (*Trails off in laughter and tears.*)

GEORGE. (*Pause.*) Well, Doctor, what do you think?

SCHWEIN. Don't speak to me, you Cad!

After the show aired at the beginning of October, I got another call from Harry.

"Jess," he said excitedly. "That was a terrific show. How would you like to be head writer of *My Favorite Husband*? I'd like to sign you for a five-year exclusive contract with CBS, whether or not the show stays on the air."

I told him I'd have to think it over. In the weeks since that first call from Harry, all of my friends had advised me not to take a job writing for Lucille Ball. When I attended a rehearsal I had noticed that the producer-director, sitting in the control room, had eight or nine prescription bottles of various shapes and sizes lined up before him. I remember making a mental note at the time that somewhere in this group there must be, shall we say, a "strong personality." True to my friends' reports, the "strong personality" had turned out to be Miss Ball.

On the other hand, something had "clicked" when she performed the broad comedy that I had written for her. I knew how lucky I had been to work for so long with the phenomenally gifted comedienne Fanny Brice —not exactly a weak-willed person herself. There was definitely something special about Lucille Ball, and I decided to take a chance.

On my first day at CBS I was introduced to Madelyn Pugh and Bob Carroll, Jr., who had been writing most of the shows since the departure of Fox and Davenport. Bob and Madelyn were two of the most worn-out

Bob, Madelyn, and I discuss a *My Favorite Husband* script with Lucy.

looking young people I had ever seen. Red-eyed and trembling, they told me that for the previous eight weeks they had been writing four and five scripts a week—rewriting for the producer-director, the network, and the star. I assured them that, in my experience, radio scripts could be written during office hours, except for the occasional emergency.

I'll never forget the look on Bob's face. In one of my favorite "Peanuts" cartoons, Charlie Brown and Linus are walking dejectedly home from a ball game. Their chins are on their chests, the gloves and a bat they carry are dragging on the ground. Charlie Brown says, "Well, you win some and you lose some." Linus turns to Charlie Brown and says, "That would be wonderful."

Bob had the very same expression as he said, "It sounds great, but frankly, sir, I don't believe you."

The following week's show was a continuation of the first *My Favorite Husband* script I had written. Bob and Madelyn and I were delighted to find that the three of us worked well together, and Bob was amazed when, true to my word, we got to showtime without having to do a major rewrite and without incurring the wrath of our redheaded star. Unfortunately, the same could not be said for the producer-director, Gordon Hughes, whose inventory of prescription drugs I had noticed a few weeks before. By the time the show went on the air that Saturday, it had finally become all too clear that Lucy was simply more than he could handle.

The Monday after the broadcast, Harry Ackerman walked into my office and informed me that he had decided to replace Gordon Hughes. Would I like to produce and direct the show in addition to my duties as head writer, for an additional $100 a week? "Sure," I told him. "Why not?"

I had three, maybe four, idyllic weeks in my new position as producer-director-head writer, and then the proverbial fan suffered a direct hit. We were rehearsing nights, so Lucy could work days in the motion picture *Sorrowful Jones*, with Bob Hope. The cast had assembled in the studio after dinner for the first reading, and halfway through the script it became apparent that we were in deep, deep trouble. The script just didn't work. And it was the only one we had. Although I had serious doubts, I assured everyone that we could fix it by morning, and excused them.

Bob and Madelyn and I worked practically all night. We were confident that we had saved the script. We weren't too proud of the very last line, but the rest of it was good, and we had all day to work on that one last line.

At daybreak, Lucy, her agent, Don Sharpe, and Es, with a change of clothes for me, all arrived at the same time. Lucy and Don followed me and my wife into my office, where Lucy took a copy of the script and settled into an overstuffed chair to read it. I could see that she was delighted as she read along. Time after time, she laughed uproariously, in that wonderful, abandoned way she had. We all laughed with her.

I thought we were home free, until she came to that last line. Well, Dr. Jekyll and Mr. Hyde were identical twins compared to the transformation Lucy served up. She screamed and she yelled. She swore. She threw the script across the room. Then she got it and tore it up in pieces and threw it again. She roared, in that horrible, abandoned way she had. She bellowed, "I won't do this ———." Well, I don't like to use the word, but it was the same stuff that hit the fan the night before.

I had never seen anything quite like it. After she finished this nonstop salvo, I walked over to her and said, "Lucy, I thought we had a team effort going here. We're happy to stay up all night or all week, and break our butts to make the script right for you. But not if you're going to ignore a major rewrite, which you loved, and crucify us over one little

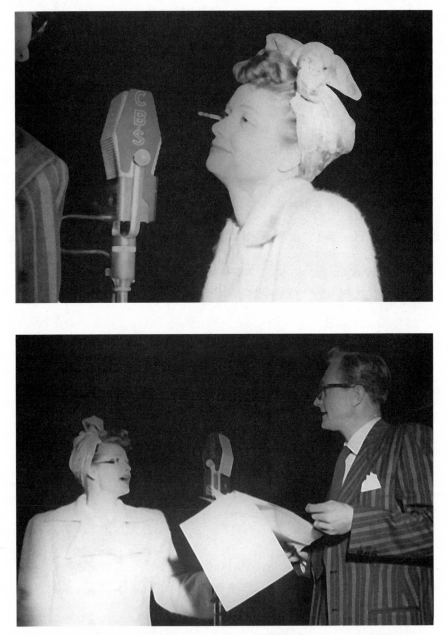

We rehearsed nights so that Lucy could work days in the motion picture
Sorrowful Jones, with Bob Hope.

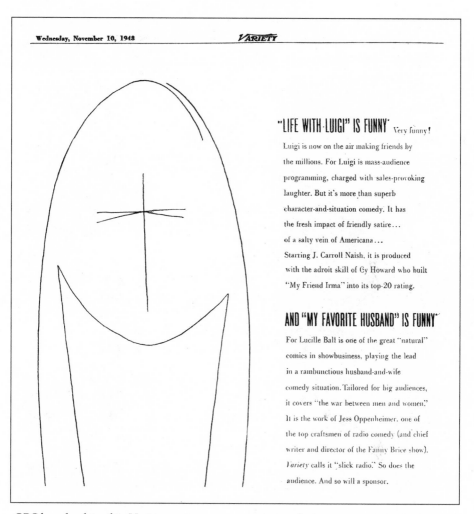

CBS bought this ad in *Variety* to try to attract a sponsor for its two sustaining programs.

line, which can easily be fixed. We need quite a bit more respect than that." I took her hand and shook it and said, "I can't say that it's been a pleasant experience working with you, but at least it's over."

I took my wife by the hand and walked out. We got about halfway down the block when Don Sharpe came running and hollering after me. "She's crying and hysterical," he said, still breathing hard from his effort to catch up with me. "She knows she was wrong. She agrees with you and wants to apologize."

I walked back to my office with Don. Lucy, still crying, asked me to forgive her and begged me to continue on the show. I told her I would come back, but only on one condition—she must apologize to Bob and Madelyn for the way she had been treating them. Lucy readily agreed.

We went down to the studio where everyone was waiting to start the rehearsal. Lucy walked over to Bob and Madelyn, who knew nothing about what had gone on in my office, and put her arms around their shoulders. As she walked them across the stage, she said, "I've been a —————," and that fan-hitting substance came up again. After the rehearsal, Bob and Madelyn came up to me and asked, "What the hell was that all about?"

When I arrived at my office the next morning, I found a glossy eight-by-ten photo of Lucy sitting on my desk. Across the bottom, Lucy had written "Dear Bossman—My love always. Lucy."

I had discovered that Lucy, despite her tough demeanor, was actually quite insecure and required somebody to lean on; she really needed to be dominated. My first inkling of this had come a week earlier, when I was directing her in a scene with her costar, Dick Denning. In the scene, Dick, normally a nice, passive fellow, really had to light into her and tell her off; he really read the riot act to her. Lucy came over to me after the first run-through with her eyes all lit up.

"Write more scenes like that!" she said. "That's great! Let him really tell me off."

Surprised by her reaction, I simply told her "Okay." But I remember thinking to myself, "And I see how *I* have to act with you in the future, too."

Once I established that kind of relationship with her, there were just no problems as far as she and I were concerned. As a matter of fact, she ultimately became so confident of our ability to fix anything that might need fixing that she practically ignored the scripts until rehearsal time.

You may not realize just what a boon that was. Most stars go over the script with a fine tooth comb thirty or forty times—and then decide it doesn't seem fresh. Just to make sure, they have it read by a series of such experts as the hairdresser, the costume designer, and the kid who delivers pizza to the set, and you end up, as Bob and Madelyn did in their earlier experience, writing four or five new scripts every week.

·   ·   ·

December brought us good news. The ratings were up, and Pat Weaver at Y&R had bought the program for General Foods, makers of Jell-O,

To celebrate our signing with General Foods, we threw a party at the studio, complete with a cake topped by boxes of Jell-O.

starting in January. Although Lucy's new, more "down-to-earth" Liz Cugat was an improvement, I decided that the show still needed a few more changes to make the characters easier for the audience to identify with. The first was to change their last name from "Cugat" to "Cooper." I also didn't feel the average listener related too well to the problems of the vice president of a bank, so we made it clear that husband George, although he had this fancy-sounding title, in fact wasn't making any more than the garage attendant down the street. This gave them the universal "average man's" problem of making ends meet. This also allowed us to have more fun with Liz's "unique" way of figuring household finances. An example:

> LIZ. You should be glad I bought that dress, George. I made twenty dollars by doing it.
>
> GEORGE. You *made* twenty dollars?
>
> LIZ. Absolutely. I bought the dress on sale at Cramer's for $39.50 and the identical dress is selling at Gordon's for $59.50—so I made twenty dollars!
>
> GEORGE. But you don't *have* that twenty dollars.
>
> LIZ. I know I don't. I spent it on a hat to go with the dress!

The show also needed another married couple, as a counterpoint to George and Liz. We decided that this should be George's boss, Rudolph Atterbury, president of the bank, and his wife, Iris, who would be Liz's best friend. Gale Gordon, best known to radio listeners at the time in his continuing role as Mayor LaTrivia on *Fibber McGee and Molly* and *The Great Gildersleeve,* had appeared on our show a few weeks before, in the part of a trial judge. The unique comic chemistry between Gale and Lucy was apparent immediately, and I decided to cast him as Mr. Atterbury.

In the part of Mr. Atterbury's wife, Iris, I cast Bea Benaderet, the wonderful comedy actress whom I had known since my days at KFRC in San Francisco, and who would later become the voice of Betty Rubble in *The Flintstones* and would star in the television series *Petticoat Junction.* Bea, who was well known as Blanche Morton on *Burns and Allen,* had been appearing almost weekly on *My Favorite Husband* in a variety of nonrecurring roles. The Iris Atterbury character opened up whole new directions for us and for the character of Liz Cooper—she finally had a real confederate to include in her wild schemes—particularly whenever the battle was "wives vs. husbands."

On one episode, Bea fell madly in love with a line we had written for her. I don't recall the line, but from the moment she first read it at rehearsal, it became her favorite of all time. She rehearsed it constantly, trying it a hundred different ways. She couldn't wait to drop that bombshell of a line on the unsuspecting public. It was going to be the biggest laugh of her career.

Bea came to me before airtime, and said, "Now, don't worry if I take a

Bea Benaderet and Gale Gordon clown it up during a run-through of
My Favorite Husband.

little extra time before I deliver that line. There's a laugh just ahead of
it, and I want to wait for absolute silence before I drop my little goody."

I agreed, and we went in to do the show.

The setup in the studio was such that the four main players shared
two microphones. As I sat in the control room, Bea and Lucy were both
facing me, while Dick Denning and Gale Gordon were facing in the
opposite direction. The scene with Bea's choice line was about twenty
minutes into the show. Just as Bea had predicted, the previous line got a
good laugh, and she looked over at me and raised her hand a little as
though to say, "Don't worry, I have everything under control."

The laugh faded and finally tailed off into complete, absolute silence.
As Bea, with the smile of anticipation on her face, drew in her breath to
deliver her bombshell, Dick Denning decided that she must have missed
her cue, and he read his next line. The program proceeded, Bea's line
was lost forever, and it was a good thing for Dick Denning that we were
on the air live. By the end of the program, she had calmed down just
enough not to kill him.

•   •   •

When General Foods bought the program, the sponsor made it clear that it wanted Lucy to be its spokesperson on the show. In addition to starting every program by saying "Jell-O everybody," Lucy was expected to do a Jell-O commercial at the end of each episode.

Lucy hated this. She just wasn't comfortable facing an open mike as herself, advertising Jell-O. Ask her to play a role and she was happy. Ask her to be Lucille Ball and she immediately became self-conscious and ill at ease. After watching her suffer through this for several weeks, I finally decided to write the "sell words" as Mother Goose rhymes, with Lucy doing all the parts: Goldilocks, the Three Bears, Jack Sprat, Jack and Jill, Little Miss Muffet, the Spider, and so forth. Not only did Lucy become more relaxed, but she also discovered, to everyone's delight, that she had a real flair for comic voices. When we did "Little Miss Muffet," Lucy, as the Spider, contorted her face into a teeth-baring grimace and came out with a high-pitched, nasal "spider voice" that had the audience howling. In later shows, whenever we wanted to evoke this sound (or this face), we would simply write "(SPIDER)" in the script. It quickly became a Lucy trademark—her embarrassed reaction to being found out.

Even with all of the changes in the show, I still had a problem—Lucy was relatively stiff working in front of an audience. She just didn't have the wildly antic quality that I was looking for. I had been trying for some time to get her and Dick Denning to loosen up and act out the jokes and reactions, to dramatize what was going on, instead of just standing there waiting to read the next line when the laugh subsided. I knew how effective this could be from watching Jack Benny do his radio program. Jack would lay his hand against his cheek, open his eyes wide, and look out at the studio audience, slowly changing his point of view, like a comic lighthouse. And as long as he looked, they laughed.

Dick Denning was a lost cause. When I tried to explain to him what I was looking for, he simply said, "If I take my eyes or my finger off that script, I'll never find my place again."

I remember telling Lucy, "Let go. Act it out. Take your time." But she was simply afraid to try. So one day, at rehearsal, I handed Lucy a couple of Jack Benny tickets.

She looked at me blankly. "What are these for?"

"I want you to go to school," I told her.

It did the trick. When Lucy came into the studio for the next rehearsal, I could see she was excited. "Oh my God, Jess," she gushed, "I didn't realize!"

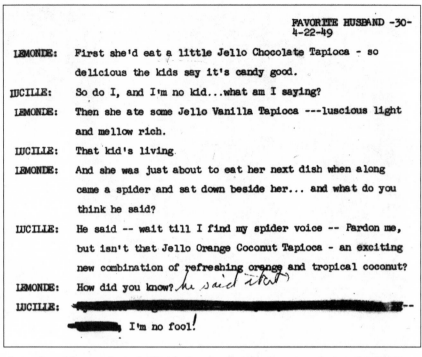

FAVORITE HUSBAND -30-
4-22-49

LEMONDE: First she'd eat a little Jello Chocolate Tapioca - so delicious the kids say it's candy good.

LUCILLE: So do I, and I'm no kid...what am I saying?

LEMONDE: Then she ate some Jello Vanilla Tapioca ---luscious light and mellow rich.

LUCILLE: That kid's living.

LEMONDE: And she was just about to eat her next dish when along came a spider and sat down beside her... and what do you think he said?

LUCILLE: He said -- wait till I find my spider voice -- Pardon me, but isn't that Jello Orange Coconut Tapioca - an exciting new combination of refreshing orange and tropical coconut?

LEMONDE: How did you know? *he said that*

LUCILLE: ████████████████████████████████ -- ██████ I'm no fool!

Lucy found her trademark "Spider" voice for the first time during this 1949 Jell-O commercial.

She just couldn't wait to get started trying out the new, emancipated attitude she had discovered. On that week's show Lucy really hammed it up, playing it much broader than she ever had before. She coupled this with her newfound freedom of movement, and there were times I thought we'd have to catch her with a butterfly net to get her back to the microphone. The audience roared their approval, and Lucy loved it. So did I.

Jack Benny eventually became one of Lucy's biggest fans, as well as her next door neighbor when she and Desi moved to Beverly Hills. And six years after I asked Lucy to attend that broadcast of *The Jack Benny Program*, Jack repaid the compliment. He required all of his writers to "go to school" by attending a special screening of *I Love Lucy*—the episode in which William Holden sets fire to Lucy's nose.

Although the radio show was doing well, Bob and Madelyn and I were always under criticism from CBS. We just weren't writing what was then considered the "in" kind of radio comedy show, where you have a series

When we broadcast My *Favorite Husband* live, I always had to keep an eye on the clock, speeding the actors up or slowing them down to make the program come out on the nose.

•   •   •

of comedy characters, each of whom comes in, does his own shtick, and then exits. Instead, we did whole stories—*situation* comedy. They kept telling us this would never fly. But we persisted, and eventually the popularity of the program just became too much for them to argue with.

•   •   •

Edgar Bergen and I confer with Dario Soria of D'Arcy,
sponsor Coca-Cola's advertising agency.

In the fall of 1949, *The Edgar Bergen Show with Charlie McCarthy* moved to CBS, sponsored by Coca-Cola. Harry Ackerman assigned me to produce and direct the Bergen show in addition to my duties on *My Favorite Husband*.

The Coca-Cola Company had for some time made it a practice to deliver free cases of Coke to practically every radio writer in Hollywood. There had never been any explanation—I just found a wooden case with twelve glass bottles of Coke on my back doorstep every week.

Shortly after I began working on the Bergen show on CBS, the deliveries stopped as mysteriously as they had begun. I assumed this was just due to some clerical mixup, so the next time I attended a meeting with someone from our sponsor, I decided to mention it.

"I've been meaning to tell you about something," I remarked after our business meeting concluded. "I've enjoyed getting free Cokes for years, but somebody must have made a mistake at the plant, because I stopped getting them just last week."

"Oh, that's no mistake," he replied. "Now that you're working on a Coca-Cola–sponsored show, we don't feel that we should have to give you free Cokes to get our product mentioned on the air."

•   •   •

One of the regular performers on both *My Favorite Husband* and the Bergen show was my good friend Hans Conried. Hans had an illustrious career on stage and screen, appearing in countless productions, but is perhaps best known by many people as the voice of Captain Hook in Walt Disney's *Peter Pan*, and Snidely Whiplash on *Dudley Doright*.

As good as he was at playing myriad and diverse characters, Hans, like Lucy, had trouble playing himself in front of the microphone. Every so often I'd be directing Hans, and his part would call for boisterous laughter as Professor Schweinkampf, or whoever he was playing. Hans was a master at this. After he did it so well, I used to kid him by saying, "Hans, I think it's time that you stop hiding behind all these characters. I think we're going to change the name of the character in this sketch to 'Hans Conried,' and we'll give you the billing on it. Now, let's take this scene again."

Hans would just choke up completely. He couldn't get himself to laugh at all—all he could manage was a coughing paroxysm. But as soon as I changed the name of the character back again, the problem would always disappear.

Once, on the Bergen show, we were doing a sketch about Robert Fulton's invention of the steamboat. There was a scene in which the boat was leaving on its trip up the Hudson River, and everyone was yelling good-byes. Hans, who played the commissioner of public works, came to me after the rehearsal and said, "Jess, there's something that I've always wanted to do in one of these crowd scenes. Would it be all right with you if instead of 'Good-bye!' or 'Good luck!', I were to yell 'Mazel-tov!'? Nobody would hear it over all of the other yelling. It would just be my own private joke." I didn't see any harm in it, so I told him he could do it if he really wanted to.

None of the other actors who made up the crowd in the riverboat sketch had lines in the next scene. Unbeknownst to Hans and me, between the rehearsal and airtime, one by one, each of them asked and received permission to be excused as soon as the riverboat started to leave. So when the show aired, just as the sound-effects man played the sound of the giant paddlewheel turning as the riverboat pulled away from the shore, all the other actors turned to go instead of yelling their good-byes into the microphone. Hans, so keyed up that he failed to notice this, was left all alone, shouting "Mazeltov!" on coast-to-coast radio.

Another actor I used regularly in various roles on *My Favorite Husband* (and later on *I Love Lucy*) was Jerry Hausner. Jerry, a familiar voice on many radio programs, had been a regular on *Baby Snooks,* as the voice of Robespierre, Snooks's baby brother.

Jerry always used to crack us all up in rehearsal, but for some reason I found myself unable to capture his brash funniness in front of the mike on the air. Once, as an experiment, I gave Jerry permission to skip rehearsals, come late to the broadcast, and simply read his lines cold, without even knowing what import they had. He got screams. From then on, whenever Jerry appeared on the show I made it a practice not to call him for rehearsals.

As I had told Bob Carroll, writing a script for a weekly radio series was something that could be accomplished during regular business hours. Being responsible for putting together *two* weekly network programs at the same time was quite another matter. I found myself working seven days a week, leaving me practically no time to spend with my wife and one-year-old daughter. Much as I enjoyed doing both shows, I decided after a few weeks to take a cut in salary and have someone else take over my duties on the Bergen show.

Es was doubly pleased with my decision. Not only did I have more time to spend at home, but within a few weeks, the Coca-Cola deliveries began again.

The TV Audition

As Lucy began to loosen up at the microphone, her highly visual antics garnered more and more attention. The *Hollywood Reporter* commented that it was "too bad that her funny grimaces and gestures aren't visible over the radio." In a 1949 feature spread on *My Favorite Husband* in *Radio and Television Life* magazine, one of the pictures of Lucy and Richard Denning at the microphone had this caption: "It could be television —Lucille and Richard Denning look like an awfully cute couple as they go through their chores as 'Liz' and 'George' on *My Favorite Husband*."

Lucy was interested in moving to television, all right—but not with Richard Denning. For years, she had been trying to promote the career of her husband, Desi Arnaz. She was unhappy because they were separated so much of the time; while she was here in Hollywood, he was always on the road with his band. This put a strain on their marriage, which was rocky enough even when they were in the same city. So when Harry Ackerman approached Lucy about transferring the radio series to TV, she tried to sell him on using Desi as her costar.

Harry wasn't particularly thrilled with the idea of using Desi on television. He was afraid that viewers wouldn't be able to understand him. But Lucy insisted that it was either Desi or no TV show. Hubbell Robinson, another CBS bigwig, nixed the idea completely, on the grounds that nobody would believe that an all-American redhead like Lucy was married to someone like Desi. Lucy had a good answer for that one—"What do you mean, nobody'll believe it? We *are* married!" But CBS remained unconvinced. Finally, Lucy told the network, "If I can't do a show with him, I'm going to travel with him." In March 1950, she and Desi formed Desilu Productions and made plans for their own vaudeville tour during our summer hiatus, to prove that the public would accept them as a team.

Bob and Madelyn wrote some sketches for Lucy and Desi's act, which was billed as "Desi Arnaz and Band with Lucille Ball." Desi got his old fishing buddy, the internationally famous clown "Pepito," to come up with some clown routines for Lucy to do. Pepito also built a Rube Goldberg-type cello for Lucy, equipped with all sorts of hidden gags.

By May, Lucy and Desi had booked their act into a string of vaudeville houses, opening in Chicago at the beginning of June. There was just one problem—their vaudeville debut was in less than five weeks, but we still had *eight* weeks to go until the end of the season. The final episode of *My Favorite Husband* wasn't scheduled to air until June 26. Fortunately, we had by this time begun taping our shows for delayed broadcast. Shifting into high gear, we managed to write, rehearse, and tape eight episodes of *My Favorite Husband* in just three weeks, one every couple of days. By May 26, we had completed the entire season's production, just in time for Lucy and Desi to keep their out-of-town commitment.

The vaudeville tour was a roaring success. *Variety* called opening night in Chicago "one of the best bills to play house in recent months. . . . If the red-headed gal wants to slide on her tummy for five or six shows a day past the initial five-week booking for this package, her agency, General Artists Corp., should have no trouble lining up dates."

Armed with the good notices that the vaudeville act had received, Don Sharpe and I took another run at convincing CBS to do a TV audition program (called a "pilot" nowadays) featuring Lucy and Desi. The answer from the network was still no. But their success as a vaudeville team was enough to pique the interest of Young and Rubicam, whose client, General Foods, was Lucy's radio sponsor. One of the Y&R men convinced Lucy and Desi not to wait for CBS to change its mind. "Produce your *own* audition program!" he told them. "That way you can sell it to the highest bidder." Unfortunately, it would also mean that neither I nor Bob and Madelyn could work on the project, because we had exclusive contracts with CBS.

Lucy and Desi took Y&R's advice. They spent a lot of their own money commissioning one independent script after another, but they were unhappy with all of them. One of the scripts had them playing themselves—the successful bandleader, Desi Arnaz, and his successful movie star wife, Lucille Ball. The story was about how *Life* magazine ruined their plans for a quiet celebration of their wedding anniversary. Although it wasn't what Lucy and Desi wanted, it did manage to spark some interest at a rival network—NBC.

The prospect of losing Lucy to NBC was finally enough to get CBS's attention. Harry Ackerman accepted the inevitable and put Desi under contract to keep Lucy and Desi together in Hollywood while a TV deal could be worked out. CBS had planned an unsponsored Sunday afternoon radio quiz show called *Earn Your Vacation*, hosted by a new young comic named Johnny Carson. Harry, just promoted to executive in charge of production for CBS radio and television, put Desi in as emcee. He changed the title to *Your Tropical Trip*, and made the giveaways vacations in the Caribbean area. The revamped program would debut on January 21, 1951.

Now it was Lucy's turn to play hard to get. Armed with NBC's overtures, she imposed her own conditions on CBS. Her agent Don Sharpe told Harry Ackerman that Lucy would make a deal with the network only if I would be her producer and head writer. She also insisted that the show be produced in Hollywood and air only once every two weeks, so that she could continue her film career. And Desilu Productions must have a 50 percent interest in the show.

Harry Ackerman came to see me just before Christmas. After describing the terms he had tentatively worked out with Don Sharpe, including my own involvement, he asked me if I would be willing to write and produce Lucy's TV show for CBS. I pointed out to him that my contract specified that I would get a substantial percentage of any new radio or television show that I created for the network. Harry offered me 20 percent. I accepted.

The agreement that Don Sharpe had made with CBS called for an audition program to be delivered to the network in less than six weeks, but we still had no series concept. Don sent me the material that had been written by outside writers earlier that fall. I read and rejected all of it, just as Lucy and Desi already had. I preferred to stick closer to the flavor of *My Favorite Husband*, which was working so well for Lucy. But we couldn't simply take the radio series and move it to the screen—even Lucy admitted that the public would never buy the notion of Desi as a small-town banker.

We held a series of brainstorming meetings at CBS Columbia Square, trying to come up with an acceptable premise for a TV series for Lucy and Desi. We were all asking ourselves, "What do you do with a comedienne and a Cuban orchestra leader?" Then one day, at one of the meetings, I hit upon an idea that I thought might work. I turned to Harry Ackerman, who was seated next to me at the conference table, and said "Why don't we do a show about a middle-class working stiff who works very hard at his job as a bandleader, and likes nothing better than to

LUCILLE BALL - DESI ARNAZ TV SHOW (AUDITION)

First Revision

MUSIC: THEME

SIMULTANEOUS WITH CARD WHICH

READS:

                                    ANNCR:

                              So and so presents LUCY starring

                              Lucille Ball and Desi Arnaz.

WE DISSOLVE TO A PANORAMIC STILL

PICTURE OF A LARGE CITY.

                                    ANNCR:

                              In that city live Lucy and ~~Larry~~ *Richar*

                              ~~Lopez.~~ *Ricardo* Of course, you know Larry is

                              the famous Latin-American orchestra

                              leader and singer and Lucy is the

                              famous - uh, well, she's the - uh -

                              her hair is very red and she's

                              married to Larry.

CAMERA MOVES FORWARD TOWARD

PICTURE..AND WE DISSOLVE TO A

CLOSER SHOT. ONE APARTMENT HOUSE

STANDS OUT FAIRLY WELL.

                                    ANNCR:

                              (AS NEW PICTURE APPEARS) In that

                              district close to theatres and night

                              clubs, where Larry works. They have

                              a modest little apartment. Here

                              they live, breath, eat and carry on

                              their never unending feud.

We had settled on names for the main characters, abandoning "Lucy and Larry Lopez" in favor of "Lucy and Ricky Ricardo." But we still needed a name for the show itself.

come home at night and relax with his wife, who doesn't like staying home and is dying to get into show business herself?" That was the nucleus. CBS liked the idea, and, best of all, so did Lucy.

Bob and Madelyn cut short a European vacation to come home and work on the pilot with me. With only a few weeks to come up with a completed script and put the whole production together, we decided to use a routine about wills that the three of us had written as part of a *My Favorite Husband* script. That routine, together with about seven minutes of physical gags and dialogue from Lucy and Desi's vaudeville act, formed the core of the audition program. In the show, Ricky has a TV audition for his band, and he sends Lucy to deliver the wills to a lawyer's office downtown to get her out of the way. Lucy inadvertently learns of Ricky's show and unexpectedly shows up in it.

That was it. There was no time spent in surveying or testing the idea with the public. All we had to go on was that Lucille Ball had been playing a certain kind of character in radio, and the public liked her.

The only other characters in the show were Pepito the Clown, played by Pepito himself, and Ricky's agent, Jerry, played by Jerry Hausner. When I called Jerry to offer him the part, he was so excited at the prospect of being a regular in a television series that he immediately called his father, told him the news, and offered to buy him his own television set.

Jerry's father was an elderly Hungarian immigrant who lived alone in an apartment on Vine Street. The only television he had ever seen was the one in the front window of Barker Brothers furniture store on Hollywood Boulevard, where every Friday night he stood outside and watched the wrestling matches. He couldn't hear a thing through the thick plate glass, of course, but with wrestling that didn't really matter. When Jerry offered to buy him a TV set, his father surprised him by declining the offer. But Jerry was even more surprised by the reason his father gave him. "Not yet," he advised Jerry. "Just wait. Wait till they get *sound*. They'll figure it out one of these days. You'll see. Just like they did with the movies."

Because of a scheduling change, we were now set to go before the TV cameras in CBS Studio A on Friday, March 2—Desi's thirty-fourth birthday. Our director would be Ralph Levy, moonlighting from his duties as producer-director of *The George Burns and Gracie Allen Show*, another live CBS sitcom. To show the audition to potential sponsors, we would make a kinescope, which was a film taken off the closed-circuit TV tube.

I was beginning to get a little nervous about the timing. Lucy was five

Lucy and Desi rehearse the opening scene of the *I Love Lucy* audition. Lucy was five months pregnant and showing quite a bit, even after we camouflaged her in baggy pajamas and a big bathrobe.

months pregnant, and showing quite a bit. What's more, Es was *nine* months pregnant. Our second child was due any day.

One thing we still lacked was a name for the show. The script on my desk simply said "So and so presents LUCY starring Lucille Ball and Desi Arnaz," but "Lucy" was just a working title. And Desi was still giving me a problem about the credits. He just couldn't understand why we had Lucy's name ahead of his. Why couldn't he be first? After about a week of going back and forth with him on this, I had finally managed to convince him on the basis that it was the "gallant" thing to do—to let the lady go first. But even then he had come back to me one more time, saying, "I tell you what, Jess, why don't we compromise and make it alphabetical?"

Because we were doing a live show, the cards bearing the title and credits had to be made up in advance. All of us had contributed possible names for the program, and I had the long list of suggestions in front of me. It was time to choose. As I sat at my desk reading it for the tenth or eleventh time, I kept coming back to the same title: *I Love Lucy.* That's the one, I decided. It would convey the essential nature of the show— an examination of marriage between two people who truly love each other. As I thought more about my choice, I realized that I had just solved another problem as well. The "I" in *I Love Lucy* was Desi. I had given him first-place billing after all.

We needed a theme song. I immediately thought of my friend Eliot Daniel, Rudy Vallee's pianist before and during the war. After getting out of the Coast Guard, Eliot had spent several years as a composer, conductor, and arranger for Disney, where his work included the Oscar-nominated song "Lavender Blue." I called Eliot at his office at Twentieth Century–Fox, explained that Lucy was doing a TV audition program, and asked him if he'd write a theme for us.

"I'll do it for you, Jess," he said, "but you'll have to keep my name out of it."

"Why?"

"Because my exclusive contract with Fox doesn't run out until next year."

"That's no problem. Your name won't appear anywhere."

"Fine. When do you need it?"

"Friday."

There was a second or two of silence.

"Okay. What's the name of the show?"

"*I Love Lucy.*"

"I'll get back to you in a day or two."

A couple of days later, Eliot came over to the studio and played the theme for me and Desi and a few others. We all loved it. He told us that he had been looking for an opening musical phrase that said *I Love Lucy*, and that as soon as he settled on the first four notes, the rest of the song practically wrote itself.

Friday, March 2, finally arrived. As I walked into my office that morning, a thought occurred to me. I had been so busy putting the show together that I hadn't even thought about the fact that I still hadn't seen a draft of my contract for the TV series. In fact, I hadn't even discussed my percentage deal with anyone since that first conversation with Harry.

I decided that I needed an insurance policy. I sat down and began to type:

I LOVE LUCY
Created by Jess Oppenheimer

This is a title of an idea for a radio and/or television program, incorporating characters named Lucy and Ricky Ricardo. He is a Latin-American orchestra leader and singer. She is his wife. They are happily married and very much in love. The only bone of contention between them is her desire to get into show business, and his equally strong desire to keep her out of it. To Lucy, who was brought up in the humdrum sphere of a moderate, well-to-do middle western, mercantile family, show business is the most glamorous field in the world. But Ricky, who was raised in show business, sees none of its glamour, only its deficiencies, and yearns to be an ordinary citizen, keeping regular hours and living a normal life. As show business is the only way he knows to make a living, and he makes a very good one, the closest he can get to this dream is having a wife who's out of show business and devotes herself to keeping as nearly a normal life as possible for him.

The first story concerns a TV audition for Ricky, where Pepito, the clown, due to an accident, fails to appear and Lucy takes his place for the show. Although she does a bang-up job, she foregoes the chance at a career that is offered to her in order to keep Ricky happy and closer to his dream of normalcy.

I took the page out of the typewriter and drove over to the Screen Writers' Guild Office on Sunset Boulevard, where I paid the one-dollar registration fee and was given a receipt and a stamped carbon copy of the typewritten page. When I got back to my office I put both items in my filing cabinet and hoped that I would never need to use them.

I wasn't the only one working without a contract that day. The lawyers, agents, and businessmen had been trying since December to get

CBS's deal with Lucy and Desi down on paper, but the contract was still unsigned as the actors took their places in Studio A on that Friday evening. Lucy was already onstage, waiting for the curtain to rise, but Desi and Hal Hudson from CBS were still arguing about some items on the as-yet unsigned contract. With only moments until curtain, Hal finally gave Desi an ultimatum: "Sign the contract right now, as is, or the show will not go on."

Desi was furious. "How much does the kinescope cost to shoot?" he demanded to know.

Hal consulted some papers he was holding. "Nineteen thousand dollars."

"Okay," Desi yelled at him. "I'll pay for it myself, and it will belong to us."

His bluff called, Hal immediately backed down. "No, that's all right, Desi," he said. "We'll go ahead and shoot it now and thrash out the contract details later."

·   ·   ·

On the following Wednesday, March 7, Don Sharpe boarded a plane for New York, carrying a completed kinescope of *I Love Lucy*, and we all anxiously waited and hoped it would sell. In the meantime we had another episode of *My Favorite Husband* to rehearse and tape by Friday.

I arrived late at the studio that Friday morning. As I walked into my office, the telephone on my desk was ringing. It was the head of the programming department at CBS in New York. He would later remember things a little differently, claiming that he loved *I Love Lucy* from the moment he first saw it. But on that Friday morning he wasn't bearing such glad tidings.

"What are you sending me, Jess?" he said. "This is the worst thing I've ever seen. How can I possibly sell this?"

It wasn't exactly the reaction I had been hoping for. But at that moment I was in such a good mood that nothing he said could dampen my spirits. I had just come from Queen of Angels Hospital, where Es had given birth to our son, Gregg, the night before.

I actually came close to missing that blessed event. What's worse, I almost made Es's doctor miss it, too. I had taken Es to the hospital just before dinnertime. This was in the days when expectant fathers just sat in the hospital waiting room until it was all over. After a couple of hours Dr. Mishell came out to tell me that it looked like it was going to be a long labor. I decided to go out for some dinner and invited him to join me.

Sure enough, as soon as we left, things started moving more quickly than expected. When we arrived back at the hospital, Dr. Mishell barely made it into the delivery room in time to catch Gregg as he came out. It reminded me of one of my situation comedy scripts, but for some reason Es didn't think it was so funny.

Two weeks later we taped the final episode of My *Favorite Husband*. There was still no buyer for the TV show, and none of us knew what we would be doing come the fall. At the close of the program Lucy gave a little speech announcing to the studio audience and our listeners that it was our last show and expressing her hope that "we'll be able to come back on the air in the not-too-distant future." She thanked everybody connected with the program for "a wonderful two-and-a-half years." It was an emotional moment, especially for Lucy, now close to six months pregnant. As she read the list of names of all of the people associated with the show, she broke down and began to cry.

Exactly one month after Lucy's tearful farewell, we got the news we had all been waiting for. Don Sharpe had succeeded in selling the show to Milton Biow, head of the ad agency that bore his name, for Philip Morris cigarettes. Biow sent word that he was on his way to Europe and that he would contact us on his return.

In the meantime, Bob and Madelyn and I rethought the pilot and realized that we had written it for Lucy and Desi only, omitting anyone for our stars to speak to and plot with, as we had in the radio show with Gale Gordon and Bea Benaderet. At first we toyed with the idea of having a lot of interaction between Lucy and Ricky and his nightclub boss. But that would mean the situations would revolve more around Ricky's job than domestic life. And that was definitely out. For the same reason, we concluded that the character of Jerry, Ricky's agent, should be dropped from the regular cast.

We finally decided to add an older couple, Fred and Ethel Mertz, whose only asset was the apartment building that the Ricardos lived in. We would reverse the roles from the radio show—in this case the younger couple would be better off financially, but not a lot more. Just as on *My Favorite Husband,* we figured that we could pursue the examination of marriage from these two different age levels and two different economic levels. We would be able to pair them off as couple against couple, women against men, or haves against have-nots, all setups that had worked for us on the radio series.

Our natural choices to play the Mertzes were Gale Gordon and Bea Benaderet, but by the time *I Love Lucy* was sold, they both had other

commitments and weren't available. So we drew up a list of likely character actors and began our search.

We were still pondering who would play the Mertzes when I got a
phone call from Milton Biow, who had just returned from his European
trip. He was obviously in a good mood. "I was thinking about the show
all the time I was away," he began. "I think it's going to be a great
program." Then, almost as an afterthought, he added, "By the way, when
are you and the Arnazes moving to New York?"

I nearly dropped the phone. "New York??? Who's moving to New
York? Nobody told me anything about that! I thought the deal called for
the show to originate from here—live—with kinnies for the cable, like
Burns and Allen and *The Alan Young Show*." I explained to him that we
had no intention of moving to the East Coast.

"Jess," he said, "I bought a show that's going to be done from New
York. I am not about to put on a program where 15 percent of the
audience see it clearly and 85 percent see it through a piece of cheese-
cloth."

What he was referring to, of course, was the fact that in those days
there was no coaxial cable that reached across the country. The part of
the audience that could pick the show up live would see it clearly, while
the rest would be watching a kinescope, a low-quality motion picture
of the program photographed off the tube when it went out live, and
then replayed later. And 85 percent of the audience was in the East and
Midwest.

None of us wanted to go to New York. I was afraid that our luck had
given out and we had no deal, but I suggested that he call CBS and
straighten it out.

It took about a week for us to settle the matter. To solve Biow's
concerns about picture quality, we argued in favor of doing the show in
Hollywood, but on film, like another new situation comedy, *Amos 'n'
Andy*, set to debut on CBS-TV the following month. Biow was skeptical,
but after screening a print of *Amos 'n' Andy*, he finally agreed, on one
condition—the *I Love Lucy* film would have to be at least equal in
quality to *Amos 'n' Andy*, or else we would have to do the program live
from New York as he had originally wanted.

The decision to film the series had solved one problem, but it created
another. Martin Leeds, CBS's director of business affairs, estimated that
filming the show would *double* the production costs—an additional
$5,000 per show. But Biow was unwilling to pay a penny more for each
episode than he had previously agreed. And instead of a show every

other week, Biow was insisting on a weekly show. Lucy would have to sacrifice her screen career to gamble on television.

Don Sharpe came up with a clever compromise. Lucy and Desi were to receive a weekly salary of $5,000 between them. Don proposed that they cut their salary by $2,000 a week if CBS would make up the remaining $3,000 budget shortfall. Since Desilu owned 50 percent of the show, Don figured this salary cut would really cost Lucy and Desi only $1,000.

Don's idea was acceptable to Lucy and Desi. But Desi saw an opportunity to make back the money by selling the films of the show overseas. If he and Lucy were going to risk everything on the show, he told Don, the film negatives must be owned 100 percent by Desilu Productions. To everyone's surprise, CBS agreed. We had a deal.

So suddenly here I was, producing a *filmed* television show, and I knew nothing about film. I'd never worked one day in a movie studio other than as a writer. As producer, I was responsible for making all the decisions and bringing the show in on time and on budget. Clearly, I needed to be educated in a hurry.

I went to a motion picture film laboratory and asked them to show me the ropes. In a two-week crash course, I learned the basics of all of the technical processes and what they cost, as well as what each person does and what he is supposed to be responsible for. In effect, I had to learn a whole new profession—a far cry from the days of radio when I glibly told Harry, "Sure I'll produce. Why not?"

We still had to decide *how* to film *I Love Lucy*. When we agreed with Milton Biow that the show would be produced on film, we deliberately left this issue open, and with good reason. *Amos 'n' Andy*, the film quality standard against which our show was to be judged, was shot on a soundstage without an audience, out of sequence, just like a motion picture. Then, after the film was edited, an audience was brought in to a theater and shown the film, and their laughter and applause were recorded and then dubbed into the film's sound track. Without any live audience reaction during the performance to go by, the actors on *Amos 'n' Andy* simply had to guess at how long to wait before proceeding with their next line. Not surprisingly, they often guessed wrong, and the audience reactions sometimes covered the dialogue. None of us wanted this to happen on *I Love Lucy*.

We held a series of brainstorming sessions to come up with a better solution. One of the ideas we had was to rehearse the show all week on CBS's Stage A and then, when we felt we were ready, bring in an audience and carefully time and record every one of their laughs. Then we would go over to a movie soundstage and film the episode—motion picture–style with one camera—leaving the appropriate timed gaps for the laughs. But all of this sounded impossibly confusing, so we quickly dropped the idea.

Apart from its complexity, the "timed laughs" method was unacceptable to us for a more fundamental reason. What we really wanted to do was to film the show in front of an audience. There is that quality, that response, that comes only from a live experience. And the American public had learned to expect this after twenty-five years of listening to studio audiences laugh on radio.

We knew from *My Favorite Husband* that an audience would give us not only the right character of laugh for the situation—it would also give us perfect timing. The audience's reaction told the actors when to stop, and then, as the laughter died down, to go ahead again. This interaction between the audience and the performers had other benefits as well. It enabled the actors to gloss over the things that weren't going so well, and then really milk it when things were going wonderfully.

For Lucy, doing the radio series in front of a live audience had been like having an opening night every week. She would get keyed up with nervous excitement and her adrenaline would be flowing, resulting in a combination of elements that just couldn't be faked. When we would do retakes after the audience was gone, I constantly found myself saying, "Come on now, project more." And Lucy and Dick Denning would say, "Well, we're screaming," and I would say, "No, even more!" And I'd fight with them about it. Then, finally, this take, in which they had insisted that they were screaming, would be cut into the tape that was made in front of the audience. The sound level would drop down to nothing. No, it just couldn't be faked, and the result would transmit itself clearly to the viewers at home. They would know whether it was a real, live performance.

So our meeting naturally turned to a discussion of the logistics of shooting the show in sequence, in front of an audience, just like a live TV show, but using film cameras instead of TV cameras. We knew that the technique of using multiple film cameras moving on dollies, pushed to various positions by grips, with the camera operator riding, had been around since the late 1920s. In those early days no one yet knew how to prerecord motion picture sound, so they used a stylus on a wax record to record the sound as the scene progressed. They had to shoot each scene in sequence, with several movie cameras shooting simultaneously, from beginning to end.

"Why," someone asked, "hasn't anyone used this method on TV?"

"They have," said a voice to my right. It was Eddie Feldman, head of Biow's radio and television departments on the West Coast. "Ralph Edwards films *Truth or Consequences* for us live, in front of an audience, with three motion picture cameras. The guy we should talk to is Al Simon."

One of the CBS executives, who had heard of Simon as a radio comedy writer, was skeptical. "What does a radio writer know about filming a TV show in front of an audience?" he asked Eddie.

"Just more than anyone else in Hollywood, that's all," Eddie countered. "He works for Ralph Edwards now. He's the guy who developed the three-camera technique that Edwards is using on *Truth or Consequences*."

"Then let's get him over here!" I said.

Eddie got Al Simon on the phone and asked him to join us at our meeting. Al came over right away. We told him our problem, and he described the technique that he had developed for Edwards with the help of RCA. Although *Truth or Consequences* was a game show, Al didn't see any reason why a comedy show couldn't be filmed the same way. By the end of the meeting, we had hired Al as our production manager.

Al's first assignment was to find us a director of photography. Lucy urged him to call Karl Freund, the brilliant, award-winning cinematographer who had photographed Lucy so beautifully in *DuBarry Was a Lady*.

When I first heard Freund's name mentioned, I thought we were daydreaming. Freund was a giant in the movie industry, with a list of film credits that included Fritz Lang's *Metropolis*, E. A. DuPont's *Variety*, and, in America, *All Quiet on the Western Front*, *Dracula*, *Camille*, and *The Good Earth*, for which he won the Oscar. I never thought that a man of Freund's stature would want to do television. But after several appeals from Lucy and Desi, this living legend stepped from the rarefied air of feature pictures and joined us in the lowly new medium of TV.

As I came to learn, Karl had a keenly inventive mind, with several patents to his credit, and the challenge of pioneering was enough to seduce him, just as it had in his early days of movies in Berlin, where he was the first man to move the camera during a scene. Whatever his reasons, I was thrilled to have him.

Al and Desi spent practically the entire summer searching for a suitable theater in which to film *I Love Lucy*, but they came up empty-handed. With less than two months to go until our network airdate in October, we were running out of time. Finally, in late August, Al got a call from his friend Earl Spicer at RCA, who had worked on *Truth or Consequences* with him.

Oscar-winning cinematographer Karl Freund was not an easy man to get along with, but he had a kind of cute quality that endeared him to us—sort of like a Prussian teddy bear.

"I just got a call from Jimmy Nasser, who owns General Service Studios," Spicer told Al. "He's heard you're looking for a place to film your show. He'd like you to consider his studio."

"Earl," Al replied, "we're not making a motion picture. We're doing the show in front of an audience. We don't need a movie studio. We need a theater."

Spicer was determined. "Listen, Al. Jimmy's a hell of a nice guy, and he's having tremendous financial problems right now. As a personal favor, would you just go over there with me and talk to him?"

"Okay, Earl. I'll do it for you. But we'll both be wasting our time."

General Service Studios was an eight-soundstage motion picture studio located not far from our offices at CBS Columbia Square. When Al got there that afternoon, he saw that Spicer hadn't been exaggerating about Nasser's financial difficulties. In addition to Nasser, they were accompanied on their tour by the bankruptcy custodian.

When Nasser showed him Stage 2, Al realized that if he could knock down a wall and create an entrance for the audience on the side street, maybe we *could* use a motion picture soundstage, after all. He asked Nasser if we could make our own entrance. "Sure," Nasser said, "if you get the necessary permits, and as long as you agree to put it back the way it was when you leave, because we have no money for construction."

"Of course we will," Al assured him.

Walking around Stage 2, Al started to see other advantages. Live TV generally used flimsy sets, which had to be "struck" quickly after each show, to make way for the next program. We had planned to do the same thing. Al figured that if we could rent the stage on a full-time basis, we could build substantial, realistic sets and leave them up all the time. And they would be available for us to rehearse in.

The more he thought about all the possibilities, the more excited Al became. He was so afraid we would lose this golden opportunity that he made a handshake deal then and there to rent Stage 2 for a year for $1,000 a week.

The news that a deal had been made to rent a motion picture studio soundstage came as a shock to Desi and me. Not only had we not been looking for a soundstage—neither of us had authorized Al to make a rental offer to anybody. But when we visited Stage 2 and took a look for ourselves, both of us immediately agreed with Al that it was just what we were (or should have been) looking for. We finally had our "Desilu Playhouse."

Three Cameras or Four?

WE WERE JUST ABOUT to sign a long-term lease with General Service Studios when I realized that I still hadn't seen even a draft of my own contract with Desilu. I decided to speak to Desi about it. When I told him about my conversation with Harry Ackerman and my 20 percent interest in the show, Desi hit the ceiling. CBS had never told him about my contractual arrangement—not even when they agreed to give up their own interest in the series.

"This can't be!" he yelled. "Lucy and I own the package. How can CBS do this? No way are we going to do the show. Forget the whole thing!"

With that, Desi stormed off the lot. When he got home, he told Lucy, "The show is off." Lucy was in shock. "We can't back out now!" she told Desi. She broke into tears and phoned me at home.

I told her my side of the story—CBS had promised me a 20 percent interest and that's the reason I agreed to do the TV audition program. When I told Lucy that the network had simply forgotten to inform her and Desi about my deal, she started to sob. "Jess," she said, "everyone knows we're doing it. If we don't go through with it, they'll say we failed. My entire career is at stake!" But I explained to her that naturally, if my understanding wasn't lived up to, I would have to back out of the show.

It looked as though the whole thing would fall apart. But after long negotiations through my attorney, Norman Tyre, Desi finally agreed to let me have the 20 percent interest. I told him I thought Bob and Madelyn should have an interest in the show as well, but he wouldn't give anyone else anything. So I gave Bob and Madelyn a 5 percent interest out of my share, which left me with 15 percent.

Things were starting to fall into place. To play the landlord, we had already hired William Frawley. Frawley was a familiar character actor

Bill Frawley—the perfect Fred Mertz.

from films, with the screen persona of the kind of sport you'd find in a pool hall—the unpolished guy with a heart of gold. He was the perfect Fred Mertz.

Marc Daniels was the ideal choice as our director, a talented professional who had won awards for his direction of live TV drama in New York using multiple cameras. On Marc's recommendation, Desi and I drove down to La Jolla one evening to see a relatively unknown actress named Vivian Vance play the leading role in *Voice of the Turtle* at the La Jolla Playhouse. By the end of the first act, Desi and I agreed that we had found our Ethel Mertz.

But on the technical side we still faced tremendous challenges. In live TV the director was only concerned with the output of one camera—

the one being sent out over the air. The product of the other two cameras, as they moved freely about to get ready for the next shot the director would cut to, never saw the light of day outside the control room. At first we thought we could duplicate this exactly by using a device that turned off two of the cameras and left running only the one the director selected.

In theory, this would not only give us a "precut" film; it would also result in major cost savings. After all, if we left all three cameras running all the time, we would have to throw away two-thirds of the film that we shot.

That was the theory. In practice, however, the stopping and starting of cameras during the actual shooting just didn't work. The mechanism couldn't maintain the necessary relationship between the shutters of the three cameras, and our film was always one or two sprocket holes out of sync.

So we reluctantly reverted to leaving all three cameras on continuously. No sooner had we done this than we made the sensational discovery that we now had three perfectly usable angles to cut back and forth between at all times! This made it possible for us to do extensive editing, and enabled us easily to cut shows to size and do all sorts of technical goodies that would have been impossible with just one usable piece of film to work with.

Once we made the decision to run all three cameras all the time, the lighting had to be adjusted so that each of the cameras would always have an acceptable picture. As if that weren't enough of a challenge, the sets and the actors all had to be lit so uniformly that we would be able to cut from one camera to another without any noticeable change. The man who was at the forefront in the solution to all these problems as they developed was Karl Freund.

Karl, despite his film background, was the first to point out that the lighting had to be flat rather than beautifully molded for one point of view at a time, as in feature production. Positioning the lights to provide flat, uniform lighting from all angles was more difficult than it may sound. Historically, in motion pictures, they would light "from the floor"—they had a lot of lamps that sat on the floor and they would move them around, while the single camera sat in one place. But we couldn't have lights standing on the floor because that would keep the audience from seeing what was going on. Even the lights that hung down from up above couldn't hang too low because they would block the audience's view. And we were lighting not for one camera, but three—one straight on and the other two coming in from the sides.

Familiar scene, unfamiliar angle: Lucy and Desi in the Ricardo kitchen, with Karl Freund's flat lighting system much in evidence.

Another problem occurred when our director took his side cameras and put them in where he got just the shot he wanted. This left the audience looking at the cameramen's backs and nothing else, because all the cameras were blocking the action. So we had Karl put longer lenses on the side cameras and move them back to allow space between them for the audience to see.

Karl was not an easy man to get along with, but he had a kind of cute quality that endeared him to us—sort of like a Prussian teddy bear. During our disagreements, and we had plenty, he always referred to me as the "old man with the young face."

But there were plenty of lighter moments as well. Once Karl was

We had Karl put longer lenses on the side cameras and move them back to allow space
in between for the audience to see.

discussing some of his latest innovations with several of us on the set,
when somebody remarked to him, "You know, Karl, your work has sold a
lot of television sets." As Karl beamed, the fellow added, "I know that I
sold mine!"

•   •   •

Somehow we managed to get through the filming of the first show,
entitled "Lucy Thinks Ricky Is Trying to Murder Her" on Saturday
evening, September 8, less than two weeks after moving onto the General Service lot. Lucy and Desi, camera-wise veterans of many motion
pictures, knew just what they were doing. Karl was a bulwark of strength.
Marc's background of live television and motion picture studies and his
insistence on "rehearsal, rehearsal, rehearsal" paid off in spades.

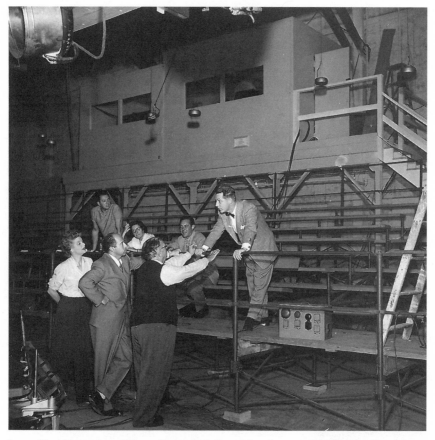

Lucy, Karl Freund, and I confer with, *left to right,* director Marc Daniels, camera coordinator Emily Daniels (Marc's wife), PR director Kenny Morgan, and announcer Johnny Jacobs a few hours before filming our initial episode, "Lucy Thinks Ricky Is Trying to Murder Her."

With the film safely delivered to the lab, I drove home to my house in Brentwood late Saturday evening with a happy feeling that I had experienced so many times in radio. The show was done—the work was over. It had come out fine. Nothing could go wrong now.

As I pulled into my garage, a disturbing thought hit me. What if one of the cameramen had missed a shot? We had no way of seeing what they were shooting. I calmed myself by remembering that it was all set in advance between the cameramen and the director to tell him if they missed anything. That was no major problem.

Three days before the first episode of *I Love Lucy* went before the cameras, we took out this full-page ad in both the *Hollywood Reporter* and *Daily Variety*.

I quietly climbed into bed. Just as my head hit the pillow I sat bolt upright and a cry of horror escaped my lips. Es, who was sleeping soundly on her three-quarters of the bed, jumped up startled, ran out, checked both the children's temperatures, and changed the little one's pajamas before she awakened sufficiently to realize that I was home. I told her it was a sneeze that had awakened her. She went back to sleep while I spent sleepless hours trying to get rid of this new idea that had occurred to me —suppose something went wrong in the film lab!

Pacing the floor, I realized more and more firmly that the work wasn't over. The road was not clear. Monday morning we would see what we had on film. We would see what we had on film *if* the cameraman got the shots, *if* a piece of grit hadn't lodged in the camera and scratched the film, *if* the film was not torn or broken or scratched in the lab, *if* the machinery didn't break down while our negative was being developed, *if* it wasn't over- or underdeveloped, *if* there was no defect in the raw film we had used to shoot the show, and a million other *ifs* based on mechanical or human error or failure, which wove the rest of the night into a tortured montage so frightening that I didn't dare shut my eyes for fear of the nightmares that awaited me.

Sunday was no better. On Monday, with red eyes and a hesitant step, I walked into the projection room as though it were the execution chamber. To my intense delight, slightly hysterical for lack of sleep, everything was there on the screen, just as we had hoped for!

Now, at last, I was able to heave a real sigh of relief. There it was. We knew we had it on film. The road ahead was really clear at last. It was just a matter of putting it together and showing it on the network—*if* it wasn't out of sync, *if* the sound was dubbed correctly, *if* the opticals came out right, *if* the negative wasn't scratched in handling, *if* the composite print was balanced correctly for light and sound, *if* the commercials came in on time, *if* we could cut our picture to come out on the nose if the commercials were longer or shorter than we expected (shorter, ha!) and *if*, with all of these things working out, we got our prints early enough to ship them to the network in time for the play date.

Luckily, I had no time to spend worrying about all of these things. As the lights in the projection room came back on, I realized that not only did we have another show to rehearse and film by Saturday, I was also due in an all-day writing session with Bob and Madelyn to come up with a story for another episode. In addition, on my desk there were draft scripts for two shows waiting for me to edit them. I also had costumes and sets to worry about and actors to audition and hire for three other

During the dress rehearsal for our first episode, I sat quietly in the bleachers, worrying about all the things that might go wrong during the filming that evening. Everything that could go wrong *after* filming hadn't yet occurred to me.

upcoming shows, not to mention supervising the cutting together of film from three cameras on the one we had just filmed. Our television premiere was more than a month away, but I was already beginning to wish that someone would un-invent television and return us all to those beautiful dream days when the picture people made pictures and the radio people did radio and none of us knew how well off we were.

Actually, the film that we had just screened came not from three cameras, but four. Desi had wanted to shoot the show like a stage play, straight through, with no intermission except for the middle commercial break. But each Mitchell camera would hold only ten minutes of film, which meant that we had to have a fourth camera (complete with camera operator, dolly grip and camera assistant) to fill in while the other cameras reloaded. This resulted in an overcrowded stage, not to mention a lot of extra expense. Worse still, it left no time for normal costume changes. Lucy, who was in almost every scene, had to wear all of her wardrobe in layers that could be shed quickly to reveal the next scene's costume as the show progressed.

Marc Daniels, sitting next to me in the screening room, made an appeal for us to abandon the fourth camera and simply pause for reloading between scenes. I wanted to get rid of the fourth camera as much as Marc did, but I pointed out to him that the last thing in the world we needed was a restless, impatient audience.

"They sit two or three hours to see a stage play," Marc persisted. "What's an extra half hour?"

"The difference is that in the theater the audience is entertained for the entire two or three hours, except for intermission," I answered. But that gave me an idea. "Okay, Marc," I said. "We'll do it with only three cameras. Desi can talk to the audience during the breaks like he did during the preshow warmup, and we'll have the band play a few songs."

Marc broke into a smile, and so did Bob and Madelyn. This little change would not only save us money and eliminate the traffic jam on the set—it also meant that we would be free to write stories with elaborate makeup and costume changes, which was impossible with the four-camera method.

By the second week, a bottleneck had developed in the editing room. Our film editors, Dann Cahn and Bud Molin, were doing a superhuman job, but with three usable angles of every shot it just took us too long to view each of them, one after another, on a standard Moviola editing machine. George Fox, our film operations manager, came to the rescue. He had had a special multiheaded Moviola machine built with three

Film editor Dann Cahn, *right,* and his assistant Bud Molin examine
the innovative "three-headed monster," a special multiheaded Moviola
machine which could run the sound track and film from all three
cameras at once.

screens, which could run the sound track and the film from all three cameras at the same time. Dann took one look at the huge, odd-looking con-
traption and asked, "Where are we going to put this monster?" The name
stuck. The "three-headed monster," as it came to be known in the industry, was a life-saver for us, eliminating hours of time in the editing room.

Among the idiosyncrasies of TV that Karl Freund instinctively understood was one that many cinematographers of the day, with their motion
picture backgrounds, couldn't bring themselves to respect. In the movie
business, the moment of truth for a director of photography came when
the dailies were run in a projection room at the studio for the producer
and other bigwigs. If it looked good in that showing, then it would look
good in every theater in the country, because the projectors were all just
about the same. But given the state of the emerging technology of TV at
the time, it seems that contrast was unavoidably added to the film when

it was played through the circuits at the networks that converted it into a broadcast signal. To get a good-looking picture on home sets, it was necessary to process the film so that when it was shown through a standard theater projector, it appeared to be badly underexposed. In other words, it looked really lousy in the projection room, but great on the tube.

Later on, as more and more television programs were produced on film, many cinematographers working on filmed shows could not bring themselves to sit next to the producer in the projection room and show him an underexposed product. They would shoot and process their film the way they had been taught, so they would have the comfort of sitting in the projection room and proudly displaying a great-looking picture. Then they'd come in the day after it was on the air looking like they'd been shot. They would accuse the networks of sabotage and so forth. Of course, it was not long before they learned to shoot it the TV way, in order to survive.

Even with his wonderful grasp of the problem, there was one issue over which I constantly crossed swords with Karl. Each episode of *I Love Lucy* had two or three shots, mostly close-ups of Lucy, that we couldn't shoot during the regular filming. After the audience left, we would use one of the cameras to pick up these shots. This one-camera shooting was precisely like making a movie. Karl, freed from the pressure of the show, and by now relaxed and mellowed by a couple of martinis, would set about doing what he was famous for—making close-ups that were beautiful, seductive works of art.

The only trouble was that these backlit, glamorous, utterly masterful pictures, however beautiful, could not possibly be cut into the rest of the film. They were completely out of key with the flat lighting of the rest of the show. Week after week I would see the dailies, tell the editor to scrap the unusable close-ups, and then go argue with Karl about it. He would stubbornly tell me I was wrong, along with several other remarks about my intelligence and lineage.

Once, when the big brass from the network was coming to see a couple of shows, I cut Karl's close-ups in just as he had shot them, and invited him to join us. The shocked reaction of the network VIPs was about the same as though I had cut in a scene from a nudist camp. I never had that trouble with Karl again. We became good friends during the Lucy years. Working with him was not only a privilege, but a thorough education.

• • •

In our sixth show, I made a cameo appearance as one of three network bigwigs who came to the Tropicana to audition Ricky's act. The other two network men were played by CBS executives Harry Ackerman, *center,* and Hal Hudson, *right.* As soon as the show aired, I went on a diet.

We filmed six *I Love Lucy* shows before the first one hit the network. Because of the technical problems we had encountered on the first one, we decided to air the second show, "The Girls Want to Go to a Night-club," as our premiere episode.

Fortunately, every possible piece of luck seemed to be breaking in the show's favor. Our time slot couldn't have been better—immediately following Arthur Godfrey, the number one show in the country. Nobody had to search around to find us. At nine o'clock on Monday night, October 15, 1951, Arthur Godfrey asked his audience to stay tuned, and we popped right onto most of the sets in the country. Talk about luck.

Ironically, some six weeks before our network debut, AT&T completed its coast-to-coast television network link. For the first time, nationwide television broadcasts could originate from the West Coast, removing the very problem that had caused us to abandon our original plan to telecast the series live from Hollywood. That change in plans had been the catalyst for all the technical innovations that would contribute so much to the success of *I Love Lucy*, the growth of the Desilu empire, and the eventual shift of the center of television production from New York to Hollywood.

As Lucy, Desi, and I watched the premiere episode, however, we were preoccupied with technical difficulties, not innovations. Partway through the show, the sound track had developed an unbelievably bad echo. Each station in the network, as a failsafe measure, had a 16mm backup print of the show, which it ran in sync with the 35mm broadcast print. If anything went wrong at the network, the station could instantly switch over to the backup print. Somehow, in the middle of our premiere, the sound on the Los Angeles backup print had inadvertently been switched on. With both sound tracks going at the same time, one three or four sprockets ahead of the other, the dialogue sounded as if it were being played over the public address system of Yankee Stadium. Fortunately, it was only a problem at the one station.

At the time, none of us had the slightest notion that we were making what would become a landmark series. We were all just in a tough job, and we were trying to do it the best way we knew how. We knew that in Lucy we had an unbelievable talent, but we were still totally unprepared for the public's response.

That week's *Variety* called *I Love Lucy* "one of the slickest TV entertainment shows to date." "If the story line wasn't exactly inspiring," the review said, "nonetheless it had a flexibility that permitted for a full-blown exposition of Miss Ball's comedic talents. On this score alone, Monday's preem was a resounding click." The *Hollywood Reporter* was even more effusive:

Every once in a rare great while a new TV show comes along that fulfills, in its own particular niche, every promise of the often harassed new medium. Such a show, it is a genuine pleasure to report, is "I Love Lucy," starring Lucille Ball and Desi Arnaz in a filmed domestic comedy series for Philip Morris which should bounce to the top of the rating heap in no time at all. If it doesn't, the entire structure of the American entertainment business should be overhauled from top to bottom.

The outstanding pertinent fact about "I Love Lucy" is the emergence, long suspected, of Lucille Ball as America's No. 1 comedienne in her own right. She combines the facial mobility of Red Skelton, the innate pixie quality of Harpo Marx and the daffily jointless abandon of the Patchwork Girl of Oz, all rolled into one. She is a consummate artist, born for television.

Half a step behind her comes her husband, Desi Arnaz, the perfect foil for her screwball antics and possessing comic abilities of his own more than sufficient to make this a genuine comedy team rather than the one-woman tour de force it almost becomes. In support are William Frawley, who is superb as the landlord of the Arnaz apartment, and Vivian Vance as his wife, a trouper who knows her way around both lines and situations.

Congratulations came pouring in from all quarters as soon as the first show aired. The show's popularity kept growing and growing until it just got completely out of hand. It seemed that I had been wrong about who the "I" in *I Love Lucy* was—it wasn't just Desi, but everyone else who tuned in as well.

The Ideal Cast

As WONDERFUL as the entire cast was, *I Love Lucy* was without question a "star" piece. The entire project rode on the radiant talent of one woman. The Lucille Ball of the 1950s was an incredible, stunning performer. In every sense, she was a star. Remove any other actor from the project and it would be diminished. Take away Lucille Ball, and it would be demolished. In fact, to my mind no combination of the supporting players could sustain interest on the screen without Lucy, unless they were talking about her.

Most comedy writers consider themselves lucky if a star realizes 60 percent of the values they've written into a script. Lucy, somehow, returned about 125 percent. Unexpected qualities appeared out of nowhere. Little, human, ordinary, recognizable values. Inflections that were exactly the way your sister or your mother, or the lady bus driver used to sound. She was everywoman. Ask her to be a tough showgirl and you got back a broad who simply could not look and move like that unless she'd been pumping out bumps and grinds in a burlesque house for twenty years. Ask her for royalty and she became a queen. And she kept astounding us that way every week.

The audience never had the feeling that they were watching her act. She simply *was* Lucy Ricardo. And if you looked carefully, you would marvel that every fiber in the woman's body was contributing to the illusion. Did Ricky catch her in a lie? She wouldn't be just a voice denying it. Her stance would be a liar's stance. Defensive. There would be a telltale picking at a cuticle, or a slight, nervous jerking of an elbow, or a finger brushed against an upper lip, which is the first place you feel the perspiration of anxiety. Her hands, her feet, her knees, every cell would be doing the right thing. This was an exceptionally talented young lady, and I don't know enough superlatives to do her justice.

People used to ask me whether Lucille Ball was funny in real life. And I had to tell them no, not funny in the way that Lucy Ricardo was. But she could come up with things that were remarkable in their ability to evoke laughs. I never heard her suggest any dialogue—she wasn't a writer, as such. But within her character, she had the ability to throw in little universally humorous things.

We could put down a line that said "Lucy gets up in the morning, she's terribly tired and goes into the kitchen, barely able to feel her way around because she can't get her eyes open, and makes a cup of coffee." That's all it would say on the paper. But it would be seven hilarious minutes on the air, because she had this incredible talent for making people say, "Oh my God, that's just the way I look in the morning." It was difficult, after watching her turn a routine transitory scene into a comedy gem, to keep from thinking what a great writer you were.

She also had a marvelous sense of what would work and what wouldn't. If she felt a scene wasn't exactly right—even if she couldn't articulate exactly what was wrong with it—we'd take another look at it. After a closer inspection, we would usually discover that she was right and we would rework the scene.

One of the many unexpected benefits of our three-camera technique was that over four days of rehearsal, a lot of good material would get developed. In a single camera situation, you have maybe one day of rehearsal, and then you film it, out of sequence, over the next few days. If you think of something on the third day of shooting on a one-camera show, even if it's a sensational idea, you can't use it because it affects something that you already shot on the first day of filming. But on *I Love Lucy*, where we didn't shoot it until the very last evening, if someone thought of something during rehearsals we'd just make the necessary changes elsewhere in the script. This gave us tremendous flexibility.

Take the famous "grape-stomping" scene in "Lucy's Italian Movie." The original script read this way:

> *The woman walks toward the big vat, and Lucy stands there a minute, and the woman looks around and indicates to her to come on, so Lucy follows her.*
>   WOMAN 1. (*Italian.*) Come on—let's get to work.
>   SUBTITLE. Come on—get the lead out.
> *Lucy follows her into the vat. The woman climbs in and starts stomping on the grapes. Lucy looks over the edge and sees what she's doing, and looks squeamish. The woman indicates with a wave of her arm to come on. Lucy cautiously climbs in and gingerly puts her foot on the grapes. Her face reflects*

*that this is a very weird sensation. The Italian woman is stomping vigorously,
and Lucy looks like she's walking on eggs.*

*The woman reacts to Lucy's delicate air, stops, and illustrates for Lucy by
stomping hard. Lucy, getting the idea, goes at it with fuller enthusiasm, like a
runner running in place, shaking every muscle. She begins to enjoy this, and
starts running around the vat, then tries trick steps, like a ballet dancer, and
perhaps like a person with one leg shorter than the other, etc.*

*Lucy reaches up to check her earring, which is loose, tightens it, then checks
the other ear, and finds that her earring is missing. She looks alarmed and realizes
it is down in the grapes. She starts feeling around with one foot, trying to find
the earring.*

*The other woman notices that she isn't working, comes over, nudges her and
indicates that she should keep stomping.*

WOMAN 1. (*Italian.*) Come on—get to work.

SUBTITLE. Quit goofing off.

*The woman starts stomping to show Lucy, suddenly gets a pained expression
as she steps on the earring. She hops up and down holding her foot.*

*Lucy quickly takes off the other earring and throws it away. She starts
stomping away as we fade out.*

The funniest part of that entire episode—Lucy's riotous fight with the
other woman in the grape vat—wasn't in the original script. It was
developed on the set during rehearsals, with our director for that season,
Jim Kern. I can't remember exactly when or how it was added. It might
have been that they called us down to the set because they felt it needed
more, that it just didn't build up to a big enough height. Or they might
have just improvised on their own. They were absolutely free to do
whatever they wanted, and when I came down to the stage, if I agreed,
it would stay in. If I didn't agree, we would have a long discussion
about it.

The only real problem we had with adding the fight to the vineyard
scene was that Lucy kept getting her hair under the water in the grape
vat. Because she colored it so much, the prop and makeup people had to
find something that wasn't going to leave her with purple hair. They
finally came up with a food coloring at the very last minute.

Lucy always did every stunt that we wrote for her, usually without
question. Occasionally, though, this took some convincing. In my favorite *I Love Lucy* episode, "L.A. at Last," when William Holden visits the
Ricardos' hotel room with Ricky, Lucy disguises herself with kerchief,
glasses, and a long putty nose. The script called for the end of Lucy's nose
to go up in flames when Holden lights her cigarette.

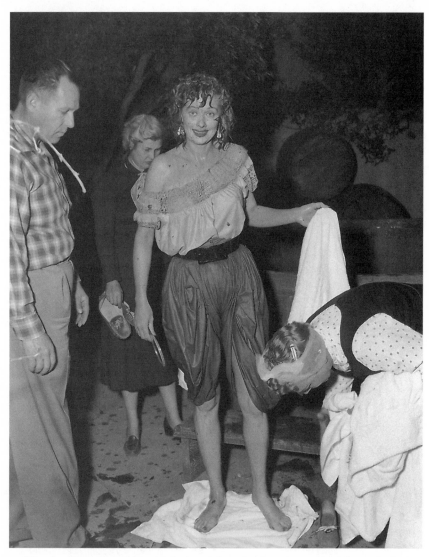

The funniest part of "Lucy's Italian Movie"—Lucy's riotous fight with the other woman in the grape vat—wasn't even in the original script.

They were absolutely free to do whatever they wanted, and when I came down to the stage, if I agreed, it would stay in. If I didn't agree, we would have a long discussion about it.

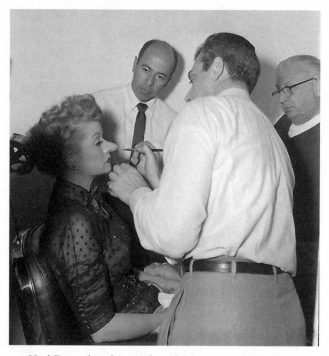

Karl Freund and I watch makeup man, Hal King, as
he gives Lucy a special putty nose designed to catch
fire when William Holden lights Lucy's cigarette in
"L.A. at Last."

It took me all week to convince Lucy that her real nose wouldn't catch
on fire. Our makeup man, Hal King, used a putty nose that wouldn't burn
and placed a candlewick in it, just to ensure her safety. Still, Lucy was
extremely nervous about it all through the rehearsal and during the final
shooting, and we all held our breath until the scene was over and in
the can.

When her putty nose caught fire, the script called for her to remove it
and dunk it in her cup of coffee. Lucy ad-libbed and picked up the cup
with both hands, dunking the end of her putty nose while it was still
attached. It was an inspired moment, entirely hers.

Some of the stunts posed big technical problems for us. "The Great
Train Robbery" episode, in which Lucy repeatedly brings the train to a
screeching halt by pulling the emergency brake, was one of the most
challenging shows to produce. You've probably seen movies or television

In "The Great Train Robbery," we actually mounted the entire Pullman car
set on huge springs, which we released whenever Lucy pulled
the emergency brake.

programs in which there is supposed to be a sudden stopping of a train, simulated by shaking the camera. In this episode we actually constructed the set—representing the entire interior of a Pullman car from one end to the other—and mounted it on huge springs. At the appropriate moment a large, coiled spring was released, and its power shot the entire set forward about four feet, literally driving the actors to their knees.

On another show, where Lucy was supposed to be lowered onto the deck of a ship from a helicopter, we put her in a harness and suspended her above the set. She didn't tell us until afterwards, but early in her movie career she had been in a similar harness and had fallen thirty feet to the ground when it failed. The impact broke several vertebrae in her back. Lucy was scared to death of the harness because of what had happened to her before, but she never said a word about it. During dinner, about an hour and a half before we shot the show, she was so overcome by the tension that she actually passed out cold. Even then, she didn't quit. She revived and gave a great performance, stunt and all. And nobody in the audience ever knew what she had gone through.

Lucille Ball was about as different from Lucy Ricardo as anyone could possibly be. To me, Lucy Ricardo represents the childish factor still a part of every adult. Most people who get into a frustrating situation may have a flash thought of some impulsive act that would be a gratifying way of coping with the situation. But they quickly put it out of their minds, the way responsible, inhibited adults are supposed to. For Lucy Ricardo, however, the impulsive thought invariably becomes the course of action. In identifying with her, the audience can vicariously enjoy exercising their own childish impulses, petty curiosities, and foolhardy but self-gratifying escapades.

Lucille Ball, on the other hand, was a hard-nosed and dedicated professional. There was only one thing that she and her TV character had in common—an overactive imagination, which sometimes got her into embarrassing situations.

Once, when we were doing the radio series, Gale Gordon didn't show up on time for rehearsal. After several people had remarked on his absence, Lucy sadly announced to the cast and crew that Gale had had a heart attack the night before. We all just sat there in shock at the news, unable to speak.

Suddenly, in walked Gale. "I'm terribly sorry for being so late," he explained, "but I was stuck in an awful traffic jam on Sunset Boulevard."

All eyes turned to Lucy.

"Well," she said sheepishly, "he *did* come over to our table at Chasen's last night and say he wasn't feeling well."

• • •

Even though the entire world loved Lucy, everyone on *I Love Lucy* didn't love everyone else. For one thing, Vivian Vance couldn't stomach Bill Frawley. Actually, they got along quite well at first. But before long Viv became upset at the fact that people so readily accepted her lovely young self as the wife of "that old man," as she called him. Though her believability in the role was actually a testament to her talent, she felt deeply insulted, thinking she would be better cast as Bill Frawley's daughter.

When Bill got wind of her complaints, he was offended, and retaliated by suggesting lines for himself that characterized Ethel as having a "figure like a sack full of doorknobs" or some other of a long list of tried and true, if unoriginal, insults. I had to be called down to the set many times to settle arguments between the two of them. Usually it was because Viv had suggested some script changes or additional bits of business. Because it was Viv who had done the suggesting, Bill would flatly refuse to cooperate, often retreating to his dressing room in a pout. But underneath his gruff exterior, Bill was really a teddy bear, and he and I had a good relationship. I would listen to his complaints and then ask him to "do it for me." He would usually agree, but he always took pains to remind me, "I'll do it for you, but not for that bitch."

We were careful to make the Mertzes like the Ricardos in some ways, yet very different in others. Lucy and Ricky were comparative newlyweds, married perhaps eleven years and still having a relatively starry-eyed love affair. Fred and Ethel, while still in love, had been married a long time and knew each other backward and forward, and they didn't much like the view from either direction.

When we cast Bill Frawley and Vivian Vance as the Mertzes, we knew only of Frawley's work as a character actor in films, and of Vance's fine performance as the lead in *Voice of the Turtle*, a straight drama. A few weeks after we started production, we had a story idea that depended on Bill and Vivian being able to sing and dance a little. I went down to the stage where they were rehearsing and sheepishly asked them if they thought they could handle it. With our luck, I shouldn't have worried. To my delight (and embarrassment for even having to ask such a question), they informed me that they each had had an illustrious career in the musical theater. So a whole, unexpected, wonderful new area fell into our laps as a gift.

Another important stroke of luck for the show was Desi Arnaz. When we started *I Love Lucy*, I thought of Desi as a big question mark. Neither

he nor anyone else knew whether he could really do this kind of thing at
all. But Desi was a quick study, and considerably brighter than many
people gave him credit for. He was conscientious and worked extremely
hard to prove his doubters wrong. In the end, to everyone's delight, Desi
proved himself to be a skillful farceur and a fine actor, providing Lucy
with a charming foil and giving the show an added dimension.

Desi was also a shrewd businessman, as he proved to CBS on more
than one occasion. Technical matters, however, were not his forte. I
remember one Tuesday morning when he came into my office complaining that we weren't leaving enough blank space on the screen around the
show's credits, with the result that one or two letters were being cut off
of some of the names.

"I didn't notice anything wrong on last night's show," I told him.
"Your new TV set must need adjusting."

"There's nothing wrong with my TV set," Desi insisted. "I tell you it's
the prints that we're sending to the network."

To calm him down, I finally had to promise him that I'd check with
the film lab. But after he went back down to rehearsals, I asked one of
our technicians to go out to Lucy and Desi's ranch in Chatsworth and
check out their brand-new TV. Sure enough, that's where the problem
was. The technician made a few simple adjustments and then returned
to the studio. Desi never even knew that he'd been there.

The following Tuesday morning, Desi was back in my office again. "I
just wanted to let you know that the film lab fixed the problem," he said,
smiling. "The credits on last night's show looked perfect." I told him I
was glad the problem had been solved. Just as he was leaving, Desi turned
back to me and added, "I told you there was nothing wrong with my TV
set."

Desi had a lot of obstacles to overcome. He was painfully aware that
CBS hadn't even wanted him on the show in the first place and had only
reluctantly agreed when it became clear that they might lose Lucy to
another network. And CBS was not alone in its opinion of Desi. When
the original pilot film was sent back to New York, Milton Biow screened
it for his good friends Richard Rodgers and Oscar Hammerstein II. After
the screening was over, Hammerstein reportedly turned to Biow and
delivered a one-line assessment of the show: "Keep the redhead, but
ditch the Cuban."

"He's her husband," Biow quickly explained. "It's a package deal. To
get her, we have to take him."

"Well, then for God's sake don't let him sing," Hammerstein replied.
"No one will understand him."

So Biow added a clause to his contract with Desilu to insure that Desi's vocals would be kept to a minimum. "It is agreed," the clause declared, "that in each program the major emphasis shall be placed on the basic situations arising out of the fictional marriage of [Lucy and Ricky Ricardo], and that the orchestra will furnish only incidental or background music except where an *occasional* script shall *require* a vocal number by Desi Arnaz *as part of the story line*."

Because of that clause, we made it a point during the first year to make any song by Desi an important part of the story. For example, Desi would be singing, and Lucy would be trying to break into the act *during* the song. But after the show got to be number one, Desi demanded that the contract be revised to ease the restriction. By that time both Biow and Philip Morris wanted the show so badly that neither was about to buck him.

Just as we had done with Lucy's radio husband, we took pains to humanize the character of Ricky Ricardo by bringing him down in earning power so the average person could identify with his problems. The "Tropicana" nightclub where Ricky Ricardo worked was a far cry from the Copacabana. Instead, we made it kind of a middle-class tourist trap patronized mostly by out-of-towners and conventioneers.

There were actually a lot more jokes involving Ricky's botched pronunciation than ended up on the screen. Seven or eight times a week he would say something during rehearsal that came out funny because of his accent, and the people on the set would throw it in. Desi was an awfully good sport to go along with this, but I had to take most of them out. I felt that the audience would get sick of "accent" jokes if we did them all the time.

Desi's accent wasn't the only aspect of his Cuban background that had an effect on the show. His Latin American upbringing influenced the story lines, as well. For instance, we could do stories all day long about Ricky being unfaithful to Lucy (or at least about her *thinking* that he was being unfaithful), but to do a story about Lucy's infidelity was quite another thing altogether, because in the Cuban culture in which Desi had been raised, it was accepted that no woman would ever dare to be unfaithful to a man.

If Desi didn't like something, we'd change it, because if he didn't like a piece of material, he was simply incapable of performing it. Sometimes it was just that he didn't understand certain things that were part of our American culture. We wrote one script, "Lucy Tells the Truth," in which Ricky bets Lucy a hundred dollars that she can't go for twenty-four hours without fibbing. The entire second half of the episode consisted of an unexpected visit to the Ricardos by an auditor from the Internal Revenue Service. Much to Ricky's dismay, Lucy answers all of the tax man's questions with the truth, the whole truth, and nothing but the truth—revealing that Ricky had "fudged" on some income tax deductions for which he no longer had receipts. If this plotline doesn't sound familiar, that's because it never made it on the air. After the first read-through by the cast, Desi flatly refused to do it, maintaining that Ricky Ricardo would never attempt to cheat the United States government in this way. A short but lively discussion ensued, but there was no changing Desi's mind. In a matter of hours we came up with an entirely new second act in which Lucy's fibs unwittingly land her a job as a knife thrower's assistant (and target).

Desi and Lucy were diametrically different kinds of performers. Each Monday morning we would assemble for a first reading of that week's script. This was usually the first time Lucy or anyone else in the cast had laid eyes on it. Desi was always much better than Lucy at these first read-throughs. He would understand the material as soon as he saw it, and give a good reading the first time through. His performance would be exactly the same, never any better or any worse, four days later.

Lucy, in contrast, was the kind of performer who needed a lot of rehearsal. If you sat in on one of our Monday morning sessions and then were asked to give your assessment, you probably would have said, "The story is fine, the dialogue is excellent, most of the cast is great, but get rid of the redhead. She doesn't know what the hell she's doing."

Lucy *didn't* know what the hell she was doing—at the first reading. But after stumbling through that first reading, she would take the material to the mat. She fought with it, examined it, internalized it, and when it reappeared, she *owned* it. Her performance would improve more and more as each day went by. And if she got enough rehearsal time there were just no heights she couldn't reach.

As running Desilu started to take more of Desi's time, he would continually be leaving rehearsals to go to a meeting or something. Many times Lucy would see him starting to leave and protest, "But Desi, we need the rehearsal!" Desi would look at her with a puzzled expression and say, "What are you talking about? We know the words!" He never could quite understand what was going on inside of Lucy's head.

For Lucy, who was basically unhappy, the only release she had was in her work. That was the only time I ever saw her really enjoy herself. Except at parties. She was a great partygoer. Lucy liked nothing better than to be at a party, playing a game of some kind. But she had an unhappy home life with Desi, and she was anxious to get away from it.

She would come in and would want to work, work, work, rehearse, rehearse, rehearse, day in and day out. This helped the show tremendously, but it was a tragic situation for her personally.

The signs of the eventual bust-up of their marriage were visible even in the early days of I Love Lucy. It was clear that something was wrong. Desi had his thirty-eight-foot power cruiser, which Lucy didn't like at all. After we would finish filming a show, Desi would go down to his boat at Corona del Mar with his drinking and card-playing buddies, and Lucy would go back to the ranch. Unless they had something to do together for publicity, they wouldn't see each other again until the following week, when they both arrived on the set for the first read-through.

Their domestic difficulties were already there before I Love Lucy, of course, but the problems just increased geometrically with the tremendous success and popularity of the show. It would have been tough enough for Lucy and Desi to adjust to all of the sudden money and acclaim even if they had had nothing else bothering them. But with all of these other things on their minds it placed an incredible strain on their marriage.

It was just destined not to work. Lucy needed to be dominated, and Desi wasn't happy in a relationship where his wife had a more powerful reputation than he did. He was deeply hurt by all the publicity that said that the success of the show was entirely due to her artistry.

A couple of months after I Love Lucy went on the air, Lucy came storming into my office. "That's it!" she yelled. "The series is over. Desi can go to hell. I'm not going to work with him anymore."

It took me a long time to calm her down. At least one source of the problems between them was easy to understand. Lucy had always been a bigger star than Desi, but at least they had been in different parts of the entertainment industry. Now they were both in the same show. With Lucy getting all of the acting acclaim and the production credit going to me, he really didn't have much to hang on to. And Lucy's relationship with him was clearly suffering as a result. I managed to quietly patch things up between them, but it was clear to me that the problem was not going to go away.

Lucy, in interviews, had long been giving Desi as much credit as she could for the success of the show. Shortly after the first of the year, she decided to take more concrete steps to balance their relative standings in the public eye. At rehearsal one day she took Al Simon aside and asked him to do her a personal favor. "I'd appreciate it," she told Al, "if you'd suggest to Desi that he be executive producer of I Love Lucy."

Not too long after that, Desi came to see me in my office. "Jess," he

There was a lot of clowning around on the set.
Whenever the script called for a fake mustache,
beard, toupee, or wig, somebody always wanted to
see how it would look on me.

said, "you and I know that after this show goes off the air I'm not going
to get a lot of other acting jobs. What I really want to do is produce, but
I need to build a reputation as a producer. How would you feel about
letting me take 'executive producer' credit on the show?"

Up to that point all of the important decisions on the show had
been reached by consensus, after extensive consultations with Desi and
everyone else concerned. But I had made it clear from the outset that if
I was going to be the producer, I would have to have ultimate control of
all of the show's creative elements. My contract spelled that out. Even
Desi could not override my decisions—only Lucy had that kind of veto
power. If Desi took the title of executive producer, I wondered, wouldn't
that cause confusion about my authority as producer of the show?

Mr. Jess Oppenheimer   -2-   September 12, 1951

        6. You agree to devote your best talents and abilities to your services as producer and head writer of the programs. In your capacity as producer and head writer you shall give all orders and make all decisions that a producer would make according to the practice of the television-motion picture industry. You will use your best efforts to cause the program to be produced within a reasonable budget determined by us after consultation with you. You may not, except for an emergency situation which may occur without sufficient time for you to consult with us, make expenditure for any program in excess of a sum equal to 5% of such show's budget without our approval. However, in the event the production costs on one or more programs exceeds the budget therefor you will use your best efforts to cause other programs to be produced under budget so that any group of 13 programs will be produced within the budget for such 13 programs. If Desi Arnaz and you are unable to mutually agree as to a material matter concerning any of the programs, a meeting shall be held as soon as possible between Desi Arnaz, Lucille Ball and you to discuss the matter and the decision of the majority of such persons shall control. Until such meeting and decision your position in the matter shall obtain.

        Please sign below to indicate your acceptance hereof.

        Yours very truly,

        DESILU PRODUCTIONS INC.

        By_____

ACCEPTED:

Jess Oppenheimer
Jess Oppenheimer

I had made it clear that if I was going to be the producer of *I Love Lucy*, I would have to have ultimate control of the show's creative elements. According to my contract, even Desi could not override my decisions— only Lucy had that kind of veto power.

In addition, Desi was not the only one wanting to build a reputation as a TV producer. This was my first, and so far quite successful, producing venture in the new medium. I was concerned that adding an "Executive Producer" credit might convey the impression that Desi, rather than I, had overall control of the show's artistic elements.

I suggested naming Desi as "Executive in Charge of Production" or "Co-Producer," but he wasn't interested in either of those titles. After a long discussion without reaching an acceptable arrangement, we finally agreed to discuss it again after we had both had more time to think about it.

•   •   •

A few days later, at the home of a friend, I was introduced to someone as the producer of *I Love Lucy*. After telling me how pleased she was to meet me and how much she enjoyed the show, this person said she had a question for me. "*I Love Lucy* is only a half hour a week," she observed. "What do you do during the rest of the week?"

Hard as it may be for today's sophisticated viewers to believe, some people in those early days of television actually thought that everything they saw on the tube was real. They assumed that each week we just filmed whatever happened to be going on at the time in the Ricardo apartment.

I had no trouble at all finding things to do during "the rest of the week." I figured out once that I was always working on something like thirteen episodes at the same time. In addition to the one we were rehearsing, there would be the show the three of us would start writing that week, the show already in rewrite by me, another show that had been shot the week before, another one in mimeograph, another one in the first editing stages, still another in final stages, and so on. For upcoming shows I held production meetings for things such as casting, costumes, sets, and props. On shows that had already been filmed there were meetings on editing, music, dubbing, publicity, you name it. Right on through to the answer print, people were continually coming to me and asking me detailed questions about this show or that. "In the rough cut of show number seventeen, in the opening scene," someone would say, "there's a close-up of Desi at the telephone, and you told me you wanted to use a two-shot of Lucy and Desi, but we can't use that angle because the boom wasn't clear." Somehow, I would always know exactly what they were talking about. Through some quirk of my brain, I could remember every bit of the footage on all of the shows. Automatically. That part was easy. The hard part was being responsible for actually putting all of these shows together, and for coming up with a new story with Bob and Madelyn every single week.

Anatomy of a Lucy Script

WHERE DO YOU GET YOUR IDEAS? That was the question that people asked me most often when I was writing *I Love Lucy*. I finally started answering them with my own question: "Where did you get the idea to ask me that?" That always stumped them.

When Bob and Madelyn and I would sit down every Monday morning to plot another *I Love Lucy* show out of thin air, we would sometimes look at one another after about a half hour of nothing and ask sarcastically, "Where *do* you get your ideas?" That's when we really wished we had the answer.

One of the first things that we discovered, after we had written just a few scripts, was that we were doing essentially the same story every week, with Lucy trying to get into Ricky's act at the club. So we started going in the direction of other, more normal domestic situations.

Another problem we had in the first few shows was remembering that we were writing for a visual medium instead of radio, where we had had to use dialogue alone to let the audience know what was happening. Every once in a while, when we were dictating a script, we would throw in some line like "Look, here comes Fred," to establish that Fred had entered the room. Our casting director, Mercedes Manzanares, who doubled as my secretary, would look up from her steno pad and say, "Hey, guys, this is *television*, remember?"

We were never trying to manufacture something funny. Instead, we were looking for a situation where Lucy's and Ricky's problems and differences of opinion were the same ones that most of our audience had encountered. We called it "holding up the mirror."

We knew that as long as we were playing around with things that everybody has lived through, we would have a captive audience who could understand and relate to the problems they were seeing on the screen. They'd just be happy that *this* time it was happening to somebody else instead of them. In my opinion, the funniest single line ever uttered on *I Love Lucy* was when Lucy summed up in an epigram what happens to a lot of marriages: "Since we said, 'I do,' there are so many things we don't." The line was not particularly funny in itself, but it gave viewers a sudden, deep insight into themselves—a shock relieved by laughter.

We tried never to get too far away from basic human behavior. We composed a list of common problems that most viewers face: diet, money, noisy neighbors, business competition, and so on. Sometimes we'd go through the list until one of these topics provided a springboard for a script.

Other story ideas would come from our personal experiences. As I mentioned earlier, this was true of both "The Passports" show, which was based on my mother's trouble in getting a passport in 1934, and "Ricky Thinks He Is Getting Bald," which grew out of my own early (but unavailing) experiments with baldness cures.

And these were by no means the only such cases. For example, Es used to hate the sloppy old clothes I wore around the house. There was one particularly awful-looking pair of beat-up old tennis shoes that she kept asking me to throw away, but I just couldn't bring myself to get rid of them. She finally found an effective way to stop me from wearing them, though—she took one of the shoes from the closet and had it bronzed.

We never actually had Lucy bronze Ricky's shoes on *I Love Lucy*. But we did have a show called "Changing the Boys' Wardrobe," in which Lucy and Ethel get so fed up with Ricky's and Fred's worn-out old clothes that they sell them to a used clothing store.

Another time, when Bob and Madelyn and I went to lunch together, Madelyn ordered a ham sandwich. Then Bob ordered veal chops. Before I could give the waiter my order, Madelyn told him, "Wait. That sounds good. I'll have the veal chops." Then as soon as I gave my order for roast beef, Madelyn said, "Wait. Forget the veal chops—I'll have the roast beef instead." That episode inspired a segment of *My Favorite Husband* entitled "Liz Changes Her Mind," in which Liz drives a waiter crazy by constantly changing her order. The scene worked so well that when we transferred it to television, in "Lucy Changes Her Mind" we left it virtually intact, even to the point of casting the same actor, the marvelous Frank Nelson, as the harassed waiter.

Our story conference for the "Freezer" show, during our first season, will give you an idea of what our Monday story sessions were like. At the time the newspapers were full of advertisements and television was full

Lucy asked me to join in this publicity shot for "Ricky Thinks He Is Getting Bald," which was inspired by my own experience with losing my hair.

of commercials with wild claims about how a home freezer "pays for itself and the meat and pays you a salary," and so on. So we decided that it would be a good idea to do a show about buying a home freezer.

Bob and Madelyn suggested that it would be funny if Lucy could get caught in the freezer. Well, although this sounded like a good situation, it seemed impossible on the face of it. We finally concluded that even if we could think of a situation strong enough to motivate Lucy to hide in a home freezer, there just wasn't one on the market that Lucy could reasonably get herself into.

But out of that discussion came a suggestion: "What if we could get one of those walk-in freezers that they have in butcher shops?" That would solve our problem. Now, this solution was a pretty big problem in itself. How would a big freezer like that find its way into an apartment house? After kicking this around for a while, we finally hit upon the notion that Ethel could have an uncle who was a butcher going out of business. That sounded fairly reasonable, so we decided to proceed in that direction and to try to write a story around it.

We started back at the beginning, with Lucy agitating to get Ricky to buy a freezer, and Ricky taking the time-honored position that they can't afford it. Then Lucy and Ethel, together, get the idea about her uncle. After talking to him they decide to go through with it on the basis that they'll save so much money by buying the meat wholesale that their husbands will love them for it. So far so good, we thought.

Then we hit a snag. We realized that if Lucy and Ethel buy a reasonable amount of meat and put it in a freezer they get for practically nothing, their husbands can't be angry with them. After considerable discussion, we decided that most people, lay people, probably don't know how big a side of beef is. We threw in an extra clincher by having Lucy tell Ethel, "Well, if a side of bacon is *this* big, then a side of *beef* must be just a little bit bigger." Anyway, we had them order two sides of beef, one for each of them, because the wholesalers only sell it by the side.

When the meat arrives, of course, there is a *tremendous* quantity, which gave us a completely new dilemma for the girls to try to work out. Here we decided to use a variation on a routine that had worked for us on the radio series (in an episode called "Selling Dresses"). Lucy and Ethel decide that they got the meat so cheaply that they can sell it below the retail price that the butcher charges, so they set up a stand just inside the butcher shop and try to snag customers away from him. Of course, the butcher discovers their plan and chases them out. Then they go home and put all the meat in the newly delivered freezer so it won't spoil. They hope that maybe they can keep Ricky and Fred away from the basement so that the boys won't even know there is a freezer down there until Lucy and Ethel figure out an answer to their problem.

Now Lucy and Ethel don't know what to do next. And neither did we. After further discussion, we finally decided that in order to create another situation, we had to have the boys know that the freezer was there. So when Ricky and Fred come home we had them tell the girls that they ran into Ethel's Uncle Oscar, the butcher, on the street, and that he told them about the transaction. The boys even think it was an excellent idea and have brought home thirty pounds of meat as a starter, and they want to go down and put it in the new freezer.

Once again, we were faced with a problem. If Ricky and Fred go down and see the freezer, the story is over and it really hasn't gone anywhere. So we had to figure out a way to keep the boys from going down there until the girls could do something about it.

Lucy, it was decided, hits on the idea of playing on Ricky's actor's ego. She tells Ethel to ask him to sing to her. Ethel doesn't think it will work, but Lucy says she thinks it will. (Of course, we *know* it will, because we're writing the script.) So Ethel tries it while Lucy rushes down to the basement, takes the meat out of the freezer, and tries to put it someplace out of sight. We figured we'd have her get caught in the freezer and when the boys and Ethel finally come down she'll be a pitiful sight, frozen stiff, with snow and icicles hanging from her.

Now we had to figure out how she gets caught in the freezer. For this to make sense, the thing would have to be a self-locking freezer that can only be opened from the outside. But it would be too expedient to present that fact just when we needed it, so we went back to an earlier scene and introduced this to the audience without making too much out of it. So later, when Lucy comes down to move the meat, the audience already knows that the freezer is self-locking when it closes and that she can't open it from the inside.

We were happy—it was about four o'clock in the afternoon and we had the story pretty well plotted out. But then Madelyn said, "That's not much of a finish. What happens? She's frozen. Do we take her out? Do we thaw her out? If we do, what's funny about it? We have to have a final high point—a final fillip that really wraps this thing up." And of course she was right. So we wiped the smiles off our faces and the three of us started looking for a climax.

The only possibility any of us could think of was to make something out of the place that Lucy hid the meat when she took it from the freezer. Out of our discussion came the idea that it would be funny if she hid it in the furnace. Now, the thought of just taking a lot of meat, even wrapped meat, and putting it in a dirty furnace is pretty unreasonable. Even in desperation it seemed like a pretty stupid thing for Lucy to do. So we went all the way back to the beginning and opened up the show with Fred coming upstairs and saying, "Don't expect any heat today. I've been fixing the furnace. I had to take all the insides out of it and put all new firebrick in and it'll take at least all day before the cement sets." This gave us a furnace that wasn't working and a nice, fresh, clean repository for the meat. So when Lucy put it there it wasn't unreasonable at all. At least, the three of *us* felt that way.

We had Lucy run down and make trip after trip from the freezer to the furnace and stack it full of meat. She gets caught in the freezer on her last trip in. When Ethel and the boys come down, they find Lucy frozen, take her out, carry her upstairs, and put an electric blanket around her. In order to help even more with the thawing-out process, Fred lights the furnace. This gave us the joke finish we were looking for. When everyone notices the smell of cooking beef coming from the heating register, Lucy leaps up and starts toward the door. Ricky asks her where she's going, and she says, "I'll explain later. . . . Just get a knife, fork and some ketchup and follow me to the biggest barbecue in the world!"

That was more or less typical of our Monday writing sessions. We usually worked until five o'clock—sometimes as late as seven—and we tried to stay as isolated as possible, because this was an important several hours. We'd just kick it around and when we finally felt we had it, I'd dictate the whole thing scene by scene into a machine while Bob and Madelyn were still there. Often we'd get other ideas as we heard it talked straight through like that. By Tuesday morning each of us would have a typed draft of the outline that I had dictated the night before. Bob and Madelyn would take this and turn it into a first draft of the script, which they would deliver to me on Wednesday at the end of the day.

I think in the five years I was on the show there might have been three times that we didn't finish developing a story by the end of the first day. We had no choice, really, because our schedule demanded that we write a new script every single week. In our first season, the three of us wrote forty shows in forty weeks. (Today a show will do about twenty-four episodes per season, using ten or fifteen writers.) If it had taken us two or three days to develop a story, there would have been no way to do the series. Of course it helped that we had a two-and-a-half year backlog of scripts from *My Favorite Husband*. Each of those radio scripts had a good solid basis for a story, whether or not we used any of the particulars. It also helped that we knew the characters so well because we had no outside writers. It was just the three of us writing every show until the fifth year, when I added Bob Schiller and Bob Weiskopf to our writing staff.

Bob Weiskopf and I had been roommates briefly in 1942, when we both wrote for *The Rudy Vallee Program*, before Bob moved to New York

It was just the three of us—me, Bob, *bottom right,* and Madelyn, *center*—
writing every show until the fifth year, when I added Bob Schiller, *top right,*
and Bob Weiskopf, *second from left,* to our writing staff.

to write for Fred Allen. I remember inviting the two Bobs down to the
set to watch the rehearsals of their first script for Lucy—the classic "Lucy
Visits Grauman's," in which Lucy and Ethel steal John Wayne's footprints
from Grauman's Chinese Theatre. "Come on down to the set and watch
Lucy perform your material," I told them. "She'll make you think you're
writers."

I always insisted that every *I Love Lucy* show have a logical foundation.
I wanted there to be a sound reason for everything in the script, because
I knew from experience that if you start with a believable premise and
take the audience one step at a time, and they know why they're being
taken there, you can go to the heights of slapstick comedy and outland-
ish situations. They'll go along with you past the point of absolute believability, as long as the pleasure of being entertained outweighs the
assault on their intelligence. But this only happens if the audience is
completely relaxed, if you've made it as comfortable as possible for
them by illuminating everything that might be considered illogical or
unreasonable.

Take the candy factory scene in "Job Switching," the first of more than a hundred *I Love Lucy* episodes directed by the wonderfully talented Bill Asher. The assembly line concept is an old one. It's been done dozens of times on other shows. But I don't think I've ever seen another show that didn't violate the logic of the moment. They'd have the conveyor belt speeding up and slowing down just for comedic effect, and for no other reason. And that's the kind of thing that turns off an audience. It suddenly reminds them that this is just for fun, rather than allowing them to be comfortable and go with it.

Even the bread scene in "Pioneer Women" is a logical extension of what *could* happen if one put in too much yeast. And the "Freezer" episode is merely an imaginative extension, having Lucy come out with icicles on her face. It's not completely illogical. But if we had had her come out of the freezer frozen in a giant block of ice, then we would have lost everyone.

It was just as important that the reason for everything be self-explanatory. I was a real stickler for this. On one of the shows we had a scene where the door to the Ricardos' living room was left open, and in the next scene that same door had to be closed. In the meantime, the only two characters in the scene were supposed to be intently watching something on the television set. Well, this led to a tremendous discussion. My position happened to be that we must find some way to close that door. We couldn't just find it closed. That would be too expedient. Someone suggested, "Well, during the time we aren't watching that scene, Ricky or Fred could've gotten up during a commercial and noticed the door was open and closed it."

"Well, sure, they could have," I said, "but there's no way for the audience to *know* that they did, and it's a bit disturbing, isn't it, if the audience doesn't happen to think, 'Oh well, I know what happened. They got up during a commercial and closed the door.' It's just a little disturbing thought that pulls some of their attention away from the comedy: 'Wait a minute—that door was open before. How did it get closed?' "

We finally solved the problem to everyone's satisfaction. The first scene was rewritten so that when Ricky entered the room he pushed the door open with such great force that it swung open, hit the door stop, and swung closed again. We accomplished this by putting a thread on the door and pulling it closed. The audience saw the door close on the screen, so when we got to the next scene there was no question how it got that way.

This kind of thing created a lot more work for us as writers. We would spend hours and hours taking all the necessary information and lacing it in while other things were happening, until we had everything logically locked down. Of course, if someone sat down to watch just the last ten minutes of an *I Love Lucy,* they might say, "My God, this is ridiculous." But someone else who had been watching from the beginning would say, "No, wait a minute. You don't understand how they got into this mess." And he could explain it logically.

Unfortunately, many of the *I Love Lucy* reruns that are on TV these days are missing a lot of the information necessary to have everything make sense. In 1958, a year after they stopped making the half-hour *I Love Lucy* shows, CBS cut about four minutes out of each of them for syndication purposes, to add more commercial time. But they didn't want to go to the expense of recutting the film using outtakes and the footage shot by the other two cameras, so all the cuts were made at either the beginnings or ends of scenes. The fellow who edited the syndication prints for CBS once told me he had a hell of a time cutting all of the shows down to the required twenty minutes and forty-five seconds; in a lot of cases there was simply no way for him to do it without hurting the story.

My insistence on having a logical basis for everything sometimes caused clashes on the set. During rehearsals for one episode I was called down to the stage because Lucy and Marc Daniels were arguing about a bit of business that Marc wanted to do that wasn't in the script. This sort of thing happened all the time and usually the improvisations and suggestions were sound and they became part of the show, but not this time.

Bobby Jellison was playing a milkman, and he was in the Ricardo bedroom. And he wanted to get over to the window. Instead of walking around the bed, Marc wanted him to get up and walk *across* the bed. Lucy and Bobby both thought it was silly, that there was no earthly reason why anyone would jump up on a bed if he could just as easily walk around it. But Marc felt that it was funny. When I came down and saw it, I had to tell Marc, "You can't do it. Not unless you can give me a good reason why he would walk on the bed." That was in February 1952. After that, Marc, who was very concerned about who was boss, would literally cringe anytime I came on the stage.

•   •   •

We started off with the cast working five days a week—from the first read-through around the rehearsal table on Monday morning until the filming on Friday night. They had no help at all in the way of cue cards, and they worked their tails off. Most of the time, by the evening of the second day, the cast did a run-through during which they tried to put down their scripts for the first time. Mostly they had to be helped a little bit, but I could see what was working and what wasn't, and I would jot down my suggestions about line readings or whatever wasn't logical. Then we had a "note session" where we'd discuss everything that I had made notes about.

We had another run-through on Wednesday at 5 P.M.—kind of a first dress rehearsal. When that was finished, usually around 6:30, we'd bring in sandwiches and I'd hold another note session. Everyone would stay for this, even the stagehands.

These were wonderful, stimulating sessions. We'd even get into the philosophy of the script, and why the characters were saying this or that. There were lots of arguments. It was almost like a little theater group session. We'd thrash everything out and change things, really digging into the characters, because we took these people seriously. We rarely got out of there much before midnight.

On Thursday I would carefully go over Bob and Madelyn's first draft script and then give it back to them with my comments. Then they would do a second draft, which they would deliver to me by the following Monday when they and I would sit down again to work on a new story. After that the script would never go back to them. The next day, Tuesday, amid my other responsibilities, I would do a final rewrite and then put the script into mimeo.

Bob and Madelyn always did a wonderful job with the script. But I made it a point, no matter how good their draft was, to redictate the entire thing from beginning to end, because that way each of the characters consistently spoke the same way each week. It didn't have to be *me*, necessarily, as long as it was filtered through one person's senses. But I felt that I knew best the mood and feel of our previous shows, and that I could bring it all into line so that nothing sounded too different or out of character.

To me, a situation comedy series is much like visiting a friend's family. You don't know what they are going to say, but you know how each person is going to react in a situation and how each of them talks. The more consistency there is, the more comfortable you are, and the more you can enjoy everything that happens. So, rightly or wrongly, the show sounded the same each time because it funneled through me.

I did this for another reason as well. Redictating the script from start

The fourth annual Emmy Awards banquet in 1952. Accepting his second
Emmy for excellence in comedy, Red Skelton remarked: "Ladies and
gentlemen, you've given it to the wrong redhead. I don't deserve this. It should
go to Lucille Ball." The entire audience rose to its feet, cheering Lucy.

to finish made me intimately familiar with everything in it. If a question
arose at any time during the production of that episode, I knew the
reason everything was in there—every line, every piece of business. So if
someone wanted to make a change, I would immediately know if we
couldn't do it because of something that had happened earlier. There has
to be one person with that sort of overview.

I remember one time that Bob and Madelyn gave me their draft and I
felt it was so good, and I was so tired, that I said, "That's just the way I
would do it. I'm going to turn it into mimeograph without any changes."
So at the first reading with the actors, questions naturally arose, and I
was completely lost. I didn't have any of the answers. I had no idea why
a certain line was in there, or a bit of business. It scared me half to death,
and I never did it again.

Even though we always got along great, Bob and Madelyn thought I
loused up all their scripts. One time, after they complained bitterly to me,
I said, "There's a good and logical reason for everything I do, everything I

change. On the next script, I'm going to keep a journal of the reasons for all of my changes. Then you'll know the reasons."

It took me a lot of time to do this, but I thought it was worth it. The following Monday, when we sat down to talk, I asked them if they had read my revision. They said that they had. "Okay," I said, "I'm going to show you line by line the reason for everything I changed." Frankly, I thought I had done a pretty masterful job, and that they would throw themselves at my feet when I finished. When I was done, I asked them, "Now, don't you agree that each of the changes was for a good reason?" "No," they replied. "We still think you screwed the whole thing up."

Straight to the Top

On March 2, 1952, Desi turned thirty-five years old, and we gave him a big birthday party. In the middle of the festivities he took me aside and asked me again to let him have the executive producer credit. His timing was excellent. My duties as producer and head writer had me so utterly exhausted that I had actually been considering quitting the show. At that moment, the prospect of having Desi take over some of my many responsibilities on the business end of things was attractive to me. What's more, Lucy had come to see me only a few days earlier, asking me to let Desi have executive producer credit as a personal favor to her, in order to help keep the peace in their marriage.

When Desi assured me that his credit would come after mine and would have no effect whatsoever on my authority as producer, I acceded to his request. We agreed that Desi would be named executive producer of *I Love Lucy* commencing with the "Freezer" show, which was scheduled to air at the end of April.

On Friday, April 18, 1952, the Nielsen ratings declared that *I Love Lucy* was now the number one show on television in America, reaching a record twenty-three million people, in nine-and-a-half-million homes. To celebrate, Desi gave a party for the cast and crew, at which he presented me with a trophy. It was, of all things, a statue of a baseball player taking a swing (something I found particularly ironic considering what an abysmal baseball player I had always been). At the base of the trophy, the inscription said: "Jess Oppenheimer: The Man Behind the Ball, 4-18-52, #1 Nielsen."

It was a nice gesture by Desi. I decided that I had probably been wrong to be so concerned about letting him have the executive producer credit.

The number of people watching the show every week had become larger than we could easily comprehend. "At the end of next week's

A nice gesture by Desi.

show," someone joked, "why don't we say, 'Thank you for watching. If you enjoyed the show, please mail us a dime.' " Everyone laughed, but I could see that at the same time they were all doing the mental calculation that just ten cents from each viewer would yield us an incredible $2.3 million a week.

The following Monday morning I came into my office to find a telephone message waiting for me. It was from Eddie Feldman at the Biow Agency. I returned the call.

"Did you talk to anyone at the *Hollywood Reporter* on Friday about Desi becoming executive producer at the end of this month?" he asked.

"No, I didn't. Desi must have had Kenny put out a press release about it. What does it say in the *Reporter?*"

"Take a look for yourself. It's on page 9, in Dan Jenkins's column."

Both trade papers were sitting on my desk. I picked up the *Reporter,* flipped to the column, and started reading:

TAKE HAPPY NOTE, gentlemen, of the five following facts about "I Love Lucy": (1) It tops the latest national Nielsen; (2) it tops the same Nielsen in the number of homes reached, a figure in excess of 9,500,000, which translates to something around 23,400,000 viewers; (3) it stars an established motion picture personality, Lucille Ball; (4) it originates in Hollywood; (5) it is on film. It's worth repeating: a Hollywood television film series, starring a motion picture personality, is as of this moment the No. 1 TV show in the nation. The credit goes to a lot of different people —to Don Sharpe for believing from the beginning (1949, that is) that Lucy and Desi could be starred together as husband and wife; to Harry Ackerman for never once throwing cold water on Desi's starry-eyed idea of not only filming the show but filming it before a live audience on a motion picture sound stage; to Jess Oppenheimer, the producer-writer who shared Sharpe's faith when everyone else was telling Lucy and Desi they were headed for career suicide; to Karl Freund, an Oscar-winning cameraman whose pioneering spirit plunged him happily and successfully into a new medium which, on form, he was supposed to sneer at disdainfully; to a crew which honestly believes "Lucy" is the greatest show on earth and works accordingly, week in and week out;

Then I saw why Eddie had called me:

and above all to Desi Arnaz, the crazy Cuban whom Oppenheimer insists has been the real producer all along and who in two weeks reluctantly starts taking screen credit as executive producer.

I stormed into Desi's office and confronted him with the column. "How can you quote me like that?" I demanded to know.

"It's like I told you, amigo," Desi answered. "I need to build a rep as a producer."

After an extended shouting match that got nowhere, I walked out. Angry as I was, I knew that there was nothing I could do about the publicity without seriously damaging both the series and Lucy's precarious marriage. And I would never do anything to hurt Lucy or the show. I was stuck, and Desi and I both knew it.

Desi's habit of taking credit for other people's accomplishments was a continuing source of friction between us (even as late as 1976, when, in his autobiography, Desi neglected to mention that *I Love Lucy* had any producer other than himself), but each of us had such great respect for the other's abilities that we never let it interfere with the show. In time, Desi became a fine producer and a very good director in his own right. And he did have his gracious moments. After *Cosmopolitan* ran a cover story which said, "Lucy's antics can't be underrated. But no show is better than its producer, and Desi Arnaz is the producer," Desi actually wrote a letter to the editor, in which he pointed out the error. "I am flattered that you call me producer of 'I Love Lucy,' " Desi's letter said. "Actually, I am executive producer. Jess Oppenheimer is producer and also head writer, which means that he does most of the work."

As the producer and head writer of the hottest new series on television, my name began appearing in newspapers and magazines on a regular basis, and I even started receiving some fan mail! I also received a congratulatory letter from Professor Terman at Stanford, who told me how happy he was for my newfound success. I wrote back to him that "I, too have been thrilled by the success of 'I Love Lucy.' It's one of the crazy things where the right combination suddenly happens, and although you're doing all the very same things for years, it suddenly goes crazy and becomes a tremendous hit."

It was now much easier for me to get a good table at popular restaurants. But although my name appeared often in the newspapers, my picture did not, so I still enjoyed relative anonymity in public. I considered this a blessing. Fans can sometimes act a little strangely when they encounter Hollywood celebrities, and I was just as happy to have such behavior directed at someone other than me.

Several instances of fans' peculiar conduct come to mind. I was having dinner once at Musso and Frank's Grill in Hollywood when I noticed Peter Lorre walking toward the exit. He stopped briefly to say hello to a friend at the bar. After exchanging greetings, Lorre continued toward the door. Another man at the bar turned to Lorre's friend and asked, "Is that Peter Lorre?" "Yes, it is," he was told. The inquisitive bar patron looked again at Peter Lorre for a moment, and then asked the friend, "Is he really that short?"

Another time, I was walking along the street with Steve Allen, when a fan came up to us. The fellow pointed at Steve and said loudly, "I know you! You're Steve Allen!"

"Yes, I am," Steve politely replied.

"Do you know how I recognized you?" the man continued.

"No, how?" asked Steve.

Beaming, the man proudly answered, "By your *face!*"

Douglas Fairbanks, Jr., once told me that his father, at the peak of his popularity as a silent-screen swashbuckler, once booked an ocean voyage in order to escape the mobs of his adoring fans in Hollywood. The senior Fairbanks and his son were taking a stroll on the deck of the ocean liner when they saw a little old man coming in their direction. Until then, the screen star had been lucky enough not to be recognized by anyone aboard ship. Not this time, though. When the man happened to look in their direction, Fairbanks saw the old gentleman's eyes light up with the spark of recognition.

"I'll bet I gave him an autograph once, and he'll of course think that I should remember him," Fairbanks whispered to his son as the man approached them. "Well, I've had it. I took this cruise to get away from this sort of thing. For once, I'm going to tell a fan exactly what's on my mind."

Sure enough, the little man walked up to Fairbanks and said, "You don't recognize me, do you?" Fairbanks lit into him for two or three minutes, berating the old gentleman about how big a star he was, how many fans he met every week, and how he could not possibly be expected to remember most of them.

The old man was visibly crushed. "I'm terribly sorry, Mr. Fairbanks," he said meekly. "Of course, you're absolutely right. I just thought there was some chance you might remember. We met last week at David Sarnoff's house. My name is Marconi."

After his embarrassing encounter with the inventor of the wireless, Fairbanks never lost his cool with an admirer again.

Only one time in my career was I ever accosted by an autograph seeker. I had just come out of the studio gate when an eager-looking middle-aged woman, complete with camera and autograph book, rushed up to me, her book and pen at the ready. I was unaccustomed to being recognized on the street and was thinking to myself that it was actually rather flattering, when the woman finally spoke. "Excuse me," she said, "are you anybody?"

Having a well-known name without a recognizable face to go with it did present some problems. It was the height of the McCarthy era, and another Oppenheimer—Dr. J. Robert Oppenheimer, the man responsible for our country's development of the A-bomb in World War II—was suddenly branded a communist by the government and suspended from atomic weapons research. Los Angeles's evening newspaper, the *Mirror*, ran a story about it, complete with a photo of Dr. Oppenheimer. Unfortunately, someone grabbed the wrong "Oppenheimer" photo, and they ran *my* picture with the story by mistake.

My photograph appeared only in the early edition. Luckily, someone at the newspaper caught the error. The correct photograph was quickly substituted, and I got a sincere letter of apology from the embarrassed managing editor of the *Mirror*, who offered to print a retraction. I decided against it, feeling that the retraction was bound to attract more attention than the original foul-up. Besides, I figured, how many people could there be who would actually think that the same man had invented both the atomic bomb and Lucy Ricardo?

To be sure, there were a number of places outside of Desilu where both my name and my face were well-known. One such place was Nickodell's, a restaurant near the studio where I ate lunch at least twice a week. One waitress in particular, an attractive young woman named Shirley, knew exactly who I was, and always seemed especially anxious to please me whenever I came in. I was not particularly surprised, therefore, when Shirley finally informed me that she was really an aspiring actress.

I don't know whether she ever made it in show business, but it was clear to me that waitressing was not this young lady's strong point. Shirley was always getting my orders mixed up. Whenever I called this to her attention she was crestfallen—so much so that finally I stopped telling her about her mistakes. But even that couldn't relieve her suffering. One day at lunch, as Shirley came to the table to take my order, I could see that she was terribly distressed about something.

"Oh, Mr. Oppenheimer," she said. "I was sound asleep last night, when at around 3 A.M. I woke up in a cold sweat, and my heart was pounding like crazy!"

"What was the matter?" I asked her.

"I suddenly remembered that on Tuesday I forgot to bring you mashed potatoes instead of french fries, like you asked!"

From then on, whenever Shirley was my waitress, I made it a point just to order the daily special.

Lucy Is "Enceinte"

THE NEWS of Lucy's impending motherhood at the end of our first season was met with utter dismay by the network and our sponsor. Harry Ackerman pronounced it a complete disaster. And both CBS and the Biow Agency were adamant about abandoning our plan to showcase Lucy's pregnancy on *I Love Lucy:* "You cannot show a pregnant woman on television!" Our arguments with them went on for weeks. Finally, the Biow Agency and Philip Morris offered a compromise: they would let us do one or two episodes about Lucy's pregnancy, but no more. Desi and I found this unacceptable.

Desi sat down and fired off a letter to Alfred E. Lyons, chairman of the board of the Philip Morris Company. In it he pointed out that until then, with the creative decisions in our hands, we had managed to give Philip Morris the number one show in the country. If Lyons agreed with the people at Philip Morris who were telling us what *not* to do, Desi told him, then Philip Morris must also take responsibility from then on for telling us *what* to do—and for whatever consequences that might have on our ratings.

The objections from Philip Morris suddenly ceased. Desi discovered later that upon receiving the letter, Lyons sent around a confidential memo, instructing his people, "Don't ——— around with the Cuban!"

Meanwhile, we still had CBS to deal with. The network had already issued a firm edict that we could not use the word "pregnant" on the show. We could say she was "expecting." She could be "with child." But never "pregnant." They were still deathly afraid that some segment of the public would find something offensive in our pregnancy shows.

I was in my office at the studio one morning, preparing for another in what seemed like an endless series of meetings on the subject, when I had an idea that I thought would go a long way toward making CBS

Alfred Lyons, *left,* and Milton Biow, *far right,* made a special trip to Hollywood in March 1952 to give us the good news that the sponsor was picking up our option for a second year. Standing between Biow and me is our director, Marc Daniels.

more comfortable. Why not arrange for a priest, a minister, and a rabbi to approve each of the "baby show" scripts, and to attend each of the screenings? If any of them found anything objectionable, we would simply remove it!

The meeting, with the network censor and two other CBS bigwigs who had flown in from New York, was a big success. Everyone was enthusiastic about the idea of having the baby shows "blessed" by local clergymen. The network executives were finally starting to get comfortable with what we had been telling them all along—we could deal humorously with pregnancy on a television show and at the same time keep the program on a high moral plane.

Lucy, Desi and I confer with Monsignor Devlin, one of the three clergymen
who "blessed" each of the "baby show" scripts.

When the meeting was over, I took the three network men to lunch
at Nickodell's. As we sat down at our table, I noticed that the waitress
coming to take our lunch orders was my old friend Shirley. I silently
prayed that she wouldn't make any serious mistakes with our meals. I
even repeated all of the orders to her, just to make sure.

After Shirley left, we continued our discussion. What had started
out as a rather tense meeting an hour or so earlier was now a relaxed
conversation, and everyone was in good humor. I had just finished telling
a joke when Shirley arrived with our food. To my great relief, I saw that
for once everything was just what had been ordered. But she was still at
a loss to remember which of us had ordered what, and started putting the
wrong dish in front of each of us.

One of the network reps, sensing that he could have a little fun,
started ribbing her about the mixup. This just flustered Shirley even
more. Suddenly, she put all of the plates down and said, "Gentlemen,

please! Don't do this to me! I get very nervous. Just ask Mr. Oppenheimer —the least little thing wakes me up in the middle of the night!"

•   •   •

At around this time a small event occurred, which went almost unnoticed but probably deserves at least a footnote in TV history. The network informed us that due to scheduling requirements, seven of its affiliates wanted to rebroadcast an episode of I Love Lucy called "The Diet," which had aired the previous October. At the time, most network programs were still broadcast live, and in the summer months a "summer replacement" program would be shown. The rerun and syndication markets had not yet been invented. But because I Love Lucy was produced on film, rerunning the show was a simple matter, if only the proper clearances could be obtained. Lucy, Desi, Bob, Madelyn, and I signed a one-page letter granting our permission for CBS to rerun the one episode, and waiving any right to payment from the rebroadcast. Not long after that, the world (at least that part of it within broadcasting range of those seven stations) saw its very first I Love Lucy rerun.

•   •   •

As we broke for our summer hiatus, we had the go-ahead from the network and the sponsor to follow Lucy's pregnancy on the screen, but we still faced a major logistical problem. Our second season would start on September 15 and last forty-one weeks. The baby was due in January, which meant that Lucy would be unavailable from mid-November until at least mid-March, right in the middle of our shooting schedule! Luckily, we had written and shot forty shows during our first year, giving us five extra shows in the can for the following season. And CBS had agreed to let us rerun ten shows from our first year if we would shoot a new opening scene for each of them, turning it into a "flashback" episode. But that still left us with twenty-six new shows to produce. The only way to get it done was to call everyone back from summer hiatus in July, six weeks early. I figured that we could get five or six of the "post-delivery" shows done before Lucy was showing too much, and then we could switch to the seven "pregnancy" shows and do them until Lucy had to stop working.

•   •   •

During the summer hiatus, when I wasn't on the golf course, I spent most of my time building things in my workshop at home. I had always

DESILU PRODUCTIONS, INC.
1040 North Las Palmas
Hollywood, California

May 27, 1952.

Columbia Broadcasting System, Inc.,
6121 Sunset Boulevard,
Hollywood 28, California.

Gentlemen: Re: I LOVE LUCY

        You have advised us that in order to re-arrange your
broadcast schedule on the I LOVE LUCY television program you
desire to re-run on seven television stations program No. 4
entitled "THE DIET" which was originally broadcast on October
29th, 1951.

        This will confirm our agreement that you may re-run this
single program on these seven stations for such purpose without
further payment to the undersigned by reason thereof.

        You agree that you will make all necessary payments to
musicians, any payments required by union agreements and any other
payments which we may become obligated to make by reason of such
re-broadcast.

        Kindly confirm your agreement to the foregoing in the place
below provided.

                            Very truly yours,

                            DESILU PRODUCTIONS, INC.

                            By _____ Pres

        We agree to the use of program No. 4 as above set forth and
waive any payments that may become owing to the undersigned by reason
of such use.

                            _____
                            Desi Arnaz

                            _____
                            Lucille Ball

                            _____
                            Jess Oppenheimer

_____   _____
Bob Carroll   Madelyn Pugh

CBS invents the rerun. But who would ever want to watch a
rerun of *I Love Lucy*?

At our 1952 end-of-the-season party we shared a secret: Lucy was pregnant. We would have to resume filming in July, not August, in order to complete enough episodes before Lucy had to stop working.

been a tinkerer; when I was nine years old I built a device for our Victrola that picked up the needle when it got to the end of the record and dropped it back down at the beginning, so that I could listen to the record again without getting out of bed.

Now that I could afford a real workshop, I outfitted myself with a complete set of power tools, including a lathe. I used to spend so much time there that a few years later, when my kids were asked what their father did for a living, they used to tell people that I was a carpenter.

Mostly I built things for around the house, or for friends. For instance, we had a blind friend who relied on her sense of touch to enable her to pour her own cup of coffee; she put her finger over the edge of the cup and stopped pouring when the coffee touched it. But she frequently scalded herself using this method. I built her a little device that fit over the edge of the coffee cup and had a little float inside attached to a stiff wire that extended beyond the rim. She just placed her finger on the outside of the cup and as it filled up, the liquid raised the float, which made the wire touch her finger when the cup was full. It wasn't exactly the electric light bulb, but I found it rewarding when one of my inventions proved useful to someone.

One night Es and I were sitting at home in our den watching a news program. It had always annoyed me to watch TV newscasters surreptitiously looking beside or below the camera to read their scripts. "If only there were something they could put in front of the lens to cue them," I used to think, "then they wouldn't have to do that." Suddenly we heard the siren of an ambulance going by. I turned to look out the window. The drapes were pulled back, but it was dark outside. All I could see was a reflection of the room.

Then it hit me. I jumped up excitedly and cried, "That's it!"

Startled, Es said, "What's wrong, Jess?"

"Look," I said, pointing at the window. "You see a reflection of the room because we've got the lights on in here and it's dark outside. But if you were outside in the dark, looking in through the window, you wouldn't see any reflection at all!"

"Yes, I know that," Es replied. "But what are you so excited about?"

"Well," I continued, "there's no reason why I can't apply the same principle to the lens of a TV camera and figure out a way of looking directly into the camera to read the script without interfering with the picture!"

During the next couple of weeks, I built a working model, which I called the "Jayo Viewer." Just as I hoped, it worked perfectly! It projected a reflection of the script (in letters $\frac{2}{8}''$ high) onto a piece of glass placed in front of the lens at a forty-five-degree angle. The actor couldn't even see the camera lens. He just saw the reflected script going by. At the same time, the camera, just like someone standing outside the window of our illuminated den, saw just the actor, and couldn't see the reflection of the script at all.

I applied for a patent (which was later granted), and held a press conference to announce my invention. The press coverage was positive, although some of the newspapers' technical descriptions left something to be desired. The *Hollywood Reporter* explained to its readers that "Jess Oppenheimer in two weeks will show his new invention, which will keep television announcers from glancing off to the side, up or down to read copy. It's a bracket attached to a tripod with a thingamajig."

When I invented the in-the-lens prompter, I was thinking mainly of newscasters. But columnist Frank Scully, writing in *Variety*, immediately predicted that the ones who would benefit most from my invention would be the politicians:

> With such a device Harry S. Truman would no longer be killing half the effect of his indignation by looking down at a script or turning a page just when he should be giving the camera the old piercing hyperthyroid look, the one which so often has aroused audiences to shout, "Give 'em hell, Harry!". . .
>
> Neither would Ike have to fiddle with his glasses and practically bury his head in a script while uttering words of no great depth. . . . All of us are less depressed when a guy says nothing but says it to our face, than when he says nothing and is reading it to us. . . .
>
> So, all in all, Oppenheimer, the lad who made one happy family out of Lucy, her husband, their landlord and his wife, is now destined to add one more boon to mankind—the elimination of sciatica from those who are forced in the interest of their diminishing liberties to watch our statesmen perform on TV.

Scully's comments proved to be prophetic. Any time the president addresses Congress or a political convention there are always one or two small pieces of glass mounted on poles at a forty-five-degree angle between him and the audience, from which he can read a reflection of his speech without anyone being the wiser. Usually there are at least two of these devices, so that he can casually shift his gaze to different parts of the room without losing his place in the script.

Most politicians would probably be surprised to learn that the earliest version of this device, on which they have come to depend for maintaining constant eye contact with the audience, was first successfully tested by Lucille Ball, on *I Love Lucy*. She and Desi used it in a commercial for Philip Morris—in an episode fittingly entitled "Lucy Has Her Eyes Examined."

•   •   •

Lucy was never comfortable doing the Philip Morris commercials—with or without an in-the-lens prompter. As on the radio series, she just couldn't get a handle on how to face the public as herself, particularly with the dull, straightforward sales talk that Philip Morris gave her to read.

Ironically, the most famous routine she ever performed was when she did a television commercial as Lucy Ricardo, during our first season. It was for a mythical health tonic called "Vitameatavegamin," containing

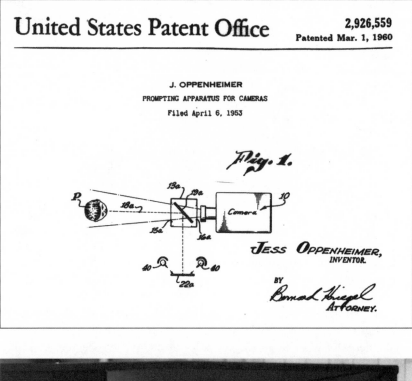

On "Lucy Has Her Eyes Examined," my in-the-lens prompter allowed
Lucy and Desi to read their lines for the Philip Morris commercial while
looking directly into the camera lens. But Lucy was still uncomfortable
doing commercials as herself.

23 percent alcohol. In the episode, Lucy manages to rehearse the commercial perfectly for Ricky's benefit, but after a few more rehearsals (each requiring her to drink some of the stuff) she gets totally bombed, with hilarious results.

The night that we filmed the show, I was watching her performance from my usual vantage point in the control room at the top of the bleachers. Lucy had the audience rolling in the aisles with her progressively drunken readings of the commercial pitch. I could barely stop laughing long enough to press the talk-back button and deliver my line of dialogue (as the off-stage "audio man"), telling Lucy to "go ahead" on her fourth time through. After Lucy, on her fourth reading, drunkenly explained, "It contains vitamins, meat, megatables, and vinerals," she was supposed to tell everyone to take a tablespoon after every meal. Then she would attempt to demonstrate this by pouring a spoonful from the bottle for herself. She had done it just this way in rehearsal and in the three previous readings. But this time she mistakenly skipped all the way to the end of the commercial, leaving out the whole bit with the bottle.

For an instant I thought we would have to retake the entire scene. But then Lucy, without missing a beat, stopped just before the very last line and went back and reconstructed what she was saying, *while* we were filming. And she did it in a way that made perfect sense and allowed her to do the bottle routine and all of the other material that she had left out. I sat there watching in utter amazement. Only Bob, Madelyn, and I knew what Lucy had done.

•   •   •

We filmed the first of the "pregnancy" shows in early October 1952. It was titled "Lucy Is Enceinte" (French for "pregnant"). In the show, Lucy visits the doctor and discovers she is pregnant. She is all set to tell Ricky when he comes home that afternoon, but he is called back to the club before she has a chance. She finally decides to visit the nightclub that evening and give Ricky the news during the middle of his show. The script for the nightclub scene went like this:

RICKY. Thank you, ladies and gentlemen. The next number—(*The maitre d' walks onto the floor and hands Ricky a note. To audience*) Pardon me. (*He reads the note.*)

RICKY. Oh, isn't this sweet. Listen. (*Reads.*) Dear Mr. Ricardo: My husband and I are going to have a blessed event. I just found out about it today and I haven't told him yet. I heard you sing a number called "We're

Having a Baby, My Baby and Me." If you will sing it for us now, it will be my way of breaking the news to him. *(To audience)* Oh, isn't that wonderful? I have an idea. I think they ought to come right up here on the floor and I'll sing it to them. *(The audience applauds.)* Come on—who sent me the note? *(He is looking around the room.)* Come on. We just want to wish you luck. *(He starts walking toward the tables and the piano player starts playing Rock-a-Bye-Baby. To first table on the side)* Was it you? *(The couple giggles and shake their heads "No." Ricky starts to sing along with the piano and ask with his eyes as he comes to each table.)* *(Singing.)* . . . in the treetop. Etc. etc. *(He sees an elderly couple—the woman is 95. He starts to ask with his eyes and quickly turns to the next table. As he is doing this Lucy comes in and sits at the empty table. Ricky sees her when he gets to the table, gives her a pantomime "Hi" between the words of the song, and, as though this is a big joke, asks her, with his eyes and expression, "You?" Lucy slowly nods her head "Yes." Ricky gives her a wink, starts to look away as he sings the next verse of the song and then does a tremendous take. What???! Lucy again shakes her head "Yes." Ricky rushes back to the table, sits down next to her and has a hurried whispered consultation with her.)* *(Whisper.)* Lucy, you aren't kidding?

LUCY. No. I've been trying to tell—

RICKY. Why didn't you tell—

LUCY. You didn't give me a chance—

RICKY. Oh, darling. *(He kisses her.)*

On the night of the filming, Lucy and Desi got to this point in acting out the script, and then this strange thing happened. Suddenly, they remembered their own real emotions when they had discovered at last that they were going to be parents, and both of them began crying. It was one of the most moving things I've ever seen.

When we reached the end of the scene, our director, Bill Asher, remarked sadly to those of us sitting in the control booth that as beautiful as that first take was, there was a problem with it—Desi, overcome with emotion, had messed up the lyrics to "Rock-a-Bye Baby." Pressing the talk-back button, he made the announcement to the audience: "I'm sorry, ladies and gentlemen, but due to technical problems we're going to have to take that scene over again."

The response to this announcement was immediate and overwhelming. The entire audience, most of whom had been crying right along with Lucy and Desi, jumped to its feet and shouted a thunderous "NO!!!"

Bowing to the audience's instincts, we used the first take on the air, complete with the messed-up lyrics. The scene became one of the classic television moments of all time. In all of the airings that it has had since

Without missing a beat, Lucy went back and reconstructed what she was saying, *while* we were filming, allowing her to do the bottle routine and other material she had left out.

then, I've never heard of anyone outside of that control booth who noticed Desi's mistake.

.   .   .

The problem of the sex of the expected baby didn't come up until we were approaching the filming of the show on which it was to be born. Normally one merely waits and lets Nature decide, but we were faced with a complicated logistical problem of filming duplicate scenes, one with a boy and one with a girl, and then, at the last minute, incorporating into the film the one that corresponded to Lucy's real baby.

Desi and I were discussing the technical and financial aspects of the problem one day when I turned to him and said, "Desi, we're going to break our backs and spend a small fortune making sure that the sex of Lucille Ball's baby and of Lucy Ricardo's baby is the same. But the two babies won't have the same name, so why do they need to have the same sex? As a writer, if I had to choose, I would give the Ricardos a baby boy. I think it would give us more comedy situations. For instance, we could have Lucy insisting on dressing him in feminine clothes, or not wanting to get his hair cut."

I could see from Desi's face as I spoke that he liked the idea of Lucy Ricardo having a boy. But his reasons were decidedly different from mine. "Look," he said, "Lucy gave me one girl, she might give me another. This is my only chance to be sure I get a son. You give me a boy on TV."

.   .   .

Three months after my conversation with Desi about the baby's sex, I sat alone in my kitchen, waiting for word from Desi at the hospital. I had written a baby boy for the Ricardo family, but at the moment that was the best-kept secret in Hollywood. Whether Nature would cooperate and give the Arnaz family a baby boy as well, nobody yet knew. I had been hanging on the phone, waiting to find out, for more than half an hour, thinking back over all of the twists and turns of fate that had led me to this moment.

Luck. There was no question about it. In everything from my not showing up on the day the police raided my childhood crap game, to the way I landed my first job in Hollywood, I had had more than my share of incredible good fortune.

My thoughts were suddenly interrupted when Desi came back on the line. "Jess!" he shouted. "Lucy followed your script! Ain't she something?"

I laughed. "Terrific!" I yelled back at him. "That makes me the greatest writer in the world!"

Then, before Desi could run out to address the anxiously waiting press corps, I added, "Tell Lucy she can take the rest of the day off!"

Afterword

I LEFT *I Love Lucy* in the spring of 1956, one year before it went off the air as a regular weekly series. Although I had faith that reruns of the 153 episodes I had produced would stay on the air for quite some time, I was concerned that if we kept on trying to turn out new ones, the show would start to go downhill. Even with Lucy's tremendous talent, there are only so many stories that you can do within a particular premise and set of characters. We had already taken them to Hollywood, and then Europe. Where were we going to take them next—to the moon?

I knew that Lucy was such a phenomenal performer, and that the other people complemented her so well, that the television audience would continue to watch the show indefinitely, simply because she was the best thing around. But we were already starting to hit areas where we'd been two or three times before, such as jealousy, or running the house on a budget, or getting into show business, and it just wasn't fresh enough anymore to please me. I sat Lucy and Desi down and explained how I felt.

"Here we have a series that is number one," I told them. "We've lasted for five years, and won every award and magazine poll imaginable. Why don't we just retire undefeated, and let there be *one* series that isn't driven right into the ground."

Despite my pleas, they ultimately decided to do just one more year of weekly episodes. But my own five-year commitment to Desilu was up, and my old friend Pat Weaver, then chairman of the board of NBC, had offered me an attractive post with the rival network as a programming development executive. The lessons that I had learned years earlier about the dangers of "staying on too long," as well as the continuing friction between me and Desi over production credit, convinced me that the time had come to move on to other projects.

After we wrapped my last *I Love Lucy* ("Return Home from Europe"), in April 1956, Lucy and Desi gave a big party in my honor at their home in Beverly Hills. It was an evening filled with tears and laughter—tears when we said our good-byes and laughter at a musical comedy revue, performed by Lucy, Desi, Bill, Vivian, and others, entitled "You Are Theirs." Lucy's lyrics in the revue even recalled that time in 1948 when I walked out (briefly) on her radio show because of Lucy's tirade over the last line of one of our scripts:

> I'll never forget the first time we met—
> He handed me a script—
> There was a light in his eyes
> that lit up his map.
> He just wasn't prepared for:
> "Who *writes* this crap?"

Knowing I would be asked to make a speech, I had had special "Oppy Awards" manufactured for the occasion, which I presented to members of the *I Love Lucy* cast and staff in appreciation of their long and devoted service on the show. The bronze statuette looked a little bit like an Oscar but more like me—a little man with glasses, very little hair, and his hands discreetly positioned in front of his crotch. Lucy, no stranger to awards ceremonies, was close to tears as she accepted her "Oppy."

At the end of the evening, after all the goodbyes had been said, Desi walked me and Es down the long driveway to where I had parked our car. As I opened the car door, Desi put his hand on my shoulder. "Pardner," he said, "You know, if you change your mind, and you can see it in your heart to do it, I wish you'd come back."

"I'll think about it, Desi," I replied, looking Desi in the eye, "but I don't think I will."

•　　•　　•

Six months after I left *I Love Lucy*, Lucy and Desi sold all of their rights in the show to CBS for what they considered an excellent price—$4.3 million. After all, they figured, the reruns couldn't last more than a few years.

For my part, I had a hunch that repeats of *I Love Lucy* would be around longer than most people expected. A year earlier, in the fall of 1955, CBS had begun airing *I Love Lucy* reruns at 6:30 P.M. on Saturdays, and in December an astonishing thing had happened. The Saturday reruns of

(*Above*) Lucy and I go "face to face" just before filming the *I Love Lucy* episode of the same name, a few weeks after I announced my decision to leave the show. (*Opposite, top*) At my farewell party Lucy (with Desi, Vivian, and Bill seated behind her) assures me and the rest of her guests that "We don't feel we're losing a producer. We feel we're gaining a parking space." (*Opposite, bottom*) Lucy was close to tears as she accepted her "Oppy Award."

I Love Lucy had placed in the top ten shows on television, tying with *first-run prime-time* episodes of *The Honeymooners*. So when CBS offered to buy out my ownership interest as well, I told them I wasn't interested. I had been lucky enough to be part of a once-in-a-lifetime phenomenon, and my instincts told me to let it ride.

I'm beginning to think that that wasn't a bad idea.

Appendixes

Index

Appendix A

A Character Is Born

Jess Oppenheimer's first script for Lucille Ball—My *Favorite Husband*, performed live October 2, 1948, on the CBS Radio Network. This program is track 1 on the included CD, and is discussed in Chapter 10.

PROGRAM # 11   OCTOBER 2, 1948

"MY FAVORITE HUSBAND"

LUCILLE BALL   RICHARD DENNING

CORY   John Heistand *ok*

KATY   Ruth Perrott *ok*

SCHWEINKAMPH   Hans Conried *P*
Writing girl

MATRON   *JEANNE ok*   Bea Benaderet
WOMAN   *Vanderpyl.*   { Doubled
PREACHER

Directed by
GORDON T. HUGHES

4 minutes

FAVORITE HUSBAND -1-
10/2/48

MUSIC:	THEME...
LEMOND:	We present MY FAVORITE HUSBAND, a new series based on the delightful stories of Isobel Scott Rorick's gay, sophisticated Mr. and Mrs. Cugat, starring Lucille Ball with Richard Denning.
MUSIC:	UP AND HOLD FOR...
	(APPLAUSE)
ANNCR:	You know, it's a long time since Liz and George Cugat took thier marriage vows. Just ten years since Liz answered the preacher.
PREACHER:	Do you promise to love honor and obey?
LIZ:	(STARRY EYED) I do.
ANNCR:	Even after five years of wedded life, Liz's answer was the same.
GEORGE:	Now let's not argue, Liz. Remember, you're my wife and you have to love, honor and obey.
LIZ:	(QUESTIONING) I do?
ANNCR:	And how many marriages can claim that ten years of marriage haven't changed one word of the loving wife's answer.
WOMAN:	(GOSSIPY) Confidentially, Liz, when you and George have an argument--who wins?
LIZ:	I do!
ANNCR:	But don't get me wrong. The Cugats, Liz, busy young matron, and George, busy young fifth-vice-president of the bank, are one of the few couples we know who live together and like it. Let's look in on them now as Liz waits for George to come down to breakfast.

FAVORITE HUSBAND -1A-
10/2/48

LIZ: Oh Katy?

KATY: Yes, Mrs. Cugat. What is it?

LIZ: Katy, you don't have to serve breakfast this morning. I'll
          serve Mr. Cugat myself.

KATY: Don't you feel well, Mrs. Cugat?

LIZ: Yes, but there's a special little favor I want from him,
          and if he thinks I cooked the breakfast it might put him
          in a better frame of mind.

FAVORITE HUSBAND -2-
10/2/48

KATY: If he thinks you cooked it, Mrs. Cugat, I don't think he'll eat it.

LIZ: Well, fix something real nice--like scrambled eggs!

KATY: I'll make a nice omellette. (LAUGHS KNOWINGLY) Oh, you can always get around a man with food. I used to get anything I wanted from my first husband, Clarence. I'd just cook him an omelette and put in a whole bottle of Tabasco sauce.

LIZ: A whole bottle?

KATY: Uh huh...and I wouldn't give him a glass of water till he said yes!

LIZ: Well, just leave out the Tabasco. I've done everything to keep George in a nice frame of mind this morning.

KATY: (LEAVING) All right.

GEORGE: (OFF) (BELLOWS) Liz! Hey, Liz. Where are my clothes? I can't find them anywhere.

LIZ: (CALLS) They're all there, George. I hung them up.

GEORGE: (OFF) What did you do that for? I had them all neatly laid out on the floor where I could find them!

LIZ: (CALLS) I'm sorry, dear.

GEORGE: (CALLS) Could it have been you who laid out my shaving brush with the tooth paste on it?

LIZ: Oh. (CALLS) I didn't mean to.

GEORGE: (CALLS) That's all right. My cheeks needed a good Ipana massage!

LIZ: Oh, Dear. If that was tooth paste on his shaving brush--what did I put on his tooth brush? Well, I won't say anything if he doesn't. Now let me see. I'll just put the paper in front of his place at the table and open it to page sixteen. There.

FAVORITE HUSBAND -3-
10/2/48

Phone ring.

LIZ: Hello? Oh, hello, Ann. Lunch? How can you think of it?

Aren't you going to the tryouts for the play? The Young

Matrons League. It's in the paper this morning. On ~~page~~ *the Society Page*
I just put it in front of George's place at the table
~~sixteen~~, And you know what Ann? Anatol Brodny is going to

be in the audience on opening night. Yes, the famous

Hollywood director. He used to live in town here. I

hope George will let me try out. Oh, oh, here he comes

I'll call you later, Ann.

SOUND:Q   HANG UP PHONE

LIZ: (HUMS GAILY) Good morning, Dear.

GEORGE: ((EARLY MORNING PRE-OCCUPATION)

LIZ: ~~Aren't you going to give me a kiss?~~

GEORGE: Mmmmm. (SLIGHT PECK)

LIZ: (PETULANTLY) That's not much of a kiss. You're not even

speaking to me.

GEORGE: I'm afraid if I open my mouth it will start lathering

again!

LIZ: (LAUGHS ~~PLEASANTLY~~ TO GET HIM STARTED)

GEORGE: (CAN'T HELP GOING ALONG. THEY BOTH LAUGH) Oh, Liz, you'r

a great ~~girl~~

LIZ: Well, I'm trying.

GEORGE: ~~You certainly are.~~ *uhm,* Well, what's for breakfast? (CALLS)

Katy!

LIZ: Oh--I told Katy to work around the house.

GEORGE: (WARILY) Are--you cooking breakfast?.

LIZ: (TRIES TO SNEAK BY IT WITHOUT ACTUALLY LYING) Well--

you're my favorite husband.

GEORGE: (HE KNOWS THIS ATTITUDE) *okay—* What do you want from me, Liz?

LIZ: (SHOCKED AT THE SUGGESTION) Me? Want? I just felt like ~~making my dear husband a wonderful breakfast.~~

GEORGE: You've felt like that before---but the breakfast never quite made it.

LIZ: Oh, it will this time. We're having an omelette.

GEORGE: How are you cooking it, by Radar?

LIZ: Oh---well, I'm keeping an eye on it. It ought to be ready just about now. ~~I'll go in and see.~~

SOUND: DOOR OPEN

KATY: Mrs. Cugat. Can I see you a minute?

GEORGE: What is it Katy? Something wrong?

KATY: Well, er---

LIZ: (A BRAVE FRONT) Yes, whatever it is, tell me. I have nothing to keep from Mr. Cugat.

KATY: Well--Breakfast won't be ready for a while because the omelette you were cooking spoiled and you had to make another one!

LIZ: (TRYING TO CARRY IT OFF) Thank you, Katy.

GEORGE: (PAUSE) I hope you didn't put too much salt in it.

LIZ: Don't be funny. Why don't you read your paper, George?

GEORGE: You mean you'll let me?

LIZ: Certainly dear. See it's all set for you. All you have to do is read.

GEORGE: (PUT OUT) Who opened this paper to the society page?

LIZ: You could do worse than read the society page. There are some interesting things there.

FAVORITE HUSBAND   -5-
10/2/48

GEORGE: There are? Well, let's see. Well! I should say. Just look
at this. (READS) At a late afternoon ceremony ~~at the~~
~~hanging gardens of her parent's home in Crestwood,~~ Deborah
Ann Rassmussen, ~~daughter of Mr. and Mrs. Irving Cantrell~~
~~Rassmussen~~, became the bride of Arthur Spondulik Cranfeather
~~Jr.~~ ~~Cranfeather Jr. is the son of Mr. and Mrs. Arthur~~
~~Spondulik Cranfeather Sr.~~

push him X

LIZ: ~~Amazing!~~ Why don't you read something else, dear?

GEORGE: No, this is exciting. The bride wore a bouffant gown of
white Chantilly lace and her head was covered by a lace cap
from which fell a large veal.

LIZ: That's veil!

GEORGE: Veal, veil. They all look silly (CONTINUES READING) the
bridesmaids wore aqua taffeta gowns, and---

LIZ: ~~Oh, George, stop being funny. There must be something~~
~~interesting on that page.~~

GEORGE: ~~Let's see. Oh yes. (READS) According to scientists, the~~
~~silkworm moth sometimes lays as many as thirty million eggs~~
~~in one season. Imagine that.~~

LIZ: ~~No, thanks, it makes me tired.~~ Why don't you try somewhere
around the middle of the page, darling?

GEORGE: (READS) Overheard at tea--People wouldn't be so incompatable
if the men had more income and the girls were more patable!
(LAUGHS) That's very good.

LIZ: Here. Give me the paper and I'll see if I can find ~~something~~

GEORGE: (INTERUPPTING) No. Here it is. Just listen to this
(READS) Williams tkos Smith in bloody battle.

LIZ: How'd that get in there?

GEORGE: I turned to the sports page!

SOUND: DOOR OPEN

FAVORITE HUSBAND -6-
10/2/48

KATY: Here's your omelette, Mrs. Cugat. I hope you don't mind that
         I took it off the stove and put it on a plate for you.

LIZ: No, it's all right, Katy.

GEORGE: It looks wonderful. Congratulations.

KATY: Thank you.
LIZ:

KATY: (EMBARRASSED) Uh (FADING) I have some work to do.

SOUND: DOOR CLOSED

GEORGE: Wait a minute, Dear wife. ~~I have a suspicion that an intrigue is taking~~
         ~~place this morning. Now~~ what's all this interest in the
         society page?

SOUND: RUSTLE OF PAPER

GEORGE: ~~Wedding announcements, routine~~--Oh, ho! ~~Methinks I have~~
         ~~found the Holy Grail~~ (READS) Young Matrons League to present
         annual play.

LIZ: Oh, really? ~~I didn't see that.~~ X very elaborate X

GEORGE: (WINDING UP ON A PET HATE) If there's one thing I can't
         understand it's why a bunch of respectable married women
         want to get up on a stage and make Jackasses out of themselves.

LIZ: I don't see anything wrong with it (TAKE) They don't make
         jackasses out of themselves.

GEORGE: Oh, come now, Liz. You know they do.

LIZ: You didn't feel this way last year. You let me be in the
         play.

GEORGE: That's what started me feeling this way.

LIZ: Oh, you think I'm a jackass.

GEORGE: I didn't say that.

FAVORITE HUSBAND   -7-
10/2/48

LIZ: You ~~interrupted~~. *implied it --- Well, didn't you?*

GEORGE: ~~(PATIENTLY CORRECTING) You inferred it. I implied it.~~
          ~~I did not.~~

LIZ: ~~Well, answer me then.~~

GEORGE: No comment.

LIZ: George Cugat. You are calling your wife a Jackass by
          keeping your mouth shut.

GEORGE: Think of the trouble I could get in *to* by opening it.
          (SUDDENLY CAJOLING) Look, why don't you forget it, Honey.
          I know what you're leading to. You want to be in the
          play.

LIZ: I do not. I didn't even hear about it until you happened
          to find it in the paper.

GEORGE: Really?

LIZ: Don't you believe me?

GEORGE: Certainly, Dear. I wonder what play they're going to do?

LIZ: John Loves Mary. (SUDDENLY REALIZES WHAT SHE'S DONE) Oh!

GEORGE: Well, forget it, Liz. The answer is no! *not after last year.*
          (laughs)

LIZ: ~~It's for a good cause, though. Charity.~~

GEORGE: ~~Charity begins at home. Be kind to your husband and don't~~
          ~~get up on that stage. The simple fact is, Liz, that you~~
          ~~can't act. I wouldn't mind if you had talent, but last~~
          ~~year. (LAUGHTER CUTS THE REMINDER OF HIM)~~ *etc.*

LIZ: That wasn't my fault.

GEORGE: You're supposed to feel at ease on the stage. Move around.
          I almost died when that fellow came bounding in and called
          "RUN FOR YOUR LIFE, THE DAM HAS BROKEN" and you just sat
          there. I know how you felt. I've had stage fright, too.

```
                                    FAVORITE HUSBAND   -8-
                                    10/2/48
```

LIZ: I didn't have stage fright.

GEORGE: Then why didn't you get up when the dam broke?

LIZ: Cause when I sat down a strap broke!

GEORG:E   Oh.

LIZ: And I'll tell you something else, George Cugat. There's
            going to be a famous Hollywood director in the audience ~~on~~
            ~~opening night~~ and I'll ~~bet~~ you ~~if he sees me~~ he'll offer
            me a contract.

GEORGE: Oh Liz, stop it. You're talking like a child.

LIZ: Come on. We'll make a bet. How much?

GEORGE: No. This is just a trick so I'll let you ~~act~~. Well, I
            have to go to the office, dear. Sorry I had to deprive you
            of a Hollywood career.

LIZ: Very funny. What has Betty Grable got that I haven't got?
            Or Lana Turner.

GEORGE: Nothing, Dear. In fact, you have something they haven't got.

LIZ: (PLEASED) I have? What?

GEORGE: Me! Well, see you later, dear. If you want me, I'll be
            at the bank.

SOUND: DOOR OPEN AND CLOSE -- TELEPHONE DIALLING

LIZ: Hello, Ann? Liz. I just spoke to George about being in the
            play. He put his foot down. Absolutely no. He was really
            definite about it. What time are we going to the tryouts?
            Of course I am. It's a challenge now. If I get the part
            think how surprised George will be on opening night. To
            say nothing of that Hollywood director. Me? Don't be
            silly. A Hollywood contract is the last thing in the world
            I want -- I'd just like to show George I could get one if I
            wanted. Goodbye, Ann

SOUND: HANG UP PHONE -- HORN HONKS OFF

FAVORITE HUSBAND -9-
10/2/48

KATY: (FADING IN) I'll get the door, Mrs. Cugat. I know that
          horn. It's Mr. Cartwright.

LIZ: Good old Corey. I'm glad he dropped by.

KATY: What does Mr. Cartwright do for a living, Mrs. Cugat?

LIZ: Nothing, Katy, he's just a very eligible bachelor.

KATY: From what I gather, he chases women for a living.

LIZ: Oh, that's not exactly fair, Katy. Women chase him for a
          living -- only none of them has caught him yet.

SOUND: DOORBELL

KATY: (FADING) Well, I'll let him in.

SOUND: DOOR OPEN

COREY: Greetings, Heaven's gift to unmarried Young America is here.

LIZ: Corey Cartwright! I'm glad you dropped by,   . I
          want you to help me with something.

COREY: You know me, Liz. Anything up to murder. And for you
          I may go a step further. (MOCK SERIOUSNESS) Who do you
          want me to rub out? Or should I say whom do you want me
          to rub out?

LIZ: (LAUGHS) You're never serious, are you? Well, you'll get
          married someday! By the way, how's your new girl friend?

COREY: Which one?

LIZ: That little red-head.

COREY: Which one?

LIZ: Her name was Mary.

FAVORITE HUSBAND   -10-
10/2/48

COREY: Which one? What was her last name?

LIZ: What a life you must lead. If I remember, it was Johnson.

COREY: Mary Johnson. That was---(FIGURING TO HIMSELF) Thirty
days hath December, April, June and Roberta. All the rest
have thirty one except Eleanor who is twenty-eight.
(THEN UP) Oh I haven't seen Mary Johnson since last August!

LIZ: Sorry I brought it up. Let's forget her.

COREY: No, I'm glad you brought it up. / She hasn't called me in
ages! I've got her name in my book. Yes, here it is.
Mary Johnson. RHRW.

LIZ: Allright. Would you mind decoding that for me.

COREY: Not at all. RH that means Red Head.

LIZ: What's the other R for?

COREY: Real! And the W is my kissing guide.

LIZ: I get it. Won't, eh?

COREY: (WISELY) No.

LIZ: Will?

COREY: No - Wow!

LIZ: You've got more on your girls than the FBI has. Next thing
you'll be giving them a loyalty check!

COREY: Enough about me and Amour.

LIZ: No, Wait a minute. If you had my name in your book,
what would it say?

COREY: I have. Here.

LIZ: Let's see. Liz Cugat. RHR. W?

COREY: Keep going.

LIZ: W.I.W.G. Holy Cow, what does that mean?

COREY: Wish I were George.

```
                              FAVORITE HUSBAND    -11-
                              10/2/48
```

LIZ: Oh, that's sweet, Corey. You're a good friend.

COREY: Now what was on your pretty mind when I came in.

LIZ: Corey, George doesn't want me to be in the play the Young

            Matrons are putting on, But I want to get a part and show

            him I can act. If I get a part will you see that George is

            out somewhere on the nights I have to go to rehearsals.

COREY: Sure. It'll be worth it to see the look on his face

            opening night.

LIZ: Gee, thanks, Corey. Now I have to rush down to the tryouts.

COREY: Me, too. I'm picking up George and we're having lunch with

            Anatol Brodny.

LIZ: Well, don't tell him you were here or anything about----who

            did you say you were having lunch with?

COREY: Whom.

LIZ: Allright. Whom is eating lunch with you?

COREY: Anatol Brodny. He's an old college chum of ours who made

            good out in Hollywood. I never thought he'd have what it

            takes. He was a real goof.

LIZ: Maybe that's what it takes. Listen, Corey, try to get

            George to bring him to the house, will you. If I can make

            an impression on him in my own home, it will be half the

            battle.

COREY: Well, I'll try, but I don't think George will go for it.

LIZ: Then you bring him. Promise me you'll try?

COREY: Promise.

LIZ: Thanks, Corey. You're a real Pal.

MUSIC: BRIDGE

SOUND: BUZZ OF MANY WOMEN'S VOICES JABBERING

FAVORITE HUSBAND -12-
10/2/48

MATRON: Let's come to order girls. Girls! Girls! To order. I'd

like you to meet the director of our little show. Miss

~~Croftsworth~~ *Worthington* - from the drama department of Sickesly

College.

SOUND: POLITE APPLAUSE.

CROFT: (EVERY VOWEL IS PEAR SHAPED AND EVER CONSONANT OVER

PRONOUNCED) How do you do. ~~It is my distinct pleasure

to make your acquaintance.~~ Before we start tryouts, I'd

like to tell you about the way I direct. I stress nat-

ur-al-ness. Every word you say must sound real, vi-tal,

and nat-ur-al. How many of us have heard an actress on the

stage say to her fiancee, Darling, I love you. (SMUG

LAUGH) How much more believable it would have been to us

if she had been natural and said, (SAME THING) Darling, I

love you. ~~So you see, our performances must be vivid and

real.~~

MATRON: (SEMI SOTTO) Isn't she wonderful, Mrs. Cugat?

LIZ: Huh? Oh, yes.

MATRON: She could have been a great actress. Doesn't she remind

you of Cornell?

LIZ: No, she reminds me more of Notre Dame!

CROFT: Well, now to the parts. We have two main parts. One is

a *beautiful* young girl of eighteen.

ALL: (AD LIB) Oh I'd love that. That's for me. Perfect for

me. I'm just the type, etc.

CROFT: The other part is a young matron of thirty-six.

ALL: DEAD SILENCE.

CROFT: (CLEARS THROAT) This is the main part.

FAVORITE HUSBAND -13-
10/2/48

LIZ: Oh well, I'll try it. But I'll have to be a pretty good
          actress to portray anyone that old! (SILLY LAUGH)

CROFT: Good. Let me look at you. Oh, my dear, you're just the
          type.

LIZ: Well, you don't have to get nasty about it.

CROFT: Now here is the scene I want you to read. You are crying
          your heart out because your lover has left you. Suddenly
          ~~as your heart is breaking~~, you hear the bark of a dog. It
          is his dog! He has come back. You run to your lover
          laughing now as hard as you were crying before. You say
          to him, Hold me in your arms, then, seeing the dog is on the
          sofa, you say to it. Leave, ~~quickly,~~ you're not supposed
          to be in here. Have you got it?

LIZ: ~~What is the matter with my lover, has the cat got his tongue?~~

CROFT: ~~We ought to talk in this scene. This is your scene. Now~~
          let's go. You are crying your heart out.

LIZ: (VERY SMALL CRY)

CROFT: You'll have to do better than that. I said you are crying
          your heart out. Like this. (TREMENDOUS WAILING CRY)

LIZ: (LAUGHS)

CROFT: What are you laughing for?

LIZ: Because my lover is coming.

CROFT: We haven't reached that part. I was showing you how to cry.

LIZ: Really? (ABASHED) I thought that was the dog.

CROFT: We will continue, but you must practise that crying if you
          wish to get the part in the final auditions. Now, you
          hear the dog. (BARKS LITTLE BARKS)

LIZ: (LAUGHS HYSTERICALLY)

FAVORITE HUSBAND   -14-
10/2/48

CROFT: You sound like you just heard a joke. This is a laugh of
           hysteria. Wild and abandoned. You must practise that,
           too. Now for your lines. Go ahead.

LIZ: Hold me in your arms. Leave quickly. You're not supposed
           to be in here.

CROFT: Not bad. Not bad at all. A little practise and I think
           you'll be ~~in contention~~ for the part.

LIZ: Oh, don't worry, Mrs. Croftsworth. I'll practise.

MUSIC: BRIDGE

SOUND: DOOR OPEN

KATY: Oh, hello, Mr. Cugat. Is there something wrong?

GEORGE: No, Katy, I just had to run home for some papers I left
           in the study. Is Mrs. Cugat home?

KATY: Yes. She went out for a while, but she came back, and
           went right into her room and closed the door. Hasn't
           come out since.

GEORGE: That doesn't sound like her. I hope she isn't sick. We
           better go and see.

SOUND: FOOTSTEPS UNDER NEXT SPEECH

KATY: She hasn't looked any too well lately.

GEORGE: Her door is still closed. I'll just kno---what's that?

LIZ: (SNEAK IN UNDER LAST SPEECH) (CRYING)

KATY: She's crying.

GEORGE: The poor kid. I better go in and see what's the matter.
           Wait a minute. Let's be sure it's not my fault. Our
           anniversary is in December. Her birthday is in August.
           Her mother's birthday is in June. I'm in the clear.

LIZ: (BACK OF DOOR) (CRIES HARDER)

KATY: Why she's crying her little heart out.

MY FAVORITE HUSBAND-15-

LIZ:	(BACK OF DOOR) (REAL BIGTIME WAIL)
GEORGE:	Come in with me, Katy. I get all funny when she cries.
LIZ:	(BACK OF DOOR) (BARKS LIKE A DOG)
GEORGE:	(PAUSE) Did you hear what I heard?
KATY:	I'm not sure. What did you hear?
GEORGE:	It's a dog! She's got a dog in there. She was probably crying because she didn't think I'd let her keep it.
KATY:	The poor sensitive soul.
LIZ:	(BACK OF DOOR) (LAUGHS LIKE THE DEVIL)
GEORGE:	She's all right now. That's all it was, Katy. She's got a dog in there.
LIZ:	(BACK OF DOOR) Take me in your arms!
GEORGE:	I better go and take a look at that dog!
KATY:	(EXCITED) I, uh, have some work to do.
~~George:~~	~~Quick --- I don't think she knows we're here.~~
~~SOUND:~~	~~GEORGE BUMPS INTO TABLE~~
~~KATY:~~	~~Ouch, I always bump that table.~~
~~GEORGE:~~	~~I don't think she heard you.~~
LIZ:	(BACK OF DOOR) Leave, quickly. You're not supposed to be here.
GEORGE:	~~She heard you all right.~~
SOUND:	GEORGE BANGING ON DOOR.
GEORGE	Let me in. Liz, let me in, do you hear?
SOUND:	BANGING AGAIN, DOOR OPENS
LIZ:	(VERY CALM) Hello, George. What's new?
GEORGE:	(BLOWING) What's new?!! What were you doing in here?
LIZ:	Me? Why I was just sleeping. You woke me up.
GEORGE:	(WHISTLES LIKE FOR DOG)
LIZ:	What's the matter with you? What are you whistling for?
GEORGE:	Nothing. Can't a fellow whistle?

MY FAVORITE HUSBAND-16-

LIZ: What are you looking under the bed for? Did you lose anything?

GEORGE: I don't know yet! What's in the closet, Liz?

LIZ: You know what's in the closet.

GEORGE: I'll just take another (GRUNTS AS HE OPENS CLOSET DOOR FAST)..look... Nothing but clothes.

LIZ: What did you expect to find -- the Toni Twins?

GEORGE: What was going on in here, Liz?

LIZ: I told you. I was asleep. Maybe I had a nightmare. That's it. A nightmare - or - it was - a daymare. It's daytime, isn't it?

GEORGE: You better lie down again, dear. Try to get some rest.

LIZ: It's nothing, George. You run along. I'll be all right.

GEORGE: Are you sure? Maybe I better stay home the rest of the day?

LIZ: No. No. I'll be fine. Honestly.

GEORGE: Well -- all right, but I'll come home early. And don't get up. Just rest.

LIZ: All right, honey. Goodbye.

SOUND: (DESK PHONE BUZZER) (CLICK)

KATY: Hello, Mr. Cugat? This is Katy. I just passed Mrs. Cugat's room, and she's acting funny again.

GEORGE: What is she doing, Katy?

KATY: The same thing. She cries a while, and then she laughs a while, and then she barks a while. She's getting pretty good at it.

GEORGE: I'm worried, Katy. I think I'll see a psychiatrist and get some advice on what to do for her.

KATY: Well, I'll keep an eye on her until you get home.

GEORGE: Thanks, Katy. I won't be long.

MUSIC: BRIDGE

GIRL: Dr. Schweinkampf will see you now, Mr. Cugat.

GEORGE: Thank you.

SOUND: DOOR OPENS, CLOSES

SCHWEIN: (VIENNESE DIALECT, WHAT ELSE?) Good afternoon.

GEORGE: Good afternoon, Doctor. My name is Cugat.

SCHWEIN: I see. Lie down, Mr. Cugat.

GEORGE: Oh, it's not for me. It's for someone else.

SCHWEIN: Of course. I understand perfectly. Lie down, Mr. Cugat.

GEORGE: But I'm serious. I came to see you about someone else.

SCHWEIN: Everyone does. Lie down, Mr. Cugat.

GEORGE: (GETTING HIS BACK UP) I won't lie down.

SCHWEIN: (SCOLDING) Xavier!

GEORGE: Look, my name is George Cugat, and I can't even carry a tune. My wife is acting strangely and I want your advice.

SCHWEIN: Certainly, Mr. Cugat.

GEORGE: And I won't lie down.

SCHWEIN: As you wish. Mr. Cugat?

GEORGE: What?

SCHWEIN: Do you mind if I lie down?

GEORGE: No.

SCHWEIN: I've always wondered what it was like. Say, it's nice here. After this I think I'll lie down and let the patient sit up. (CATCHES HIMSELF) Oh, pardon me, Mr. Cougar, what were you saying?

MY FAVORITE HUSBAND -18-

GEORGE: It's Cugat. I want to tell you about my wife. She locks.
            herself in her room.

SCHWEIN: This is very common with married people.

GEORGE: But you don't understand. She laughs, and then she cries,
            and then she barks like a dog.

SCHWEIN: Hmm, that's not quite so common. In fact it sounds like a
            serious case of manic depressive psychosis aggravated by
            alternate canine insanity, prompted by a subconscious
            desire to put on the dog.

GEORGE: That sounds awful.

SCHWEIN: Tell me, Mr. Cugat. Do you have a large income?

GEORGE: I do moderately well. I'm fifth vice president of a bank.

SCHWEIN: Very interesting.

GEORGE: Do you think that has an effect on my wife?

SCHWEIN: No, but it will have an effect on my bill! I'll tell
            you what I want to do, Mr. Cugat. I don't want to alarm
            your wife. I'd like to see her in her home environment.
            Why don't you call her up and tell her you are bringing
            a friend home. A business acquaintance. I'll come over
            this evening -- if you like I'll come to dinner.

GEORGE: You'll come to dinner?

SCHWEIN: Thank you, I'd be glad to come!

GEORGE: All right, Doctor. Anything you say.

MUSIC: BRIDGE

SOUND: TELEPHONE RINGS   PICK UP

MY FAVORITE HUSBAND --19--
10/2/48

LIZ: Hello?

GEORGE: (VERY CONCERNED) Hello, dear. How are you, Honey?

LIZ: I'm fine.

GEORGE: Dear -- I - I'm bringing a friend home for dinner. ~~Will it~~ *an aud earing of them*
be all right?

LIZ: (VERY NICE) Of course, dear. ~~Why didn't you tell me sooner?~~

GEORGE: ~~Well, I -- I just ran into him today. He's -- an old~~
~~college chum.~~

LIZ: (LEADING) Did ~~you meet him at lunch?~~

GEORGE: (GRABBING AT IT) ~~Yes. Yes I did. I met him at lunch.~~

LIZ: What's his name?

GEORGE: ~~His name? Well, his name is~~ *feel for it X* uh, I ~~know it as well as~~ *ait Jones, will see you*
~~my own -- It's~~ uh --. *later, dear*

LIZ: What's ~~your~~ name?

GEORGE: ~~Huh? Oh stop it, Liz. His name is Art Jones.~~

LIZ: ~~That's a tough one to remember.~~

GEORGE: We'll see you later, dear.

LIZ: All right.

SOUND: (HANG UP PHONE)

LIZ: (CALLS) Katy. Oh, I can see his little game. Katy.

KATY: (COMING IN) Yes, Mrs. Cugat?

LIZ: There'll be one extra for dinner, Katy. (CONFIDENTIALLY) My
husband thinks he's going to play a little trick on me.

KATY: He does?

LIZ: *yes* ~~Does he?~~ He's bringing a big Hollywood director home, only he
wants me to think he's somebody else. Then, tomorrow he'll
Lord it over me and say "See, a Hollywood director in your
own home, all to yourself all evening, and you didn't make any
impression" That's what he thinks. No impression, eh? I'm
going to make a <u>dent</u>! X

MUSIC: BRIDGE

GEORGE: Well, here we are, Doctor.

SCHWEIN: One moment before we go in. Don't be nervous, Mr. Nougat.

~~I'm telling you.~~

GEORGE: That's Cugat.

SCHWEIN: It doesn't matter. Now don't worry if she seems to act
normal. I can ~~tell~~ _{diagnose} her condition by subtle little actions
and movements. Don't do anything to arouse her.

GEORGE: All right. Here we go.

SOUND: DOOR OPEN

GEORGE: (OVERSWEET SINGSONG) Liz. Li-i-i-zzz. Oh, there you are.
Liz, I'd like you to meet an old friend of mine -- Uh --
Art Jones.

SCHWEIN: How do you do, Mrs. Cugat.

LIZ: (OVERSEXY, ALMOST MAE WEST) Hulldooo, I'm certainly glad
~~you come up to see me.~~ ~~How about a drink, boys?~~

GEORGE: Now Liz, please ----

SCHWEIN: ~~(SOTTO) Mr. Cugat. I'll handle this.~~

GEORGE: ~~That's what I'm afraid of.~~

LIZ: There's a sofa over there, Mr. Jones. Why don't you get out
of that hard chair and slip into something more comfortable?

GEORGE: Maybe Mr. Jones likes that chair, darling.

LIZ: (SUDDENLY SWITCHING INTO HIGH HYSTERICAL DRAMA) Darling?
Now you call me darling. (DRAMATIC LAUGH) But what am I
when we're alone? Your slave. (STARTS CRYING) You beat me
with a cane and push my poor broken body down the stairs.
Oh, I don't care for myself, but you pushed the children
after me!

GEORGE: The children? I did not.

FAVORITE HUSBAND --21--
10/2/48

LIZ: Then where are they? (BREAKING DOWN) Oh, I can't stand it, putting on this sham in front of your friends. (FADING) I'm leaving, leaving this life of hypocrisy. (HYSTERICAL) Leaving, do you hear? (TRAILS OFF IN LAUGHTER AND TEARS)

GEORGE: (PAUSE) Well, Doctor, what do you think?

SCHWEIN: Don't speak to me, you Cad!

GEORGE: Now wait a minute.

SCHWEIN: I would suggest you come to see me every day, Mr. Cugat. You have a serious condition.

GEORGE: I tell you this is ridiculous. We have no children.

SOUND: DOOR BELL RINGS

GEORGE: She's making this all up -- Wait a minute till I get the door.

SOUND: DOOR OPEN

LIZ: (PATHETIC OLD LADY, BUT OLD) Violets? Will you buy my violets, Sonny? Give a poor old lady a break.

GEORGE: Liz! Take that shawl off your head and come in here.

LIZ: Oh, thank you, sir, I will buy some flowers so I can buy a room and board, I haven't eaten in three weeks. (COUGHS MADLY)

GEORGE: All right, come on in a little.

SCHWEIN: Just a moment. Here you are, Old Lady. Fifty cents. Keep it

LIZ: OH, blessings on you, sir. I knew there was some kindness left in the world. (FADING) Blessings. Blessings.

SOUND: DOOR CLOSE SLIGHTLY OFF

SCHWEIN: I apologise, Mr. Cugat.

GEORGE: Now things sound different, eh?

FAVORITE HUSBAND --22--
10/2/48

SCHWEIN: Yes. You should both come and see me. Now quickly. You
           have a maid?

GEORGE: Yes.

SCHWEIN: Ring for her. We'll find out how your wife has been acting
           around the house today.

GEORGE: I am ringing. I don't know why she doesn't answer. Darn
           this bell, maybe it's broken.

SOUND: DOOR OPEN

LIZ: (COMING IN)(BROAD COCKNEY) All right, All right, I'm
           coming, Guvnor, Don't get 'ot about it.

GEORGE: Oh, no!

~~LIZ: I see we love sommy   low are you, M'lordy; lay about a~~

GEORGE: Liz. Now stop this. It's ridiculous.

LIZ: (COCKNEY) Oh, you don't like me as a cockney, eh? Per'aps
           you'd like me better as a South Sea Island Native?

GEORGE: Liz, get up off the floor. What are you doing?

LIZ: (DEEP SEXY VOICE) Me Tondeleyo!

GEORGE: That does it.

LIZ: Me love white man. You do not like me?

SOUND: DOOR BELL RINGS

GEORGE: Me answer doorbell.

SOUND: DOOR OPENS

COREY: Well, here's Cartwright, a man of his word.

GEORGE: Hello, Corey.

COREY: Where's Liz?

GEORGE: Over there on the floor.

COREY: Oh yes. (LAUGHS SORT OF EMBARRASEDLY) I don't know what you're doing on the floor, Liz -- but let me present this fellow with me. Mrs. George Cugat -- Anatol Brodny.

LIZ: I'm pleased to -- ANATOL BRODNY? (SHRIEKS) Then who's this character?

SCHWEIN: Allow me to present myself, Mrs. Cugat. Rheinhold Schweinkampf, Psychiatrist.

LIZ: Ooooh!

SOUND: BODY FALL

GEORGE: Help me with her, Corey. She's fainted.

MUSIC: BRIDGE

SOUND: (TELEPHONE DIALING - BUZZ ON FILTER)

GEORGE: (FILTER) Hello.

CROFT: Hello, may I speak to Mrs. Cugat, please?

GEORGE: Mrs. Cugat is upstairs resting. This is her husband. May I help you?

CROFT: This is Mrs. Croftsworth, the director of the young Matron's Play. I called to tell Mrs. Cugat that she got the main part. Congratulations, Mr. Cugat.

GEORGE: I think you'd better forget about my wife for that part, Mrs. Croftsworth. After the experience she had tonight she assured me she has given up the theater for good.

CROFT: Oh, that's too bad.

GEORGE: Well, goodbye, Mrs. Croftsworth.

CROFT: Goodbye, Mr. Cugat.

SOUND: PHONE CLICK ON FILTER

LIZ: (FILTER)(WHISPERING LOUDLY) Mrs. Croftsworth. Mrs. Croftsworth.

CROFT: What? Hello?

LIZ: This is Liz Cugat. I've been listening on the telephone
           upstairs in the bedroom.

CROFT: Then you heard what your husband said.

LIZ: Yes, but don't pay any attention to it. I'll see you
           at rehearsal in the morning.

MUSIC: CURTAIN -- APPLAUSE

MY FAVORITE HUSBAND
45 seconds

ALLOCATION

ANNCR: It's easy to take a chance just once. It's easy, when
          you're behind the steering wheel, to tell yourself
          it's okay this one time to cheat the traffic laws
          or safety rules just a little bit. You can talk
          yourself into such a decision in about the time it takes
          to slide past a stop sign .. or the time it takes to
          dash onto a grade crossing with a train approaching --
          or the time it takes to start around another car on a
          hill, or the time it takes to challenge another driver
          for the right-of-way at an intersection. Yes, such
          a decision is a matter of seconds. But says the
          National Safety Council, that is enough time for an
          accident to happen!
          And accidents do have a way of happening that one time
          when you're sure they won't. Sometimes you get by with
          taking a chance. But, sometimes you don't. Drive
          safely, don't gamble with lives.

MUSIC   _____

LIZ: (SLEEPILY) George. Gee-oorrr--ggge.

GEORGE: Me sleeping.

LIZ: Oh George. Wake up and speak to me.

GEORGE: (COCKNEY) I'd like to Lady. But I'm so tired, y'know.

LIZ: Well -- if you won't talk to me -- kiss me.

GEORGE: (OLD MAN) I'm an old man. I don't go in for that kind
of stuff.

LIZ: (OLD LADY) You could kiss an old lady like me. It
wouldn't hurt you none. (NATURAL) Kiss me, George,
speak to me in the language of love.

GEORGE: Allright. C'm here.

LIZ: MMmmmmmmmmMMMMmmmmmmmmMMMMMMMM! (LAZILY) Was that the
language of love, George?

GEORGE: Uh huh.

LIZ: Don't say anything, George, let's just talk!

MUSIC: THEME

          (APPLAUSE)

MY FAVORITE HUSBAND -26-
10/2/48

LEMOND: You have just heard "My Favorite Husband"...starring
LUCILLE BALL with RICHARD DENNING.

Also heard in tonight's cast were JOHN HEISTAND, RUTH
PERROTT, HANS CONREID, BEA BENEDERET AND RUTH RICHABY.

The program was produced and directed by GORDON T. HUGHES.

Script was by Jess Oppenheimer.

Original music was by MARLIN SKILES and was conducted by
WILBUR HATCH.

LUCILLE BALL will soon be seen in the Paramount picture
"Sorrowful Jones."

Stay tuned to CBS for the Camel Caravan with Vaughn
Monroe, a sparkling half hour musical featuring the week's
most popular tunes, as determined by Variety. The vocal
group known as the Moon Maids will assist popular
bandleader and singer, Vaughn Monroe, in presenting this
music you've made a must--on the Camel Caravan, which
follows immediately over most of these CBS stations.

Bob Lemond speaking...

MUSIC: OUT

LEMOND: THIS IS CBS...THE COLUMBIA...BROADCASTING SYSTEM.

Appendix B

The Unperformed *I Love Lucy*

Original, unperformed script for act 2 of *I Love Lucy* #72 ("Lucy Tells the Truth"), written by Jess Oppenheimer, Madelyn Pugh Davis, and Bob Carroll, Jr. This script, discussed in chapter 13, is the only *I Love Lucy* script that Lucy or Desi ever refused to perform.

```
                 I LOVE LUCY - SHOW NO. 72

                 (Lucy Tells the Truth)


                                          Filmed:

                                          Released:

            CAST                             SETS

     LUCY...........Lucille Ball       Ricardo L. R.

     RICKY..........Desi Arnaz         Appleby L. R.

     ETHEL..........Vivian Vance       Ricardo B. R.

     FRED...........William Frawley



     CAROLYN........

     HARRIET........

     MR. MILLER.....

     MAN............

     BABY...........

     MESSENGER......
```

Fade in on Ricardo living room. There are plates, baby cup, napkins, etc., spread all over the coffee table. Fred and Ricky are there. Ricky has the baby in his lap.

RICKY. Come on now, show Uncle Fred how I taught you to wave bye bye.

FRED. *(Waving at the baby.)* Bye bye, Bye bye. *(Ricky waves)*.

RICKY. Bye bye.

FRED. Looks more like he's teaching us how to wave bye bye.

RICKY. Well, he did it this morning. *(To baby.)* Look, old man, you'll have to learn to perform on cue if you want to be my son. *(Note: If the baby waves bye bye or cries, we'll alter the foregoing accordingly.) (The front door opens. Lucy comes in adlibbing hellos and goes right over to the baby and picks him up.)*

LUCY. Hi, honey. Were you a good boy?

RICKY. He was an angel.

FRED. Where's Ethel?

LUCY. She'll be right in. *(To Ricky.)* Did you feed him?

RICKY. I followed your instructions to the letter.

LUCY. *(Surveying the utensils.)* It looks like you fed a whole nursery full of babies. *(She starts out with Little Ricky toward the bedroom.)* Come on, young man. It's time for beddy-bye. *(She exits. Ethel comes in the front door.)*

ETHEL. Hi.

FRED. How was the bridge game?

RICKY. *(Suddenly remembering.)* Oh, yeah. How did we do? Is the bet all over?

ETHEL. Not at all.

RICKY. What?

FRED. *(Simultaneously.)* Not at all?

ETHEL. She didn't tell one fib all afternoon.

RICKY. I don't believe it.

FRED. What did she do—tape her mouth shut?

ETHEL. I wish she had. She not only told the truth, she became brutally frank and told us exactly what she thought of us without our asking. *(Ricky starts to laugh as he gets the picture.)*

RICKY. *(Laughing.)* That must've gone over big.

ETHEL. There was such a chill in the room, I felt like I was being quick frozen.

FRED. *(Laughing.)* Oh, I would've liked to have been there. *(He and Ricky laugh.)*

ETHEL. When you two hyenas are through laughing, you can go and dig up one hundred bucks between you.

RICKY. She can't keep it up.

FRED. Not Lucy. (*Lucy enters.*)

LUCY. What's so funny?

RICKY. Ethel was just telling us what happened when you told the girls the truth.

LUCY. Oh. Everybody got a little miffed but I can't help it. I feel wonderful telling the truth. I should've done it a long time ago.

ETHEL. I don't feel so wonderful finding out you hate to play bridge with me.

LUCY. I wouldn't if you just kept quiet once in a while. (*Fred laughs.*)

ETHEL. Oh, shut up, Fred. You're no rose.

LUCY. I'll say he's not.

ETHEL. Yeah.

LUCY. Why don't you buy Ethel a new dress once in a while?

ETHEL. Yeah.

LUCY. If you weren't such a tightwad she wouldn't go around looking so tacky.

FRED. Tightwad???

ETHEL. Tacky???

FRED. Come on, Ethel. We don't have to stay here and be insulted. (*They start to leave.*)

RICKY. Now wait a minute, Ethel, Fred. I don't blame you for being huffy but remember, after all, we're the ones who forced Lucy to tell the truth.

FRED. Oh sure.

RICKY. Well, now, think it over. Maybe a little truthful criticism is good for us.

ETHEL. That's easy for you to say. She hasn't said anything about you yet. (*Ricky turns to Lucy with a heroic gesture.*)

RICKY. Go ahead, Lucy. Tell me my faults. Tell me what you really think of me.

LUCY. (*Pause.*) I think you're the handsomest, the most wonderful, the cleverest, the most talented man in the whole world. (*Ricky turns to Ethel and Fred.*)

RICKY. You see? The truth didn't hurt me.

ETHEL. Oh brother! (*She starts to turn.*)

LUCY. Wait a minute, Ethel—(*The phone interrupts her. Lucy answers it.*) Hello? This is Mrs. Ricardo . . . I see. . . . (*She looks at Ricky.*) Well, he has to be at the club at 9:30 . . .

RICKY. Who is it?

LUCY. . . . Tomorrow evening? Yes, that'll be fine.

RICKY. Who is it? (*He tries to take the phone away from her. She holds on to it tightly as she finishes.*)

LUCY. . . . All right, see you then. Goodbye, Mr. Miller. (*She hangs up.*)

RICKY. Who was it? That was for me, wasn't it?

LUCY. Mr. Miller. He wants to see us tomorrow night and go over a few things.

RICKY. What kind of things? Who is he with?

LUCY. The Bureau of Internal Revenue.

RICKY. What???

LUCY. Is something wrong, dear? He just wants to ask us a few questions about the income tax return.

RICKY. Well, I can't be—(*Take*) Us???

LUCY. Yes.

FRED. What do you think about telling the truth now, Ricky? (*Laughs.*)

ETHEL. (*Laughing.*) Yeah.

RICKY. Look, Lucy, there's no reason for you to be here tomorrow night. It'll be awfully boring. Why don't you go to a movie with Ethel and Fred?

LUCY. No, I want to stay here and help you.

FRED. Yeah, let her stay. She'll be a big help.

RICKY. Look, honey, I'll tell you what. You go to the movies and we'll just forget all about that bet and I'll give you the hundred dollars.

LUCY. Why, Ricky Ricardo, are you trying to bribe me?

ETHEL. For shame! (*Fred makes a "shame on you" gesture, rubbing one finger on the other.*)

RICKY. Look, I'm not trying to bribe you. I've got nothing to hide. It's just that—I don't have receipts for everything and I sort of guessed at the amounts and if you told him a different amount, then I would—

LUCY. Now I really have to stay. Maybe I can remember some of the amounts that you've forgotten. After all, when you're dealing with the United States Government you don't tell anything but the absolute truth.

RICKY. (*A little sick.*) Yes, dear.

FRED. Well, let us know how you make out, Ricky.

ETHEL. Yeah. And no matter what happens, you can count on us. Tightwad and Tacky will come up to see you every visiting day. (*Fade out.*)

Fade in Ricardo bedroom. Lucy is having a little trouble fixing her hair. Ricky is pacing up and down nervously. The door bell rings. Ricky jumps.

LUCY. That must be the Income Tax man. Get it, Ricky. I just can't get my hair right tonight.

RICKY. All right. (*He starts out and then looks back in.*) Take as long as you want with your hair, honey. It looks awful now. You fix it. (*He leaves.*)

We see Ricky coming into the living room and opening the front door. A man, who looks like he is from the Income Tax Bureau, is standing there.

MILLER. Mr. Ricardo?

RICKY. Yes?

MILLER. I'm Mr. Miller.

RICKY. (*Jumping in.*) From the Income Tax Department.

MILLER. That's right. I'm not too early, am I?

RICKY. No—no. (*Ricky gives an apprehensive glance toward the bedroom. Quickly.*) What do you want to know?

MILLER. Could we sit down?

RICKY. Oh, sure, sure. (*Ricky takes him by the arm, leads him over by the couch and sits him and takes his brief case and tries to get him to open it.*)

MILLER. Would you mind if I take off my hat and coat?

RICKY. Will it take that long?

MILLER. (*Taking off his hat and coat.*) No, it's not very complicated. (*Ricky lights a cigarette nervously. Miller, very deliberately, opens the brief case, takes out some papers, looks at each one to identify it and lines it up on the coffee table.*)

RICKY. (*As Miller is doing this.*) Anything special? Nothing wrong, is there? (*Nervous laugh.*)

MILLER. And, now, I guess we can get started. (*As he says this, Lucy enters from the bedroom.*)

RICKY. Too late.

MILLER. What?

RICKY. Nothing. Mr. Miller, this is my wife. Mr. Miller is from the Income Tax Department.

LUCY. Oh yes.

RICKY. We won't need her, will we, Mr. Miller? (*He shakes his head no.*)

MILLER. I always like to have the wife around. Sometimes it helps to establish things.

RICKY. Yeah. (*Lucy sits on the arm of the sofa on one side of Mr. Miller and on the opposite side from Ricky.*) Well, let's get it over with.

MILLER. Relax, Mr. Ricardo. This is just routine. Now, here's an item we'd like to know a little more about. Entertainment. You claimed— *(looks at the paper)* $1,500.

LUCY. *(Whistles at how large an amount it is. Ricky gives Lucy a withering look.)*

RICKY. Now, I've got my receipts here. *(He goes over to the desk and takes a bill file and pulls out a piece of paper.)* Here's a statement from the Tropicana Club where I work. You know I'm entertaining people, buying drinks and things every night of the week.

LUCY. Except Monday.

MILLER. *(Looking at the paper.)* $900. Well, that's fine as far as it goes. What about the rest of it? *(Ricky thinks a minute.)*

RICKY. Oh, I know—

LUCY. *(Still part of the same thought from her last sentence.)* We never go anywhere on Monday night. *(Ricky deflates a little.)*

MILLER. What were you going to say, Mr. Ricardo?

RICKY. Nothing. She got there first. *(He is frantically going through the papers and pulls out another one.)* Oh, here. Here's one for a press party I gave. $110.

MILLER. *(Writing it down.)* Well, that leaves an unsubstantiated amount we'll have to charge you for. Now, here's another item—a business wardrobe.

RICKY. *(Very defensively.)* Well, you know I'm an entertainer. That's one of the main things, the way we look up on the band stand. I have to buy a lot of clothes and they have to be the very best—

MILLER. *(Calming him down.)* It's all right, Mr. Ricardo. We understand these things perfectly. We just like to substantiate.

LUCY. You don't have to worry about that. We have a lot of arguments about the amount of money he spends for clothes. It's more than I do. That's one amount I know by heart.

MILLER. Well, that's good. *(He consults the sheet again.)* Twelve hundred dollars.

LUCY. *(Disbelief.)* Twelve hundred dollars???

RICKY. Well, there are four suits of clothes in there. *(Lucy counts on her fingers.)*

LUCY. That's right. Four suits.

RICKY. At $200 apiece.

MILLER. Two hundred apiece. *(He looks at Lucy. She shakes her head "no.")*

RICKY. Oh, I guess I forgot. They were $200 suits but they were on sale and he let me have them for $175.00 (*Miller looks at Lucy and she shakes her head "no" again.*) (*Very phony.*) Those weren't the ones where I got all four at once and he let me have them for—of course, those were the ones. What got into me? $150.

MILLER. Well, I'm glad you remembered. (*Jotting something down.*) It's funny how these things sometimes slip our minds. (*Laughs. Ricky laughs with him but fades off into an "I'd like to kill Lucy" finish.*) Well, I guess that's all we had to disc—— Oh, there's one little thing here—that business trip to Louisville, Kentucky.

RICKY. Now, that you don't have to worry about. (*Going through his bill file.*) We played a weekend date at the _____ Theater.

MILLER. And stayed a whole week?

RICKY. Well, you know, getting set up. We never had played that theater before. You know how it is.

MILLER. Well, I guess so. What were those dates again?

RICKY. (*Thinking.*) Uh—it's easy to check. That was the week they were running the Kentucky Derby.

MILLER. Oh.

RICKY. Now look, I know what you're thinking but it's not true. That was a legitimate date. Not only that, but I was on a percentage and it rained and nobody came to the show and I ended up in the red.

LUCY. He's right.

RICKY. (*Pointing to Lucy.*) There.

LUCY. I remember distinctly. If we hadn't been hot at the race track, we would've lost money! (*Miller looks over the sheet.*)

MILLER. I—don't—see any—race track winnings declared here, Mr. Ricardo.

RICKY. Oh, are you supposed to put that down? I thought on account of all the money you lose, the money you won was ha ha, tax free.

MILLER. I'm afraid, ha ha, not. What was the amount?

RICKY. Ask Miss Big Mouth there. She knows everything.

LUCY. It was $562. (*Happily.*) Remember the daily double?

MILLER. (*Starting to put his things away.*) Well, I think that takes care of everything. I'll take this back to the office and we'll let you know how much you owe us, Mr. Ricardo.

RICKY. Yeah, do that.

MILLER. Well, thank you very much for being so cooperative, both of you. Goodnight. (*He leaves. Ricky closes the door and turns on Lucy with homicide in his eye. Lucy's attitude is directly the opposite from what you'd expect it to be. She is laughing. Ricky advances menacingly.)*

RICKY. Go ahead, laugh. It may be your last. *(She doesn't back up or look scared. She just smiles cutely.)* What's so funny?

LUCY. Oh, Ricky, you don't think I'd really do a thing like that, do you?

RICKY. What do you mean?

LUCY. That man wasn't from the Income Tax Department. He was— *(Notices the time)* Oops, it's 8 o'clock! *(She holds out her hand.)* Pay me my bet. One hundred bucks, please.

RICKY. What? Have you gone crazy?

LUCY. I'll explain while you're making out a check for me. Go ahead. *(Ricky goes to the desk, takes out a check book and starts writing.)* I wanted to prove that you lied sometimes too. So I went down to the Actor's Guild, gave them a copy of your Income Tax and had them send an actor out to pretend he was the Income Tax man.

RICKY. *(Already finished writing the check.)* You mean he was an—?

LUCY. Yes. *(They both laugh.)*

LUCY. He knew he had to get out by 8 o'clock because the real Mr. Miller is due.

RICKY. Boy, he was a good actor. I'll have to use him sometime.

LUCY. Yeah. Give me my check.

RICKY. Okay. *(He starts to give it to her and pulls it away.)* Wait a minute. You weren't telling the truth when you said he was from the Income Tax Bureau.

LUCY. I didn't say it. You did.

RICKY. *(Thinks it over.)* Well, all right. *(He hands her the check. The door bell rings.)*

LUCY. There's your Income Tax man now, dear, and I'm going to leave you strictly alone and you can tell him anything you want to. *(Ricky opens the door. A man is standing there.)*

MAN. Mr. Ricardo? I'm Mr. Miller from the Income Tax Department.

RICKY. *(Overly warm.)* Well, come right in, Mr. Miller. We've been expecting you. I'd like you to meet my wife.

MAN. How do you do, Mrs. Ricardo? *(He gives her a great big obvious wink. Lucy does a tremendous take.)*

LUCY. What was the wink for?

RICKY. Wink?

LUCY. You're from the Bureau of Internal Revenue, aren't you?

MAN. No, I'm the Income Tax man.

RICKY. *(Under his breath.)* Oh no! *(Accusingly to the man.)* Have you ever heard of the Actor's Guild?

MAN. *(To Lucy—snapping his fingers.)* Darn it, he knows. Gee, I'm sorry. I would've gotten here sooner but they gave me the wrong address.

LUCY. *(Spider.)* Ooooooooh. *(She tears up the check as we fade out.)*

Appendix C

"The Freezer"

Script for *I Love Lucy* #29 ("The Freezer"), written by Jess Oppenheimer, Madelyn Pugh Davis, and Bob Carroll, Jr. First broadcast April 28, 1952, on the CBS Television Network. The writing of this script is discussed in chapter 14. Track 12 on the included CD is a portion of the sound track of this episode.

```
        I LOVE LUCY - Show No. 29

              THE FREEZER


                              Filmed: March 21, 1952
                              Air:  April 28, 1952



                        CAST

        LUCY . . . . . . . . . . . . . Lucille Ball

        RICKY . . . . . . . . . . . . Desi Arnaz

        ETHEL . . . . . . . . . . . . Vivian Vance

        FRED . . . . . . . . . . . . William Frawley
                        and
        1ST DELIVERY MAN . . . . . . Frank Sully
        2ND DELIVERY MAN . . . . . . Bennett Green
        3RD DELIVERY MAN . . . . . . Joaquin Escaruga
        BUTCHER . . . . . . . . . .
        1ST WOMAN . . . . . . . . . Kay Wiley
        2ND WOMAN . . . . . . . . . Barbara Pepper
```

We open in the Ricardo kitchen. It is morning and Ricky is seated at the counter reading the paper and drinking orange juice. Lucy is just finishing frying some eggs and she slides them off the pan on to a plate and sets it in front of Ricky.

LUCY. Here you are, dear. (*She sits down next to him and starts drinking her orange juice. Ricky picks up a fork and starts to cut the eggs and does a take as he sees the plate.*)

RICKY. What's the matter, Lucy? Just two eggs?

LUCY. You never eat more than two eggs.

RICKY. I know but where is the bacon?

LUCY. Bacon happens to be 75¢ a pound.

RICKY. Lucy, where is the bacon?

LUCY. As far as I'm concerned, it's still on the hog.

RICKY. But I can't eat eggs like this. They—they're absolutely naked.

LUCY. Well, look the other way when you eat them.

RICKY. Come on now, honey, what is this? (*Lucy pops a piece of toast out of the toaster and starts buttering it.*)

LUCY. I'm economizing.

RICKY. Well, that's a good attitude. I know meat is expensive but why do you have to cut down on food? I need my strength.

LUCY. Where else can we cut down? We have to pay the rent, lights, gas, water, phone—

RICKY. That's true.

LUCY. Of course, we could always cut off the phone and learn to send messages on your conga drum.

RICKY. Now this is nothing to kid about. (*Starts thinking.*) There must be someplace we can cut down.

LUCY. I've thought it all out and there's no other place. The discussion is closed. Now, go ahead and eat your breakfast.

RICKY. Wait a minute—what about the money you spend each month on clothes and the beauty parlor?

LUCY. I said the discussion was closed now. Eat your breakfast. (*Ricky gives her a look.*)

RICKY. Well, I'm opening it again.

LUCY. (*Huffily.*) Well! If you want to make your own rules—!

RICKY. If you would cut down on hairdressing and the new clothes, we could afford meat once in a while.

LUCY. Well, okay, if you think you'd like steaks served by an ugly brunette wearing a flour sack.

RICKY. You're exaggerating.

LUCY. I'm not exaggerating. There's a lot better way to save money and still have meat.

RICKY. How? (*Lucy takes up a piece of the paper which is already folded and shows it to him.*)

LUCY. Right here, see? (*Reads.*) Save money with a home freezer. Get your meat wholesale.

RICKY. I might have known there was something in back of this.

LUCY. But it won't cost us a cent, Ricky. It says right here. (*Reads.*) This freezer pays for itself.

RICKY. Good! We'll get one.

LUCY. Really?

RICKY. Absolutely. As soon as it gets through paying for itself, tell it to give us a call and come on over.

LUCY. You know what I meant.

RICKY. Well, it's out of the question. I can't afford a freezer right now, even one that pays for itself.

LUCY. Well, what are we going to do?

RICKY. We're going to take the meat money out of your clothes budget.

LUCY. But, Ricky—

RICKY. You'll be able to figure it out some way, dear. I'll see you later. (*He kisses her.*) Goodbye.

LUCY. (*Sadly.*) Goodbye. (*Ricky leaves. Lucy sits there a second then reaches over and pulls the plate of eggs in front of her. Looking at the eggs.*) It's all your fault. This wouldn't have happened if you hadn't been sitting there with your big fat yolks showing! (*She sits there with her head disgustedly cupped in her hands. The back door opens and Ethel comes in.*)

ETHEL. (*Brightly.*) Good morning! (*She walks bouncily up to the counter as she talks.*)

LUCY. (*Mad.*) Oh yeah? Since when? (*Ethel turns without missing a step and goes back to the door.*)

ETHEL. (*Same gay tone.*) Goodbye.

LUCY. No, come back.

ETHEL. (*At the door.*) If I wanted to be with someone grumpy, I'd have stayed downstairs with Fred. He's mad because the furnace is on the blink.

LUCY. I'm sorry, Ethel. (*Ethel comes back in.*) I just had a very discouraging session with Ricky. He wants me to spend more money on meat.

ETHEL. That doesn't sound like Ricky.

LUCY. —and less money on clothes.

ETHEL. That sounds like Ricky.

LUCY. I tried to talk him into buying a home freezer but he said he couldn't afford it. (*Fred enters. He is a little smudged as though he had just been inspecting the furnace.*)

ETHEL. I asked Fred to buy us a home freezer too.

LUCY. What did he say?

FRED. I'll tell you what I said. I said you could take your—(*Ethel puts her hand over his mouth.*)

ETHEL. Please, there are ladies present.

FRED. I just came up to tell you don't try to turn the heat on today. I have to put all new fire brick in the inside of the furnace and we won't have any heat until the cement is dry. This whole house may be a home freezer by tonight. (*He leaves. Lucy starts taking the dishes off the counter and putting them in the sink. She takes the paper and puts it on the louver ledge.*)

LUCY. Why do men always act like men. Gee, it wouldn't cost them anything to buy a freezer and we could buy our meat wholesale and always have it when we wanted it.

ETHEL. Yeah. (*Lucy picks up a cup of coffee and starts to drink it. Ethel gets a sudden exciting thought and pounds Lucy on the shoulder as she talks, making Lucy spill her coffee.*) I've got it—I've got it!

LUCY. Well, you don't have to drop it in my coffee.

ETHEL. You don't understand. I've got an Uncle Oscar.

LUCY. Yeah.

ETHEL. He's a butcher and he's got a big cold chest.

LUCY. Well, why doesn't he wear a sweater? (*Ethel gives Lucy a look.*)

ETHEL. Well, if you don't want to hear this—

LUCY. I do—I do.

ETHEL. Well—he's retiring from the butcher business—

LUCY. And he's having a remnant sale.

ETHEL. Okay, Lucy, see you around. (*She gets up to go. Lucy pulls her back.*)

LUCY. Tell me, Ethel, I'll be quiet. (*Ethel looks at her doubtingly. Lucy picks up a doughnut and sticks it in her mouth.*)

ETHEL. Well, my Uncle Oscar has this old freezing chest—you know, the kind you walk into and hang up the meat. (*Lucy nods her head.*) He'll sell it for practically nothing. If we could buy it and keep it in the basement, we would have a real home freezer.

LUCY. (*With a mouthful of doughnut.*) That sounds wonderful.

ETHEL. I'll call him right now. (*They both get up and go into the living room.*)

Living Room.

LUCY. (*As they walk and as Ethel is dialing.*) Oh, that's just a great idea. I wonder how much he'll sell it for?

ETHEL. (*Into phone.*) Hello . . . Uncle Oscar? This is Ethel . . . fine. Say, Unc, how much do you want for that big old freezer of yours?—For me. —Well, that sounds like a fair price. (*To Lucy.*) He'll give it to us for nothing.

LUCY. What?

ETHEL. All we have to do is pay for the hauling and installation.

LUCY. (*Excited.*) No!

ETHEL. It'll be about $50.

LUCY. Sold.

ETHEL. (*Into phone.*) We'll take it. When can we have it installed? This afternoon?—Oh, that'll be wonderful. Goodbye, Uncle Oscar. (*She hangs up.*) Lucy, we now own a freezer. (*They shake hands.*)

LUCY. Well, let's get started. (*She picks up the paper from the louver ledge, finds the ad she showed to Ricky and starts dialing.*)

ETHEL. What are you doing?

LUCY. Ordering meat! The sooner we get the meat in the freezer the sooner we start saving money.

ETHEL. Wonder how much we ought to get?

LUCY. Twenty or 25 pounds—maybe 30.

ETHEL. Gee, that sounds like a lot of meat.

LUCY. (*Into phone.*) Hello? . . . This is Mrs. Ricardo at 623 East 68th Street. I would like to order some meat for our freezer . . . beef . . . I see. (*To Ethel.*) Ethel, it's only 69¢ a pound.

ETHEL. Why, filet is $1.89.

LUCY. I'd better order before he realizes what a bargain he's giving us. (*Into phone.*) Oh, that'll be fine. Oh—by the side? . . . Well, just a minute. (*To Ethel.*) That's the price by the side. How big is a side of beef?

ETHEL. Well, a side of bacon is about this big. (*She holds her hands up about two feet apart.*)

LUCY. Oh, that's okay! (*Into phone.*) We'll take a side. Two sides. (*To Ethel.*) One for each of us. (*Into phone.*) Can you deliver it this afternoon? . . . Fine . . . Goodbye. (*She hangs up.*) In the meantime, we'll go downtown.

ETHEL. What for?

LUCY. With all the money we're going to save on that meat, we can afford to buy ourselves some new dresses. (*They leave as we fade out.*)

Fade in on the Ricardo living room. As the front door opens Lucy and Ethel, wearing coats and carrying suit boxes, enter. They are gay.

LUCY. I can hardly wait to try my dress on.

ETHEL. Neither can I. I'll go down to my apartment and—(*We hear a knocking on the back door.*)

LUCY. Someone is at the back door. (*Getting the thought.*) Oh, it must be the meat. Come on. (*They go through the swinging door into the kitchen.*)

The girls come into the kitchen and Lucy goes over and opens the back door. A deliveryman is standing there. He steps in with two armloads of packaged cuts of meat.

DM. Johnson's Meat Company. Did you order this?

LUCY. Yes, we did. Put it on the counter, please. (*He deposits the meat on the counter, turns and starts for the door.*) Gee, it's sure a lot, isn't it?

DM. Oh, there's more. (*About this time, a second man comes in with a similar armload of meat. The deliveryman indicates where to put it and he deposits it on the counter.*)

LUCY. My goodness, that—(*A third man comes in with a similar load of meat and the second man leaves. The girls watch wide-eyed as the third man adds to the pile of meat on the counter and leaves.*)

LUCY. Wait a minute—are you sure this is all for us?

DM. This is only the beginning, lady. (*He also leaves.*)

LUCY. A side of beef couldn't be this big.

ETHEL. I'll bet there's been a mistake.

LUCY. Yeah, this must be a side of elephant. (*The second man reenters with a load of meat, followed by the third man. Lucy runs over and slams the back door. The deliveryman comes up and tries to get in. Both his arms are full and he sort of knees the door.*) Ethel, what've we gotten into? What is all this going to cost?

THIRD MAN. (*Pointing to the deliveryman outside the door.*) He's got the bill. (*Lucy opens the door. The deliveryman comes in.*) You got the bill, Joe? (*The deliveryman unloads his arms, takes out a bill and hands it to Lucy.*)

LUCY. Ethel, we're getting 700 pounds of meat.

ETHEL. (*Weakly.*) At 69¢ a pound—

LUCY. It's $483! Oh, this is ridiculous. (*To the deliveryman.*) Look, there's been a mistake. You'll have to take most of this meat back.

ETHEL. Yes, all but 30 pounds.

DM. Sorry, lady, once a side of beef has been cut, we can't take it back.

LUCY. Come on, Ethel, we've got to get busy. (*She opens a drawer and takes out a bottle of ordinary paper glue.*)

ETHEL. What are we going to do?

LUCY. We're going to paste this beast back together again. (*She picks up several pieces of meat and tries to fit them together like a jigsaw puzzle.*) Come on, Ethel, look for a piece that fits this.

DM. Look, lady, if you pasted it together and taught it to walk, I couldn't take it back. My orders are to deliver the meat here. (*Lucy and Ethel look at each other helplessly. The deliveryman surveys the laden counter.*) Well, that's one side—let's go down and get the other one. (*Lucy and Ethel practically collapse as the three men march out.*)

ETHEL. Oh, my goodness, Lucy, what are we going to do?

LUCY. Ricky and Fred will kill us.

ETHEL. Of course at the regular prices we've saved our husbands almost $500.

LUCY. I hope you can explain it to them before their hands tighten around our throats.

ETHEL. Do you suppose we could sell some of it?

LUCY. To whom?

ETHEL. How about the butcher down at the corner?

LUCY. He gets it cheaper than this. (*Gets a sudden thought.*) But what about the customers?

ETHEL. Customers?

LUCY. We could go someplace where we're not known and get the customers before they buy from the butcher. We could sell them meat for 79¢ a pound.

ETHEL. Sixty-nine.

LUCY. Well, we might as well make a little something on it.

ETHEL. Oh no, Lucy, we can't sell it like that. It wouldn't be right. It wouldn't be fair. It wouldn't be—(*The door opens and the three men come in with their arms loaded. Ethel takes one look.*) You win, Lucy. On to the butcher shop. (*We fade out.*)

Middle Commercial

Fade in on the butcher shop. The counter is in sight and the butcher is in back of it. Four or five people (we can use the three deliverymen) are standing in line. Ethel and Lucy enter looking furtively around. Ethel is pushing a baby carriage which has the hood pulled down. Lucy stops her.

ETHEL. Hey, my foot is all wet. (*She lifts her foot and shakes it.*) Are you sure you haven't got a baby in here?

LUCY. The ice must be melting. Now be quiet. (*To the last woman in* line.) Psst—psst. (*The woman looks around.*) (*Pitch man voice.*) Comere! (*The woman looks over to Lucy.*) Are you looking for meat?

WOMAN. Yes.

LUCY. Tellya what I'm gonna do. Step in a little closer. I don't want to block the traffic. (*She takes the woman and pulls her closer.*) Now, whatcha lookin fer? Sirloin, New York, filet, chuck, chops, round, rump or ribs, you name it, we got it.

WOMAN. Well, I don't understand—

LUCY. We got a special on porterhouse steak today—79¢ a pound.

WOMAN. No, really, I—(*She starts to turn away and does a take*) seventy-nine cents?

ETHEL. Get them while they last. (*She reaches in and takes out a package and hands it to the woman.*)

WOMAN. How many pounds is this? (*Lucy reaches into the carriage, pulls out a bathroom scale, sets on the floor and squats to see the weight.*)

LUCY. Three pounds.

WOMAN. I'll take it.

LUCY. Take care of the little lady, Ethel. (*Lucy turns to the next woman at the end of the line.*)

LUCY. Psst—psst. Comere. (*The lady walks over.*) (*Pitchman.*) Are you looking for some meat—you're tired of paying high prices—you want a bargain—tellya what I'm gonna do. (*The first woman taps Lucy on the shoulder. Lucy looks at her.*)

WOMAN. Is this choice meat?

LUCY. Absolutely. Give the lady her choice, Ethel. Any one she wants. (*Lucy turns back to the second customer.*)

WOMAN. But you don't understand. (*Lucy kicks her sort of upwards.*)

LUCY. Get away, kid, you bother me. (*To second woman.*) I got any cut you want at 79¢ a pound.

2 WOMAN. How can you afford to sell it so cheap?

LUCY. An excellent question. It's simple. We do all our own roping, branding, butchering and marketing.

ETHEL. You tell 'em, Tex.

2 WOMAN. Well, I'll take a couple of filets—

LUCY. All right.

2 WOMAN. A couple of T-bones—

LUCY. Yes ma'am.

2 WOMAN. And a rib roast. (*While this is going on the butcher has sighted them and has walked around to this side of the counter and is coming toward them. Lucy sees him. She slams down the hood of the carriage, pushes the woman gently away.*)

LUCY. Sorry, madam, we're closing temporarily. Watch the paper for our new location. Start the carriage, Ethel. (*They run out of the scene.*)

BUTCHER. (*Calling after them.*) Hey, come back here. Hey—(*We fade out.*)

Fade in on the basement of the Mertzes' apartment house. We see the furnace, a pretty good size one, with lots of pipes leading upwards from it. (With future shows in mind, this should be designed so the fellows can disconnect the pipes from whatever apartment they want to listen in to). We also see the freezer, the walk-in type used in butcher shops which has the upper half of the door in glass. A chair is propping the door of the freezer open. Lucy staggers on to the scene with an armload of meat, opens the freezer door a little further with her elbow, leaving the chair to keep the door from closing. As she disappears Ethel comes in staggering under an armload of meat. As she approaches the freezer, Lucy comes out empty-handed.

ETHEL. This is the last. (*Lucy holds the door further open for Ethel to enter.*)

LUCY. Thank goodness. Boy, 700 pounds is a lot of meat to carry. (*Ethel disappears in the freezer and Lucy pulls the chair out and wearily sits down on it. The door closes. We see Ethel trying to open the door. She bangs on it but we don't hear anything. Lucy sees her and gets up and opens the door by turning the key, which is already in the lock.*)

ETHEL. It gets cold in a hurry in there.

LUCY. Yeah. (*She takes the key out of the lock and puts it in her pocket.*)

LUCY. You know, this is dangerous not being able to open it from the inside. We'd better have the lock taken off tomorrow.

ETHEL. Good idea. Well, we did it. It's all in there.

LUCY. (*Smiling.*) Yes. (*Serious.*) What are we laughing for? We still have to explain all that meat to Ricky and Fred.

ETHEL. Yeah. (*Ethel pulls up a little packing box and sits down. Lucy is on the chair. They both sit there thinking.*)

LUCY. You don't suppose they'd believe that a cow wandered in here and fell apart?

ETHEL. No.

LUCY. I guess not. (*They both continue to think. We hear the muffled voices of Ricky and Fred ad libbing something about wondering where the girls are.*)

RICKY & FRED. (*Ad libbing.*)

LUCY. What's that?

ETHEL. It's Ricky and Fred.

LUCY. They're coming down here.

ETHEL. No—they're not. (*She points to the furnace.*) They're up in the apartment. We can hear them through the furnace pipe. (*Ethel goes to the furnace and reaches for the door.*)

LUCY. Look out—it's hot. (*Ethel opens the door.*)

ETHEL. Don't you remember—Fred cleaned it all out. (*Ethel sticks her head in the furnace.*)

LUCY. Oh, yeah. What's Ricky doing home already? (*Ethel pulls her head out.*)

ETHEL. They're looking for us! What are we going to tell them?

LUCY. I don't know but we can't let them find us here. Come on. (*She takes Ethel's hand rushing off scene almost snapping Ethel's head off and we fade out.*)

Fade in on the living room. The front door is open. Ricky is reading a paper. Fred comes in the front door closing it after him.

FRED. They're not in my apartment either.

RICKY. Well, wherever they are, they'll be back soon and we can tell them about our surprise. (*The door to the kitchen opens and Ethel and Lucy come in.*)

LUCY. (*Mock surprise.*) Well! Ethel! Look who's here.

ETHEL. (*Like greeting a long lost relative.*) Ricky and Fred! (*Ricky and Fred get up—they have something on their minds.*)

RICKY. Lucy—Ethel—we want to talk to you.

LUCY. (*Almost backing away.*) What about?

FRED. I ran into Uncle Oscar today—

LUCY. Start packing, Ethel.

RICKY. Now wait a minute—we're not mad. We think it's a great idea you got that freezer from him.

FRED. That was a real smart business deal.

LUCY. (*A complete reversal.*) Yeah, how about that?

FRED. In fact, we thought you had done so well getting the freezer that we want to do our share too.

RICKY. (*Getting around in back of the sofa.*) So, we're going to start things off—(*He holds up a large package.*) With 30 pounds of meat!

ETHEL. Gee, swell.

LUCY. Keen.

RICKY. Did you ever see so much meat?

LUCY. No—boy, it's sure a lot, isn't it, Ethel? Heh-heh.

FRED. Well, let's go down and put the meat in the freezer.

RICKY. Yeah, we're anxious to see it. (*They start toward the door.*)

LUCY. No, wait. (*They stop.*) As long as we're going down I bought a couple of steaks I want to put in too. We can do it all on one trip. Come on, Ethel, help me. (*They go into the kitchen.*)

In kitchen.

LUCY. (*Frantic whisper.*) Look, you stall them while I go get that meat out of the freezer.

ETHEL. How can I stall them?

LUCY. Listen, if I can hide 700 pounds of meat, you can keep two husbands occupied for a couple of minutes.

ETHEL. Well—

LUCY. Talk to them, dance with them, get them to sing. That's it—ask Ricky to sing.

ETHEL. Sing? Oh, he won't do it.

LUCY. Won't he? You go take care of the ham while I take care of the beef.

ETHEL. Good luck. (*Lucy leaves and Ethel goes back into the living room.*)

Living room.

FRED. What's the delay?

RICKY. Where's Lucy?

ETHEL. Well—I'll tell you, fellows—the freezer is a little dirty and Lucy went down to clean it up before you see it.

RICKY. What do we care what it looks like. We understand.

FRED. Yeah. Come on.

ETHEL. Wait a minute. You know, Ricky, I don't think there's anyone in the world who sings as well as you do. Would you sing a song for me?

FRED. Sing? Now?

ETHEL. Yes.

FRED. What's the matter? Are you crazy? We got a new freezer to look at and we got to put this meat away.

RICKY. Now, just a minute, Fred. If Ethel wants to hear me sing that bad, it would be a shame to deprive her of it.

FRED. Oh no! (*Ricky goes and picks up his guitar.*)

RICKY. What would you like to hear, Ethel?

ETHEL. Anything with a lot of choruses. (*Ricky starts to sing something as we fade out.*)

Fade in on the basement. Lucy comes running into the scene up to the freezer and tries to pull the door open. Then she remembers the lock, takes the key out of her pocket and unlocks the door, pulls the chair up to prop it open and goes inside. She comes out with an armload of meat, looks frantically around for someplace to hide it. There doesn't seem to be anyplace till her eyes light on the furnace. She goes over, opens the furnace door, looks in, satisfied that it is clean enough, drops the meat in, goes back into the freezer, comes out again with more meat, puts it in the furnace, starts back into the freezer, as we fade out.

Fade in on the Ricardo living room. Ricky is just finishing a song. Ethel applauds in an overboard manner.

ETHEL. Bravo—bravo! Sing another one, Ricky. Isn't he *great,* Fred?

FRED. Yeah.

RICKY. What would you like to hear now?

FRED. How about that catchy number "Let's Vamoose to El Freezo"?

RICKY. Now, here's one you'd like, Ethel. (*He starts another number as we fade out.*)

Fade in on the basement. Lucy is staggering out of the freezer with a load of meat. She is dog-tired, her knees will hardly hold her up. She staggers over to the furnace and tries to put the meat in. The furnace is full and she has a hard time pushing and shoving to get the meat in. She staggers back to the freezer. She has trouble getting around the chair, trips over it, stumbles into the freezer knocking the chair either in with her or back away from the door. The door swings closed. Lucy recovers her balance and makes a desperate lunge for it but she is just too late. We see her banging on the door and yelling help but we cannot hear anything. She places her face up against the glass and tries to look from one side to the other to see if anyone is around, then she starts to act cold by first shivering a little, then slapping her arms against her sides, then she starts walking from one side of the door to the other. As she does this, we hear voices of Fred, Ethel and Ricky approaching. Just as they enter, Lucy starts walking the long way of the freezer, that is, directly away from the door, and she disappears. Ricky, Fred and Ethel come in and inspect the freezer.

RICKY. Hey, this is all right.

FRED. Yeah, big and roomy. I'll bet you could get a whole side of beef in there. (*Ricky has gone toward the door to peer in but this remark turns him around*)

RICKY. Are you kidding?—You could get 10 sides of beef in here. (*As he is saying this, Lucy comes back into view and stands with her face right opposite Ricky's. Now Ricky turns back to look in. Screams.*)

ETHEL. Lucy!

RICKY. *(To Lucy.)* That's not very funny, Lucy. Come out of there. *(Lucy makes a gesture asking him to open the door. He tries to.)*

ETHEL. Good heavens, she's locked in.

RICKY. Well, where's the key to this thing? Where's the key?

ETHEL. *(To Lucy.)* Where's the key? The key? *(She pantomimes the motion of unlocking. Lucy looks stricken, looks in her pocket and pitifully holds up the key.)*

FRED. *(As though to solve everything.)* There it is! *(Ricky gives him a look.)* *(Realizing.)* Oh, let me try some skeleton keys on it. *(He takes a bunch of keys out of his pocket, tries several. Lucy watches him closely by putting her face flat on the glass.)* Nope, no go. *(He steps back. Lucy starts to cry.)*

RICKY. *(Calling.)* Honey, don't cry. *(Lucy takes a handkerchief, dabs her eyes, looks amazed and breaks something off her cheek. Holds up an icicle which has been concealed in the handkerchief.)*

ETHEL. Her tears are freezing.

FRED. I'll go get some tools. *(He rushes off scene. Lucy starts jumping up and down and slapping her arms.)*

RICKY. She'll use up all the oxygen in there.

ETHEL. Oxygen?

RICKY. Yes. *(To Lucy, forming the words carefully.)* Don't jump around, Lucy. Save your strength. Lie down. *(Lucy looks puzzled.)* Lie down. *(He pantomimes to her to lie down by lying down on the floor himself. Lucy doesn't quite know why but she lies down dropping out of sight from the glass door. Fred comes rushing in with a crowbar and starts trying to jimmy the door.)*

FRED. This ought to get it.

RICKY. Hurry up.

ETHEL. Oh, poor Lucy.

RICKY. How is it coming?

FRED. It's starting to give a little. *(Lucy's head slowly reappears and we see a female replica of Jack Frost—icicles hanging from every conceivable place. Her hair is covered with a cap of snow, eyebrows, eyelashes etc., all white with frost, or as much as we can accomplish in this short space of time. When she drops out of sight she can sneak off to one side and be made up. Ethel sees this hoary apparition.)*

ETHEL. *(Screams. Lucy sinks out of sight again. The door finally opens with a splintering sound and they rush into the freezer and reappear, the three of them carrying Lucy. She is as stiff as a poker.)*

RICKY. Let's rush her upstairs.

ETHEL. *(As they leave the scene.)* Gently now, going around corners. You might snap an arm off.

After scene or last scene. Up in the apartment, Lucy is on the couch, with a blanket wrapped around her . . . Ricky is hovering over her attentively. Ethel is just coming in with a steaming cup.

ETHEL. Here, have some more hot tea. *(Lucy accepts it weakly.)*

LUCY. Thank you.

RICKY. Are you sure you're going to be okay, honey?

LUCY. Yeah, I'm going to be all right.

ETHEL. One thing we can be sure of—that freezer really freezes.

RICKY. Yeah—our meat's going to be good and cold down there. *(Fred comes in the front door.)*

FRED. How's our little fast frozen redhead?

LUCY. Oh, I'm going to be fine, Fred.

RICKY. *(Sniffs.)* Hey . . . what're we having for dinner?

LUCY. What'd you mean?

FRED. *(Sniffs.)* Something smells great—like a barbecue.

RICKY. *(Sniffs.)* Yeah . . . I smell it too.

ETHEL. Smells delicious. Must be coming from next door. *(She points to the register and goes toward it, sniffing as does Fred.)*

LUCY. *(With terrible thought.)* Fred—where were you just now?

FRED. Lighting the furnace, why?

LUCY. Oh no! *(Lucy leaps up, starts toward the door.)*

RICKY. Lucy—where are you going?

LUCY. I'll explain later. . . . Just get a knife, fork and some ketchup and follow me to the biggest barbecue in the world. *(She starts out the door and curtain.)*

Appendix D

"Vitameatavegamin"

Script for Lucy's fourth reading of the "Vitameatavegamin" commercial in *I Love Lucy* #30 ("Lucy Does a TV Commercial"), written by Jess Oppenheimer, Madelyn Pugh Davis, and Bob Carroll, Jr. First broadcast May 5, 1952, on the CBS Television Network. Lucy's "rearrangement"

```
I LOVE LUCY - Show No. 30

(Lucy Does A TV Commercial)

                              March 28
                    Filmed:  April 4, 1952
                    Air:  May 5, 1952


              CAST


LUCY.................Lucille Ball

RICKY...............Desi Arnaz

ETHEL...............Vivian Vance

DIRECTOR............ Ross Elliot

JOE (PROPMAN)....... Jerry Hausner
```

of this material during her performance is discussed in chapter 16. This is track 10 on the included CD.

JOE. Say Ross, the audio man wants to get a level on her.

ROSS. Miss McGillicuddy.

LUCY. Huh?

DIRECTOR. Do you mind doing it again?

LUCY. It's perfectly all right.

DIRECTOR. Okay in the control room?

VOICE. Go ahead.

DIRECTOR. Now we're going to time it this time. All right, Miss McGillicuddy, go.

LUCY. You know you're awfully nice.

DIRECTOR. Thank you. Would you go ahead, please?

LUCY. Well—I'm your Vita—veeda—vigee—vat girl. Are you tired, run down, listless? Do you pop out at parties—are you unpoopular? Well, are you? The answer to ALLLLL your problems is in this li'l ole bottle. Vita-meeta—vegamin. (*She looks real pleased with herself for getting it right.*) Contains vitamins, meat, metagable, and vinerals. With—(*She looks at the bottle.*) Vitametavegamin you can spoon your way to health. All you do is take one of these full—vita meedy mega meenie moe a mis (*She holds up the spoon.*) . . . after every meal. (*She has a lot of difficulty getting the spoon under the neck of the bottle, keeps pouring so that it doesn't hit the spoon but goes on the table. Finally, she puts the spoon down on the table, takes the bottle with both hands and pours it into the spoon. She puts the bottle down, looks at the spoon to see that it's full, beams back at the audience, turns back to the table, picks up the bottle and drinks out of it. As she puts the bottle down, she notices the spoon again, picks it up and puts it in her mouth. She forgets to take it out. With spoon in her mouth.*) It tastes like candy. (*She takes the spoon out of her mouth. By now, she is leaning, practically sitting on the table.*) So why don't you join the thousands of happy, peppy, people and get a great big bottle. (*She opens her mouth but realizes that she'd better not try it again. Holds up the bottle.*) This stuff.

Appendix E

Compact Disc Contents

Track   *Description*

1.   **A Character Is Born**

   Episode 11 of *My Favorite Husband* ("Young Matrons League Tryouts"), starring Lucille Ball as Liz Cugat, with Richard Denning as George Cugat, Ruth Perrot as Katy, the maid, John Hiestand as Corey Cartwright, Bea Benaderet as Mrs. Wirthingill, and Hans Conried as Dr. Schweinkampf. Broadcast live, October 2, 1948, on the CBS Radio Network. Written by Jess Oppenheimer. Produced and directed by Gordon T. Hughes. Appendix A is the script of this episode, Jess Oppenheimer's first script for Lucille Ball. Discussed in chapter 10.

2.   **Lucy Meets Gale Gordon**

   Excerpt from episode 26 of *My Favorite Husband* ("Valentine's Day"), starring Lucille Ball as Liz Cooper, with Richard Denning as George Cooper, Hans Conried as Mr. Dabney, the butcher, and Gale Gordon (in his first appearance on the series) as Judge Skinner. Broadcast live, February 11, 1949, on the CBS Radio Network. Written by Jess Oppenheimer, Madelyn Pugh Davis, and Bob Carroll, Jr. Produced and directed by Jess Oppenheimer. Discussed in chapter 10.

3.   **The Driver's License**

   Excerpt from episode 51 of *My Favorite Husband* ("Reminiscing"), starring Lucille Ball as Liz Cooper, with Richard Denning as George Cooper, and Frank Nelson as the Driver's License

Clerk. Broadcast July 1, 1949, on the CBS Radio Network. Written by Jess Oppenheimer, Madelyn Pugh Davis, and Bob Carroll, Jr. Produced and directed by Jess Oppenheimer.

4.   **The Home Economics Lesson**
     Excerpt from episode 90 of *My Favorite Husband* ("Selling Dresses"), starring Lucille Ball as Liz Cooper, with Richard Denning as George Cooper. Broadcast May 28, 1950, on the CBS Radio Network. Written by Jess Oppenheimer, Madelyn Pugh Davis, and Bob Carroll, Jr. Produced and directed by Jess Oppenheimer. Discussed in chapter 10.

5.   **Lucy Promotes Desi**
     Closing credits from episode 115 of *My Favorite Husband*. Broadcast January 20, 1951, on the CBS Radio Network, with Lucy interrupting announcer Bob LeMond to promote the debut the following day of Desi's new CBS Radio Program, *Your Tropical Trip*. Discussed in chapter 11.

6.   ***My Favorite Husband* Outtakes**
     Recorded before a studio audience at CBS Columbia Square in Hollywood in early 1951. Voices heard include those of Bob LeMond, Lucille Ball, Richard Denning, and Jess Oppenheimer (speaking from the control booth). Never broadcast. Appendix F is a transcript of this track.

7.   **Lucy Says Good-bye**
     Closing credits from the final episode of *My Favorite Husband*, broadcast March 31, 1951, on the CBS Radio Network, with Lucy's tearful good-bye to the audience, cast, and crew. Discussed in chapter 11.

8.   **The Restaurant Scene—Radio Version**
     Excerpt from episode 50 of *My Favorite Husband* ("Liz Changes Her Mind"), starring Lucille Ball as Liz Cooper, with Richard Denning as George Cooper, Gale Gordon as his boss, Rudolph Atterbury, Bea Benaderet as Iris Atterbury, and Frank Nelson as the waiter. Broadcast June 24, 1949, on the CBS Radio Network. Written by Jess Oppenheimer, Madelyn Pugh Davis, and Bob

Carroll, Jr. Produced and directed by Jess Oppenheimer. Discussed in chapter 14.

9. **The Restaurant Scene—TV Version**
Excerpt from episode 49 of *I Love Lucy* ("Lucy Changes Her Mind"), featuring the voices of Lucille Ball, Desi Arnaz, Vivian Vance, William Frawley, and Frank Nelson. First broadcast March 30, 1953, on the CBS Television Network. Written by Jess Oppenheimer, Madelyn Pugh Davis, and Bob Carroll, Jr. Produced by Jess Oppenheimer and directed by William Asher. Discussed in chapter 14.

10. **Vitameatavegamin**
Excerpt from episode 30 of *I Love Lucy* ("Lucy Does a T.V. Commercial"), featuring the voices of Lucille Ball, Ross Elliot, Jerry Hausner, and Jess Oppenheimer (speaking from the control booth). First broadcast May 5, 1952, on the CBS Television Network. Written by Jess Oppenheimer, Madelyn Pugh Davis, and Bob Carroll, Jr. Produced by Jess Oppenheimer and directed by Marc Daniels. Appendix D is the script of this scene. Discussed in chapter 16.

11. **The Sales Pitch—Radio Version**
Excerpt from episode 90 of *My Favorite Husband* ("Selling Dresses"), featuring the voices of Lucille Ball, Florence Halop, and Vivi Janiss. Broadcast May 28, 1950, on the CBS Radio Network. Written by Jess Oppenheimer, Madelyn Pugh Davis, and Bob Carroll, Jr. Produced and directed by Jess Oppenheimer. Discussed in chapter 14.

12. **The Sales Pitch—TV Version**
Excerpt from episode 29 of *I Love Lucy* ("The Freezer"), featuring the voices of Lucille Ball, Vivian Vance, Kay Wiley, and Barbara Pepper. First broadcast April 28, 1952, on the CBS Television Network. Written by Jess Oppenheimer, Madelyn Pugh Davis, and Bob Carroll, Jr. Produced by Jess Oppenheimer and directed by Marc Daniels. Appendix C is the script of this episode. Discussed in chapter 14.

13.   ***I Love Lucy* Lost Scenes**

Opening "flashback" scenes from (a) the initial CBS Television
Network rebroadcast of episode 5 of *I Love Lucy* ("The Quiz
Show"), on October 2, 1952 (the first-ever nationally broadcast
rerun of *I Love Lucy*); (b) the initial CBS Television Network
rebroadcast of episode 4 of *I Love Lucy* ("The Diet"), on February
9, 1953; and (c) the initial CBS Television Network rebroadcast
of episode 91 of *I Love Lucy* ("The Club Dance"), on December
26, 1955. Featuring the voices of Lucille Ball, Desi Arnaz, Vivian
Vance, and William Frawley. Discussed in chapter 16. These
"flashback" scenes were omitted from all subsequent reruns of
these episodes.

Appendix 4

My Favorite Husband Outtakes (1951)

What follows is a transcript of track 6 on the included CD, recorded before a studio audience at CBS Columbia Square in Hollywood in early 1951. Participants include Bob LeMond, Lucille Ball, Richard Denning, and Jess Oppenheimer (speaking from the control booth).

LEMOND. It's time for My Favorite Husband starring Lucille Ball.

LUCY. Jell-O everybody! (Opening theme.)

LEMOND. Yes, it's the gay family series starring Lucille Ball, with Richard Denning, transcribed and brought to you by the Jell-O family of red letter desserts. (Jell-O jingle.)

LEMOND. And now Lucille Ball with Richard Denning as Liz . . .

OPPENHEIMER. (From booth.) Hold it please.

LEMOND. . . . and George Cooper. . . . What's the matter? Don't you like my work?

OPPENHEIMER. The guy taping stuff over at Recorders forgot to reset the machines again. Everybody tell jokes to each other.

LUCY. (Laughs.)

LEMOND. (To studio audience.) Oh, I'll uh . . . I'll explain this to you.

LUCY. (Laughs.) Hello, Mother. Hello, Mother.

VOICE. From the top.

LUCY. I didn't get a chance. That's what they get for rushing.

OPPENHEIMER. We're having a little trouble with Radio Recorders.

DENNING. (Laughs.)

LEMOND. What do you want to do? Want to play music a while?

OPPENHEIMER. Why don't you do a striptease, Bob.

LEMOND. (Laughs.) Well . . .

LUCY. Is it gonna be that long? (*Audience laughter.*)

LEMOND. Let's introduce some more people. That voice you hear back there, the one in the middle, "Curly" . . . (*Audience laughter.*) . . . that's our producer and director and writer of the show. He writes the show along with the two people sitting up in the top there, Madelyn Pugh and Bob Carroll, Jr. Right in here is Jess Oppenheimer. How about a hand for all of them. (*Applause.*)

OPPENHEIMER. System in fifteen, Bob.

LEMOND. This is CBS, the Columbia Broadcasting System.

Index

Italic page number denotes illustration.

Academy Awards, 91, 110, 145, 146
Ackerman, Harry: Arnaz TV career and, 132, 134; on Ball pregnancy, 198; cameo appearance of, *160*; *The Edgar Bergen Show* and, 129; *Hollywood Reporter* on, 194; *My Favorite Husband* and, 4, 5, 114, 115, 117, 119; 20 percent interest issue and, 148; mentioned, 139, 143
Alan Young Show, The (TV program), 142
Allen, Fred, 95, 186
Allen, Gracie, 68
Allen, Steve, 195–96
All Quiet on the Western Front (film), 145
Ameche, Don, 95
Amos 'n' Andy (radio program), 78, 95
Amos 'n' Andy (TV program), 142, 143
"Anniversary Song, The," 110
Armed Forces Radio, 106
Arnaz, Desi: acting by, 171–72, 174; in "Be a Pal," *151*; Benny and, 127; caricature of, *154*; clowning by, *177*; in conference, *167*; credits issue and, 138; Devlin and, *200*; at Emmy Awards banquet, *190*; executive producer issue and, 175, 177–79, 192, 194–95, 212; first rerun and, 201, 202; *Hollywood Reporter* on, 161, 162; Hudson and, 140; intermission entertainment by, 157; lighting for,

151; in "Lucy Has Her Eyes Examined," 205, 206; in "Lucy Hires an English Tutor," 6; in "Lucy Is Enceinte," 207–8, 210; on "Lucy Learns to Drive" set, *167*; in "Lucy Thinks Ricky Is Trying to Murder Her," 152; in "No Children Allowed," *152*; at parties, *203, 213, 214*; in pilot episode, *137*, 141; pregnancy issue and, 5–6, 198; salary of, 143; on "The Saxophone" set, *203*; script refused by, 173–74, 249–57; singing by, 172–73; son born to, 3, 210–11; Stage 2 and, 147; theme song and, 139; trophy presented by, 192, *193*; 20 percent interest issue and, 148; Vance and, 149; vaudeville act of, 132–33, 136; on "Young Fans" set, *177*; *Your Tropical Trip* and, 134
Arnaz, Desi, IV, 3, 210–11
Asher, Bill, 187, 208
Astaire, Fred, 40–41, 88–91, 92, 98
Astaire Packard Hour. See *Packard Hour* (radio program)
Astor, Mary, 102
AT&T (firm), 161

Baby Snooks (radio program): discontinuation of, 113, 114; with Brice in title role, *112*; genius of Brice

Baby Snooks (radio program) (*continued*) in, 112; Hausner and, 131; *My Favorite Husband* and, 4–5, 115; restaurant scene in, 32–33; spanking episode in, 111

Bachelor's Baby, The (play), 63–64

Ball, Lucille: in "Be a Pal," *151*; Benny and, 127; caricature of, *154*; clowning by, *176*; commercials and, 126, 127, 205–7, *209*; in conference, *153, 167*; contract negotiations of, 134, 140; on "The Courtroom" set (1955 repeat opening), *176*; M. Daniels and, 188; Devlin and, *200*; at Emmy Awards banquet, *190*; executive producer issue and, 175, 192, 194–95; on "Face to Face" set ("The Ricardos Are Interviewed"), *215*; first rerun and, 201, 202; Freund shots of, 145, 159; in "The Freezer," 277; in "The Great Train Robbery," 168-70; *Hollywood Reporter* on, 132, 161–62, 194; kiss given by, *215*; in "L.A. at Last," 127, 165, *168*; lighting for, *151*; in "Lucy Changes Her Mind," 181, 277; in "Lucy Does a TV Commercial" (Vitameatavegamin), 205, 207, *209*; in "Lucy Has Her Eyes Examined," 205, 206; in "Lucy Hires an English Tutor," 6; in "Lucy Is Enceinte," 207–8, 210; on "Lucy Learns to Drive" set, *167*; in "Lucy's Italian Movie," 164–65, *166*; in "Lucy Thinks Ricky Is Trying to Murder Her," 152; in *My Favorite Husband, ii*, 4–5, 114–31, 132, 141, 144, 275–77, 279–80; in "No Children Allowed," *152*; Oppenheimer children and, 7; at parties, *203*, 213, *214*; pregnancy of, 5–6, 136–38, 198–200, 201, *203*; publicity shot of, *182*; salary of, 143; script unperformed by, 249–57; on "The Saxophone," set, *203*; sixth season desired by, 212; son born to, 3, 210–11; "Spider" and, 126, 127; on "Staten Island Ferry" set, 7; talent of, 163–64; temperament of, 119–22; TV

set of, 172; 20 percent interest issue and, 148; unhappiness of, 174–75; vaudeville act of, 133, 136; veto power of, 177, 178

Bal Tabarin (San Francisco), 64

Barker Brothers (firm), 136

Barrymore, John, 97, 100

Bat, The (play), 59–62

Bates School (San Francisco), 17

Behr, Gwen, 92, 94

"Bei Mir Bist Du Schön" (song), 110

Bell, Book and Candle (film), 107

Beloin, Ed, 94

Benaderet, Bea, 36–37, 124-25, 141–42, 275, 276

Benny, Jack: F. Allen and, 95; Ball and, 126, 127; Boasberg and, 93–94; Emmy Awards and, 40; Harris and, 88; Josefsberg and, 10; Paley and, 78; mentioned, 98

Bence, Bob, 49–50

Bergen, Edgar, 65, 95–96, *129*, 130

Berlin, Irving, 82

Big Street, The (film), 114

Biow, Milton: Arnaz and, 172–73; demands of, 142–43; Feldman and, 145; in Hollywood, *199*; purchase by, 141

Biow Agency, 141, 193–94, 198

Blue Monday Jamboree (radio program), 18–19; Doakes and Doakes on, 37–38; "Interviews with Interesting People," 41–45; "kidley" routine and, 49–51, 56; sound effects for, 19–21

Boardman, True, 86

Boasberg, Al, 93–94

Brice, Fanny: Ball and, 117; *My Favorite Husband* and, 4, 121; portrait of, *112*; salary dispute of, 5, 113; Streisand and, 32; writing for, 111–13

Broadhurst Theatre (New York), 109

Browar, Herb, 154

Brown Derby (Hollywood), 98

Burns, George, 68

Burns and Allen (radio program), 124

Burns and Allen (TV program), 136, 142

Bury the Dead (play), 67

Butterworth, Charlie, 88, 89, 95

Caesar, Sid, 107

Cahn, Dann, 157, *158*

Cahn, Sammy, 107, 108

Camille (film), 145

Cantor, Eddie, 56

Capitol Records (firm), 106

Capra, Frank, 98

Carroll, Bob, Jr.: "Desi Arnaz and Band with Lucille Ball" and, 133; drafts by, 189, 190–91; first rerun and, 201, 202; 5 percent interest of, 148; "The Freezer," 181–85, 259–72; idea development by, 180–81; "Lucy Does a TV Commercial" (Vitameatavegamin), 207, 273–74; Mertz characters and, 141–42; My *Favorite Husband* and, 117–19, 122, 127–28; pilot script by, 136; pregnancy issue and, 6–7; staff additions and, *186*; three-camera shooting and, 157; unperformed script by, 249–57; mentioned, 131, 154, 155, 179, 275–77, 280

Carson, Johnny, 15, 134

CBS Radio Network: *The Edgar Bergen Show*, 129; My *Favorite Husband* (See My *Favorite Husband* [radio program]); programs bought by, 78; timing by, 38; Weaver and, 84

CBS Television Network: *Amos 'n' Andy*, 142, 143; Arnaz and, 172; audition proposed to, 133, 136; contract negotiations with, 134, 140, 143, 148; executives of, 159, *160*; pregnancy issue and, 3, 5, 6, 198–99; reruns of, 201, 202, 213, 216; syndication by, 188

Chaplin, Ethel, 110

Chaplin, Saul, 110

Chase and Sanborn Hour (radio program), 95, 96

Choon Marie (ship), 53–54

Christian Science, 30

Coast Guard, 100–102; *Baby Snooks* and, 111, 112; Daniel and, 138; group photograph, *101*; recruitment for, 107

Coca-Cola Company, 129–30, 131

Cohn, Harry, 109–11

Cohn, Joan, 110

Cole, Nat King, 107

Columbia Broadcasting System. *See* CBS Radio Network; CBS Television Network

Columbia Pictures Studios, 107, 108, 109–11

Community Center Players, 56–57, 58–62, 65, 67, 75–76

Connecticut Yankees (band), 100

Conried, Hans, 6, 130–31, 275

Cook, Ira, 106, 107

Cosmopolitan (periodical), 195

Crawford, Joan, 98

Crosby, Bing, 88

Cuban culture, 173

Cummings, Bob, 15–16

Cuneo, Larry, 154

Daily Variety (periodical), 69, *154*. See also *Variety* (periodical)

Daniel, Eliot, 102, 138–39

Daniels, Emily, *153*, 154

Daniels, Marc: in conference, *153*; hiring of, 149; Lyons-Biow visit and, *199*; milkman scene and, 188; rehearsal demands of, 152; three-camera shooting and, 157; mentioned, 154

D'Arcy (firm), 129

Davenport, Bill, 114, 117

Davis, Bette, 98

Davis, Joan, 100

Davis, Madelyn Pugh: drafts by, 189, 190–91; first rerun and, 201, 202; 5 percent interest of, 148; "The Freezer," 181–85, 259–72; idea development by, 180–81; "Lucy Does a TV Commercial" (Vitameatavegamin), 207, 273–74;

Davis, Madelyn Pugh (*continued*)
  Mertz characters and, 141–42; *My
  Favorite Husband* and, 117–19, 122,
  127–28; pilot script by, 136;
  pregnancy issue and, 6–7; staff
  additions and, *186;* three-camera
  shooting and, 157; unperformed script
  by, 249–57; vaudeville act and, 133;
  "Vitameatavegamin," 207, 273–74;
  mentioned, 154, 155, 179, 275–77,
  280
Day at the Races, A (play), 74
Dead End Kids (film troupe), 96
Dempsey, Jack, *101*
Denning, Richard: anger portrayed by,
  122; Benadaret and, 125; introduction
  for, 115; *Radio and Television Life* on,
  132; rehearsing *My Favorite Husband,*
  120; reserve of, 126; retakes by, 144;
  voice of, 275–77, 279
"Desi Arnaz and Band with Lucille Ball"
  (vaudeville act), 133, 136
"Desilu Playhouse" (General Service
  Studios), 147
Desilu Productions (firm): AT&T
  network link and, 161; 50 percent
  interest of, 134, 143; first rerun and,
  202; formation of, 132; Oppenheimer
  contract with, 148, 178, 212; time
  demands of, 174; mentioned, 154
Destry Rides Again (film), 99
Devlin, Monsignor, *200*
Dietrich, Marlene, 98–99
Disney, Walt, 138
Doakes and Doakes (vaudeville act),
  37–38
Don Lee-Columbia Network, 38,
  41
"Don't Go in the Lion's Cage Tonight"
  (song), 37, 38
Dorsey, Jimmy, 102
Dorsey, Tommy, 102
Dracula (film), 145
DuBarry Was a Lady (film), 145
Dudley Doright (TV program),
  130
DuPont, E. A., 145

Earn Your Vacation (TV program), 134
Easter Parade (film), 91
*Edgar Bergen Show with Charlie
  McCarthy, The* (radio program), 129,
  130–31
Edwards, Ralph, 145
Edward VIII (king of England), 57
Eisenhower, Dwight D., 3, 205
Eleventh Naval District Coast Guard
  Band, 102
Emmy Awards, 39–41, *190*
Empress of Japan (ship), 53
Evening with Fred Astaire, An (TV
  program), 40
Everett, Tom, 78–82

Fairbanks, Douglas, Jr., 196
Fairbanks, Douglas, Sr., 196
Father Knows Best (TV program), 39
Feldman, Eddie, 145, 193–94
Ferber, Edna, 69, 71–72
Fibber McGee and Molly (radio program),
  124
Fleischmann Hour (radio program),
  100
Flintstones, The (TV program), 124
Fonda, Henry, 114
"Fort Taft" (Taft Building), 106
Fox, Della, 154
Fox, Frank, 114, 117
Fox, George, 154, 157–58
Francis, Anne, 69
Frankel (proprietor), 54–55
Frawley, William: casting of, 148-49; H.
  Cohn and, 109–10; at farewell party,
  213, *214;* *Hollywood Reporter* on, 162;
  in "Lucy Hires an English Tutor," 6;
  Vance and, 171
Fred Astaire Packard Hour, The. See
  Packard Hour (radio program)
Freeman, Everett, 111
Freud, Mayfair, 57, 58
Freud, Ralph, 56–58; in *The Bachelor's
  Baby,* 63–64; in *The Bat,* 60, 61, 62;
  criticism by, 68; Oppenheimer family
  and, 76; writing jobs from, 67

Freund, Karl: close-ups by, 159; in conference, *153*; contrast problem and, 158; film career of, 145; *Hollywood Reporter* on, 194; lighting by, 150, *151*; personality of, *146*, 151; side cameras and, 151, *152*; watching Lucy in makeup, *168*; mentioned, 154

Front Page, The (play), 34

Fulton, Robert, 130

Funny Girl (film), 111

Funny Girl (musical), 32

Garden, J. B., 71–72

Gardiner, Reginald, 98

Garland, Judy, 98

General Artists Corporation, 133

General Foods Corporation, 93, 122–23, 126, 133

General Service Studios, 146–47, 148, 152, 154

George Burns and Gracie Allen Show, The (radio program), 124

George Burns and Gracie Allen Show, The (TV program), 136, 142

Germany, 46, 47

"G.I. Jill" broadcasts, 106

Glenn, Glenn, 154

Gobel, George, 15–16

Godfrey, Arthur, 160

Golden Gate Bridge (San Francisco), 65

Golden Gate Theater (San Francisco), 74

Good Earth, The (film), 145

Gorcey, Leo, 96

Gordon, Gale, 124, *125*, 141–42, 170, 275, 276

Grauman's Chinese Theatre (Hollywood), 186

Great Gildersleeve, The (radio program), 124

Great San Francisco Earthquake (1906), 29–30

Great Stock Market Crash (1929), 28

Green, Johnny, 88, 90, 91–92

Greene, Felice, 154

Green Spot (Victorville), 93

Grier, Jimmy, 102

Griffith Park (Los Angeles), 107, 108–9

Gulf Oil (firm), 98

Gulf Screen Guild Show, The (radio program), 98–99, 100

Hall, Rand, 103

Hammerstein, Oscar, II, 172

"Happiness Boys" (performers), 22

Happy-Go-Lucky Hour, The (radio program), 38–39

Harding Golf Course (San Francisco), 107–8

Hare, Billy, 22

Harrington, Tom, 78, 82, 86

Harris, Phil, 88, 94

Harry (janitor), 36

Hatch, Wilbur, 154

Hausner, Jerry, 131, 136

Hecht, Ben, 34, 69

Hepburn, Katharine, 114

Heredeen, Mildred, 86

Herman, Woody, 102

Herst, Jerry, 89–90

Hickox, Andrew, 154

Hiestand, John, 275

"Hillier the Great" (magician), 57

Hitler, Adolf, 47

Hit Parade (radio program), 91

Hoffa, Portland, 95

Holden, William, 127, 165

Holliway, Harrison, 34, *42*; "Interviews with Interesting People" and, 41, 43–45; introduction to, 19; "kidley" routine and, 49–50

Hollywood Mardi Gras (radio program), 94–95

Hollywood Reporter (periodical), 132, 154, 161–62, 194, 204

Honeymooners, The (TV program), 216

Hoover, Herbert, 18

Hope, Bob: Carson and, 15; Crosby and, 88; in *Sorrowful Jones*, 119, 120; Trustees' Award for, 40; L. White and, 9

Horace (restaurant companion), 85–86

Howard, Cy, 121
Hudson, Hal, 140, *160*
Hughes, Gordon, 119

I Love Lucy (TV program): advertising
  for, *154*; audience of, 192–93; "The
  Audition," *160*; "Be a Pal," *151*; cast
  of, 163–75; "Changing the Boys'
  Wardrobe," 181; "The Courtroom"
  (1955 repeat opening of), *176*;
  departure from, 212–16; "The Diet,"
  201; executive producer issue and,
  175, 177–79, 192, 194–95, 212; "Face
  to Face" ("The Ricardos Are
  Interviewed"), *215*; filming of, 142–
  47, 149–60, 164; "The Freezer," 181–
  85, 187, 192, 259–72, 277; "The Girls
  Want to Go to a Nightclub," 160;
  "The Great Train Robbery," 168–70;
  "Job Switching," 187; "L.A. at Last,"
  127, 165, *168*; luck in, 4, *160*, 171;
  "Lucy Changes Her Mind," 181, 277;
  "Lucy Does a TV Commercial"
  (Vitameatavegamin), 205, 207, *209*,
  273–74; "Lucy Has Her Eyes
  Examined," 205, 206; "Lucy Hires an
  English Tutor," 6; "Lucy Is Enceinte,"
  207–8, 210; "Lucy Learns to Drive,"
  167; "Lucy's Italian Movie," 164–65,
  166; "Lucy Tells the Truth," 32, 173–
  74, 249–57; "Lucy Thinks Ricky Is
  Trying to Murder Her," 152, 153, 156;
  "Lucy Visits Grauman's," 186; "Mertz
  and Kurtz," 176; naming of, 138; "No
  Children Allowed," *152*; "The
  Passports," 48–49, 181; pilot for, 135,
  136–38, 140, 141; "Pioneer Women,"
  187; pregnancy issue and, 3, 5–8,
  198–200, 201, 203; press reviews of,
  161–62; registration of (concept), 2,
  139; reruns of, 201, 202, 212, 213,
  216; "Return Home from Europe,"
  213; "Ricky Thinks He Is Getting
  Bald," 92, 181, *182*; "The
  Saxophone," *203*; "Staten Island
  Ferry," 7; theme song for, 138–39;

writing of, 180–91; "Young Fans,"
  177; mentioned, 109, 131
"Interviews with Interesting People"
  (radio program), 41–45
"It's Music City, Sunset and Vine"
  (song), 107

Jack Benny Program, The (radio
  program), 97; Ball and, 126, 127; CBS
  purchase of, 78; Wilson and, 95
Jacobs, Johnny, *153*, 154
Japan, 3, 52–54, 55, 100
"Jayo Viewer" (invention), 204–5, *206*
Jellison, Bobby, 188
Jell-O (product), 122–23, 126, 127
Jell-O Program (radio program), 93
Jenkins, Dan, 194
Jessie Bonstell Players, 57
Joe (uncle), 107
Johan van Oldenbarneveldt (ship), 53
Jolson, Al, 96–97
Jones, Ernie, 22
Josefsberg, Milt, 9–10
Judgment Day (play), 59, 61
Julius Kahn Playground, 23

Karger, Freddie, 108
Kay Jewelers (firm), 68
Kennedy, Arthur, 69
Kern, Jim, 165
KFRC (radio station), 34, 35–38; former
  employees of, 84, 124; switchovers by,
  38–39, 41. *See also Blue Monday
  Jamboree* (radio program)
KHJ (radio station), 38–39
King, Hal, 154, *168*
Kobe (Japan), 53–54

La Jolla Playhouse, 149
Lang, Fritz, 145
"Lavender Blue" (song), 138
Lee, Don, 38, 41, 42, 45
Lee, Thomas, 51
Leeds, Martin, 142

LeMond, Bob, 115, 276, 279–80
Levy, Ralph, 136
Lewis, Jerry, 107
Lewis, Ted, 102
Liemert Park (Calif.), 100, 102
Life (periodical), 133
Lifebuoy Program (radio program), 96–97
Life with Luigi (radio program), 121
Lincoln Park (San Francisco), 107–8
Lindbergh, Charles A., 51
Livingstone, Mary, 94
Loesser, Frank, 62–63
Lorre, Peter, 195
Los Angeles Civic Light Opera
    Company, 62–63
Los Angeles *Mirror* (newspaper), 197
Lowell High School (San Francisco), 16
Lubitsch, Ernst, 98
Lund, Art, 62–63
Lyons, Alfred E., 198, 199

MacArthur, Charles, 34
MacGuire, Arnold, 35–37
Manzanares, Mercedes, 154, 180
Marconi, Guglielmo, 196
Martin, Dean, 15 .
Martin, Freddy, 102
Marx, Chico, 74
Marx, Groucho, 74–75
Marx, Harpo, 162
Marx, Maxine, 74
Marx Brothers, 74
Max, Ed, 77
Maxwell, Robert, 102
Mayflower Hotel (Washington), 39
McCarthy, Charlie. *See* Bergen, Edgar
McCarthy, Joseph, 196
Menjou, Adolphe, 96
Merced Country Club (San Francisco),
    107
Mercer, Johnny, 107
Metro-Goldwyn-Mayer. *See* MGM
Metropolis (film), 145
M.G.B. (columnist), 79
MGM (firm), 91
Mirror (Los Angeles newspaper), 197

Mishell, Dr., 140–41
Mitchell cameras, 157
Molin, Bud, 157, *158*
Montgomery, Robert, 98
Moran, Eddie, 84–86
Morgan, Frank, 98, 99
Morgan, Ken, *153*, 154, 194
Morgan, Ralph, 98
Morrow, Bill, 94
Most Happy Fella, The (musical), 62–63
Mother Goose rhymes, 126
Motion Picture Relief Fund, 98
Moulin Rouge (Hollywood), 39, 40–41
Moviola editing machine, 157–58
Mr. and Mrs. Cugat (Rorick), 115
Murphy, George, 98
Music City (firm), 106–7
Musso and Frank's Grill (Hollywood),
    195
My Favorite Husband (radio program),
    114–31; advertisement for, 121;
    audience of, 144; *Baby Snooks* and, 4–
    5, 115, 121; first Oppenheimer script
    for, 115–17, 219–47; last episodes of,
    133, 140, 141; "Liz Changes Her
    Mind," 181; outtakes from, 279–80;
    press reviews of, 132; script backlog
    of, 185; "Selling Dresses," 183; TV
    possibilities of, 134; *Variety* on, 121;
    wills episode of, 136; "You Are
    Theirs" and, 213
My Friend Irma (radio program), 121
"My Time Is Your Time" (song), 100

Naish, J. Carroll, 121
Nasser, James, 146, 147, 154
NBC Radio Network, 38, 93, 100
NBC Symphony, 102
NBC Television Network: Arnaz-Ball
    pilot and, 133, 134; promotional
    program of, 15–16; *The Ten
    Commandments*, 68–73; Weaver and,
    34, 212; Werner and, 18
Nelson, Frank, 181, 275–76, 277
New England Mutual Life Insurance
    Company, 66

Nickodell's Melrose Grotto
(Hollywood), 85–86
Nickodell's restaurant (Hollywood), 197,
200–201
Nielsen ratings, 192, 194

Odets, Clifford, 67
Office of War Information, 106
O'Keefe, Walter, 95
O'Meara, Carroll, 86
Oppenheimer, Estelle Weiss (wife): at
farewell party, 213; in Honolulu, *108;*
"Jayo Viewer" and, 204; marriage of,
107; mother-in-law of, 32; *My Favorite
Husband* and, 119, 121; old clothes
and, 181; pregnancies of, 114, 138;
sister of, 100; sleep of, 155; son born
to, 140–41; time for, 131; vision
anecdote and, 105; wrong number
and, 113
Oppenheimer, Gregg (son), *7,* 140–41
Oppenheimer, James (father), 26–30,
75; driver's license for, 105;
naturalization of, 46–48; radio
receivers and, 22, 23
Oppenheimer, Janice (sister): in D.C.,
67, 75; dishwashing by, 10; driver's
license for, 105; graduation by, 46;
homecoming of, 56; portrait of, *11;* in
Singapore, 55; upset father and, 26–
27
Oppenheimer, Joanne (daughter), *7,*
113, 131
Oppenheimer, J. Robert (physicist),
196–97
Oppenheimer, Stella (mother):
academic concerns of, 16–17; *The
Bachelor's Baby* and, 63; bridge job
and, 65; correspondence of, 80; crap
game earnings and, 24–26; crap table
felt supplied by, 23; in D.C., 67;
driver's license for, 104–5; Hollywood
move and, 75; homecoming of, 56;
honesty test of, 10–11; KFRC visit
and, 20; "kidley" routine and, 50, 51;
naturalization records and, 46–47,

181; personality of, 30–33; portrait of,
11; stock sales and, 27, 28
Oppenheimer, The Trunk Man (firm),
28–30
"Oppy Awards," 213, *214*
Oriental Hotel (Kobe), 53
Oscars (Academy Awards), 91, 110, 145,
146
Ozzie and Harriet (radio program), 114

Pacific Lighting Gas Supply Company,
27
Packard Hour (radio program): hiring for,
81–82, 94, 97; *Jell-O Program* and, 93;
script review for, 88-89; submissions
for, 78–79; summer broadcasts of, 92;
writers for, 77, 84
Packard Motor Car Co., 94
Palace Theater (New York), 109
Paley, William, 78
Pangborn, Franklin, 98
"Peanuts" (comic strip), 118
Pearce, Al, 38
Pearce, Cal, 38
Pearl Harbor attack (1941), 100
"Pepito" (clown), 2, 133, 136
Perrot, Ruth, 275
Peter Pan (film), 130
Peterson, Austin, 84, 86
Petticoat Junction (TV program), 124
Philip Morris Company, 141, 154, 161,
173, 198, 205, 206
Pugh, Madelyn. *See* Davis, Madelyn
Pugh

Queen of Angels Hospital (Hollywood),
140–41
Quine, Dick, *101, 107*

Radio and Television Life (periodical), 132
"Radio Rogues" (nightclub act), 64–65
Raffles Hotel (Singapore), 54
Ralph Freud Playhouse (Los Angeles),
58

Rathbone, Basil, 98
RCA Corporation, 145
Robinson, Hubbell, 132
Rodgers, Richard, 172
Rogers, Ginger, 88
Romero, Cesar, *101*
Roosevelt, Franklin D., 18
Rorick, Isobel Scott, 115
Rosalie (musical), 88
Rosenbloom, Maxie, 100
Ross, Lanny, 95
Rudy Vallee Program, The (radio broadcast), 100, 102, 185

Sacramento immigration office, 48
San Francisco Earthquake (1906), 29–30
San Francisco Jewish Community Center. *See* Community Center Players
San Francisco passport office, 46–47
San Mateo Junior College, 17
Sarnoff, David, 196
Schiller, Bob, 185, *186*
Scott, Lee, 154
Scott, Raymond, 102
Screen Guild Show, The (radio program), 98–99, 100
Screen Guild Theatre (radio program), 99
Screen Writers' Guild, 2, 139
Scully, Frank, 205
Sealtest (firm), 100, 102
Sechrist, Andy, 90
Shall We Dance (film), 88
Sharpe, Don: Ackerman and, 134; audition proposal of, 133; Biow and, 141; *Hollywood Reporter* on, 194; kinescope carried by, 140; *My Favorite Husband* and, 119, 121–22; salary proposal of, 143; mentioned, 154
Sharpe, Jack, 89–90
Shaw, Irwin, 67
Shirley (waitress), 197, 200–201
Show Boat (novel), 69
Sides, Miss (receptionist), 78, 81, 83
Silverstein, Charlie, 107

Simon, Al, 145–46, 147, 154, 175
Simpson, Wallis, 57
Sinatra, Frank, 100, 107
Singapore, 52, 54–55
Skelton, Red, 110–11, 162, 190
"So Rare" (song), 89–91
Soria, Dario, *129*
Sorrowful Jones (film), 119, 120
Spars (military auxiliary), 102
Spicer, Earl, 145–46
Stabile, Dick, *101*
Stafford, Hanley, 111
Stage Door (film), 114
Standard Gas and Electric Company, 27
Stanford-Binet IQ test, 16
Stanford University, 17–18, 34, 46, 49, 104
Stark, Ray, 69, 111, 114
Stauffer, Joe, 78, 81–83
Steinbeck, John, 69, 70
Stewart, Jimmy, 99
Stock Market Crash (1929), 28
Stoloff, Morris, 108
Strangers When We Meet (film), 107
Streisand, Barbra, 32
Styne, Jule, 108
Sullivan, Ed, 40
Swallow, John, 96
Sweeten, Claude, 38, 39, 41
Swing Time (film), 88

Taft Building (Hollywood), 106
Tars and Spars (film), 107, 108
Ten Commandments, The (TV program), 68–73
Terman, Lewis, 16, 17, 195
Texaco Star Theater (radio program), 96
Thibault, Conrad, 88
Thomas Lee Artist Bureau, 51
Thompson, Maury, 154
"Three Radio Rogues" (nightclub act), 64–65
Thurber, James, 70, 73
Times Building (Los Angeles), 111
Today (TV program), 34
Together We Serve (radio program), 102

Tokyo, 52–53
Tonight Show (TV program), 15, 34
Toscanini, Arturo, 102
Truman, Harry S., 205
Trustees' Award, 40
Truth or Consequences (TV program), 145
Twentieth Century (play), 109
Twentieth Century-Fox Film Corporation, 138
Tyre, Norman, 148

UCLA Theater Arts Department, 58
Union Carbide Corporation, 27
University of California, 31, 46, 58
University of San Francisco, 17–18
University of Southern California, 104
U.S. Coast Guard. *See* Coast Guard
U.S. Office of War Information, 106

"Vagabond Lover, The" (song), 100
Vallee, Rudy, 100, 102, 105–6, 138
Vance, Vivian: audience view of, *152;* casting of, 149; at farewell party, 213, *214;* Frawley and, 171; *Hollywood Reporter* on, 162; in "Lucy Hires an English Tutor," 6
Van Nostrand, Jack, 86
Variety (film), 145
Variety (periodical), 121, 133, 161, 205. See also *Daily Variety* (periodical)
Voice of the Turtle (play), 149, 171
Von Zell, Harry, 86

Waiting for Lefty (play), 67
Wallichs, Glenn, 106
Waring, Fred, 102
Waves (military auxiliary), 102
Wayne, John, 186
Way We Were, The (film), 111

Weaver, Sylvester L., Jr. ("Pat"), 34, 84, 122, 212
Weede, Robert, 62–63
Weiskopf, Bob, 185–86
Weiss, Estelle. *See* Oppenheimer, Estelle Weiss (wife)
Werner, Marty, 106
Werner, Mort, 18–20, 34, 56, 106, 107
Western Union Corporation, 47
White, Francia, 88
White, Lester, 9
Whiteman, Paul, 102
"Who Knows" (song), 88
Wilmington Patrol Base (Los Angeles), 100, 102, 104
Wilson, Don, 95
Wizard of Oz, The (film), 98
Wolfe, Nat, 86
Wood, Trudy, 88
World of Suzie Wong, The (film), 107
Writers' Guild. *See* Screen Writers' Guild

"You Are Theirs" (revue), 213
Young, Loretta, 98
Young, Robert, 39, 40–41
Young and Rubicam (firm), 77, 106; application to, 78–81; Christmas party of, 86; General Foods and, 93; *The Gulf Screen Guild Show* and, 98; hiring by, 81–82; *Hollywood Mardi Gras* and, 94; KFRC veterans with, 84; *My Favorite Husband* and, 122–23; night work for, 104; pilot proposal by, 133; teletype machine of, 87
Your Tropical Trip (TV program), 134, 276
Yucca Loma (ranch), 92–93, 94

Ziegfeld Theatre (New York), 39–40

The Television Series

Robert J. Thompson, *Series Editor*

Other titles in The Television Series include:

Bonfire of the Humanities. David Marc
Lou Grant: *The Making of TV's Top Newspaper Drama*. Douglass K. Daniel
Prime Time, Prime Movers: From I Love Lucy *to* L.A. Law.—*America's Greatest TV Shows and the People Who Created Them*. David Marc and Robert J. Thompson
Storytellers to the Nation: A History of American Television Writing. Tom Stempel
"Deny All Knowledge": Reading The X-Files. David Lavery, Angela Hague, and Marla Cartwright, eds.